LANGUAGE AND ITS STRUCTURE
Some Fundamental Linguistic Concepts

LANGUAGE

RONALD W
LANGACKER
University of California at San Die

AND
ITS STRUCTURE

Some Fundamental
Linguistic Concepts

HARCOURT, BRACE & WORLD, INC.
New York / Chicago / San Francisco / Atlanta

LANGUAGE AND ITS STRUCTURE:
Some Fundamental Linguistic Concepts
Ronald W. Langacker

© 1967, 1968 by Harcourt, Brace & World, Inc.

ISBN: 0-15-549191-1

Library of Congress Catalog Card Number: 68–27167

Printed in the United States of America

Preface

Language and Its Structure is intended as a concise, readable, and up-to-date introduction to the nature and structure of language as viewed by modern linguists. It is an introduction to language, not to the discipline of linguistics. Consequently, it does not attempt to examine and contrast the views of competing linguistic schools or to introduce their arsenals of technical vocabulary and notations, but rather to present as clearly and simply as possible the fundamental insights about language to which every well-educated person should be exposed.

Part One is introductory. Chapter One points out the reasons why language is worthy of study and concludes with a thumbnail history of language study. Chapter Two, which touches on a number of different topics, lays the groundwork for the more detailed discussion of language structure in Part Two. Chapter Three deals with dialect geography, social attitudes toward language, and writing.

Part Two is a non-historical examination of language structure. Lexical items are discussed in Chapter Four, as well as the ways in which the components of a language are organized to pair meanings and sound sequences. Chapters Five and Six are devoted to syntax and phonology respectively, emphasizing the English language in the interest of clarity and coherence.

Part Three concerns the relationships between linguistic systems. In Chapter Seven, the historical relationships between earlier and later stages of a single language are discussed. Chapter Eight treats genetic relationships, while Chapter Nine examines the sense in which all languages can be said to be related, namely in their surprisingly extensive structural similarities.

Some linguists may be bothered by my discussion of lexical items; indeed, I am one of them. It is becoming increasingly clear that the whole matter of lexical items needs to be rethought, particularly their relationship to syntactic rules. In the meantime, notions such as the morpheme concept are useful if not pushed too far. Few people working in generative grammar will be surprised that I have abandoned the notions of deep structure and interpretive semantics, although some will disagree with me in this regard. In any case, it would certainly not be appropriate to fight the battle of deep structure in a book of this type.

Many people have contributed in one respect or another to this book. In particular, I would like to thank John Ross, Leonard Newmark, and Julian Boyd for their constructive comments, as well as my wife Peggy, who has helped in many ways.

R. W. L.

Contents

Basic

Concepts

CHAPTER ONE

By Way of Introduction

THE IMPORTANCE OF UNDERSTANDING LANGUAGE

Language is everywhere. It permeates our thoughts, mediates our relations with others, and even creeps into our dreams. The overwhelming bulk of human knowledge is stored and transmitted in language. Language is so ubiquitous that we take it for granted, but without it, society as we now know it would be impossible.

Despite its prevalence in human affairs, language is poorly understood. Misconceptions about it are legion, even among well-educated people, and not even professional linguists can claim to understand it fully. A person is radically mistaken to assume that the nature of language is self-evident or to conclude that we know all about a language just because we speak it. Gradually, however, we are learning about this rather remarkable and purely human instrument of communication. The purpose of this book is to summarize a significant portion of what we know about language for the benefit of those with little or no previous training in linguistics.

There are a number of reasons why an accurate appreciation of language is worth acquiring. First, many serious problems in today's world involve language in an essential way. To what extent are language differences barriers to understanding? Is a universal language feasible or desirable? Should we undertake a massive reform of English spelling? How should children be taught to read? Should the writers of dictionaries bow to popular usage? Is it worthwhile for the government of a multi-lingual nation (like India) to try to impose one language on all speakers as an official national language? If so, which one? At what level should foreign languages be taught in our schools? To what extent are the members of minority groups and the lower classes handicapped in their social and economic advancement by their speech? It is not our concern here to provide answers to these very difficult questions, but anyone interested in finding valid answers to them should not set out without at least a minimal understanding of language.

Second, insights about language are of immense intellectual significance, with direct and indirect relevance to other disciplines. Philosophers, for example, are greatly concerned with language. It is important for our view of man to know whether language is entirely a learned entity or whether it is largely innate. Language, in other words, could be one of the testing grounds on which to settle a long-standing debate between rationalists and empiricists. The rationalist claim is that people are born with innate ideas, that much of psychological organization is "wired" into the organism and genetically transmitted. Empiricists, on the other hand, claim that a person is born, psychologically speaking, as a blank slate and that psychological organization is determined almost entirely by experience, not genetically transmitted. Both rationalists and empiricists have turned to language to find support for their views on this important question, which we will examine in more detail in Chapter Nine.

Philosophers are also curious about language as an instrument of philosophical analysis. Are human languages viable as the media of philosophical inquiry and theory? Can philosophical errors be attributed to the misuse of language? What is the relationship between language and logic?

Language is also relevant to psychology in a number of ways. In fact, since language is largely a mental phenomenon, its study may be considered a branch of psychology. Any adequate theory of human psychology must give some account of our thought processes; language is of central importance here because so many of our thoughts assume linguistic form.

4

Many, if not most, of our concepts are given verbal labels of some sort. Thus the relationship between language and concept formation is of great interest to psychologists. Language also provides a significant test for theories of psychological organization. Languages are highly structured, and we have learned to identify and describe their structures in considerable detail. Any theory of psychological organization, therefore, must adequately accommodate the kinds of structures we know to be characteristic of human languages.

The other social sciences may also benefit to some extent from knowledge about language and the descriptive techniques suited to it. Since the structure of language is more obvious than the other kinds of structures that the social scientist takes an interest in, he may well learn something from an examination of it.

Third, an introduction to the nature of language is important to anyone interested in possible practical applications of the results of linguistic research. Fundamental insights about language should certainly prove valuable to anyone studying or teaching a language (even the native language of the student or teacher). Accurate machine translation, if it can be accomplished at all (and this appears quite doubtful at present), can hardly be programed without a reasonably sophisticated knowledge of language on the part of the programer. Anthropologists must know the language of a people for their investigation of its culture to be most fruitful. Missionary work in uncivilized areas requires a great deal of practical and theoretical knowledge about language. The language of the natives must be learned quickly and well, and considerable understanding is needed to devise and teach an adequate writing system for the native tongue.

Finally, an accurate appreciation of language is valuable if only because no one can be considered truly well educated if he lacks a clear understanding of the instrument of so much of his instruction. Since language permeates virtually all human affairs and is central to so many of them, an appreciation of language can hardly be considered peripheral. An introduction to language really needs no other justification. A person wishing to know and understand himself must in some measure come to understand the character of the linguistic system that plays such a fundamental role in his mental and social life. Language should be understood because it's there.

LINGUISTICS

Linguistics is the study of human language. A linguist who becomes interested in a particular language attempts to take it apart to see how it works, just as a mechanic may, purely out of curiosity, take apart an unfamiliar motor. A mechanic who has taken a motor apart will probably put it back together again; since a linguist takes a language apart only figuratively, his subsequent task is not one of reassembly, but rather one of description. A linguistic description of some language is called a **grammar** of that language. A grammar, then, is a set of statements saying how a language works. It includes, for example, a description of the principles for combining words to form grammatical sentences.

The linguistic description of languages is often undertaken with no ultimate practical goal in mind. **Descriptive linguistics,** in other words, is akin to pure science. A physicist is likely to investigate some aspect of the physical world that interests him with no intention whatsoever of turning the results of his research to practical application; he investigates it because it intrigues him, because he wishes to contribute to human knowledge. Similarly, linguists are interested in one particular aspect of psychological reality, namely the psychological phenomenon we call language. The desire to know more about this phenomenon is ample justification for investigating it.

Descriptive linguistics involves the description of a language at one point in time. **Historical linguistics,** on the other hand, is the study of language history. Historical linguists study the changes that occur in a language through time (and all living languages change through time, however imperceptibly), seeking to reconstruct earlier stages of it where written records are not available and to determine precisely what changes have taken place in the course of its historical development. Other branches of linguistics include **anthropological linguistics,** the investigation of languages as part of the investigation of their associated cultures; **psycholinguistics,** the study of linguistic behavior and the psychological mechanisms responsible for it; **sociolinguistics,** the study of the functioning of language in society; **phonetics,** the analysis of speech sounds with respect to their articulation, acoustic properties, and perception; and **applied linguistics,** the attempt to put the insights resulting from linguistic research to practical uses, particularly in the area of language teaching.

A THUMBNAIL HISTORY
OF LANGUAGE STUDY

The study of language has a long history, although linguistics as we now know it has come into being mainly in the last century and a half. Man has probably wondered about language for as long as he has had it. Cultures very often reflect man's natural concern with language. In some cultures, knowing the real name of a being is believed to give the possessor of this knowledge a certain power over that being. In some Australian tribes, a word similar to the name of a person must be suppressed and another word substituted for it when that person dies. The language of religious rituals is quite commonly considered sacred; any change in the words themselves or even in their pronunciation is felt to threaten the efficacy of the ceremony.

Our own culture is no exception. The Old Testament contains explanations for the origin of language and its diversity: Adam was called upon to name every living creature, and linguistic diversification is related in the story of the Tower of Babel. More recently, many Roman Catholics opposed the decision to allow the Mass to be conducted in the vernacular rather than in Latin. A modern form of "word magic" can be found in the world of marketing, where considerable emphasis is laid on finding a suitable name for a new product, or in the realm of standards of conduct, where a college student may be expelled for using a four-letter word.

A significant linguistic tradition developed in India long ago, but it was not known in the Western world until the nineteenth century. The religious hymns of the Hindus were composed in Sanskrit around 1200–800 B.C. Over the centuries, Sanskrit of course changed. The Hindu priests, however, believed that the efficacy of their religious practices could not be assured unless their renditions of the ritual hymns were completely faithful to the original with respect to both text and pronunciation. Hindu grammar consequently developed as an attempt to preserve the religious language in full detail. The classic work of this tradition, dated around 400 B.C., is attributed to a grammarian named Pāṇini. To this day, Pāṇini's grammar has not been surpassed as a concise and insightful description of Sanskrit. It has dominated Indian grammar throughout the centuries.

Western grammatical tradition can be traced to the ancient Greeks, who raised the question of whether there is something essential in the relation between a word and the thing to which it refers or whether the

7

relation is an arbitrary one. For example, is there some way in which the word *fish* is specially (or uniquely) suited to the creatures we angle for with hook, line, and sinker, or is the fact that we call these creatures *fish* just an accident of linguistic history? To the Greeks we trace the notion that the elements of a language can be classified into "parts of speech," such as nouns, verbs, and conjunctions. We can also find in their work the idea of case.

The grammatical practice of the Romans was based squarely on that of the Greeks. Throughout the medieval period, Latin occupied a central position in the world of education and scholarship. When one studied grammar, one usually studied Latin grammar. Even in modern times, Latin grammar has often been used as a model for the description of other languages. As a result, there is an essentially unbroken grammatical tradition stretching from the twentieth century all the way back to ancient Greece. Children are still being taught about parts of speech.

Modern linguists have often tended to slight what they call **traditional grammar** and to underestimate the insights of medieval and early modern students of language. Traditional grammarians have been charged with confusing speech and writing, with slavishly copying the dogmas that previous grammarians have expounded, with trying to force all languages into the Latin mold, and with trying erroneously to equate language and logic. There is more than just a grain of truth in these accusations. Many of us can remember learning in school to conjugate English verbs according to a paradigmatic scheme suited to Latin but not to English:

I praise	*we praise*
you praise	*you praise*
he, she, it praises	*they praise*

There is no point in learning to parrot six present-tense verb forms for English *praise*, because there are actually only two:

I, you, we, they praise
he, she, it praises

To find out why a six-form display was adopted for English, one has only to look at Latin, where a six-form display is proper:

laudō	'I praise'	*laudāmus*	'we praise'
laudās	'you praise'	*laudātis*	'you praise'
laudat	'he, she, it praises'	*laudant*	'they praise'

Nevertheless, the insights of traditional grammar are deeper, and its contributions greater, than its critics tend to realize. It is much easier to make sweeping criticisms than to evaluate with care and understanding many centuries of work. As our theories of language structure become more sophisticated, we become more conscious of the fact that traditional grammarians were not so far off the track. There is indeed some close (though not fully understood) relation between language and logic. Linguistic elements do fall into classes, like nouns and verbs, although there are many more such classes than traditional grammarians realized. Linguists have come to the conclusion that all human languages are similarly designed, but many traditional grammarians anticipated them long ago by engaging in the investigation of **universal grammar**. Traditional grammar books are not really wrong, but they do share with all other attempts to describe languages, including the most advanced, the inevitable fault of being incomplete.

Our understanding of language took some long strides during the nineteenth century. Most importantly, scholars came to appreciate what it means for one language to be **related** to another. They established that most of the languages of Europe and northern India are related as members of a single language **family**, which is known as the Indo-European family. It has been claimed, and not without reason, that the discovery of the relationship and historical development of these languages is to be classed with the truly great products of human intelligence. These philological advances, it is interesting to note, can be attributed in part to the influence of the linguistic tradition of ancient India. Previously unknown in the West, this tradition came to the attention of philologists when they realized that Sanskrit was related to the major European languages. The analytic techniques that had long ago been applied in the description of Sanskrit have been a significant factor in the evolution of modern linguistics.

In addition to their view of linguistic relationship, the nineteenth-century philologists contributed other insights. They discovered that changes in the sound system of a language are regular, in a special sense we will examine later, and not idiosyncratic, as one might suspect. They recognized the extent and importance of the **borrowing** of linguistic traits from one language into another. The advances they made constituted a beginning, not a routine culmination of any antecedent tradition of historical linguistics. Their techniques are now being applied to language

9

families around the world, and the avenues of research that they opened up are far from being exhausted. In Chapters Seven and Eight we will examine language change and relatedness more fully.

A language is a complicated system that changes slowly through the centuries. To understand the changes that occur in such a system, the linguist must first have some knowledge of the structure of the system at one or more points in time. Descriptive linguistics, then, is logically prior to historical linguistics, though it emerged as a distinct and self-conscious discipline only in the twentieth century.

For several decades, descriptive linguists laid the heaviest emphasis on the sound systems of languages, paying relatively little attention to meaning or to **syntax** (the principles for combining words to form grammatical sentences). There were several reasons for this emphasis. The preceding tradition of historical linguistics relied most heavily on the sound systems of languages; descriptive linguists inherited this tendency, along with the inclination to look for regularities in sound systems. At the same time, interest was growing in the description of the unknown and poorly known languages of the world, particularly the languages of the American Indians. In studying an unknown language, one of the first things a linguist has to do is master its sounds and devise a notation for transcribing utterances. In addition, the strong but unfortunate influence of behaviorism in psychology left its mark. The pseudoscientific doctrine that only overt, externally observable behavior is valid evidence in psychological investigation reinforced the tendency of linguists to concentrate on sound systems and to ignore the more abstract domains of meaning and syntax.

In recent years, linguists have recognized that an understanding of meaning and syntax is crucial to an understanding of language. (Traditional grammarians recognized this centuries ago and in fact anticipated many modern "discoveries" in these areas.) They have also recognized that language is basically a psychological phenomenon, one that cannot be studied fruitfully just by observing linguistic behavior. The resulting approach to the investigation of language, a movement known as **generative grammar**, provides the basic orientation of this book. Generative grammar is very much in keeping with contemporary views on the philosophy of science and also, as we have just seen, with the ideas of traditional grammarians. It represents both a revolution in grammatical thinking and a reaffirmation of the validity of structural insights about language that have been accumulating for many centuries.

Our purpose here is not to examine the intricacies of competing linguistic theories in order to show how they differ. Rather than wandering aimlessly through theoretical disputes and terminological thickets, we will attempt to say as simply and directly as possible what language is and how it is put together. Because we want to understand ourselves, it is important that we try to understand this psychological entity which permeates our mental and social life. To the extent that linguistics sheds some light on the nature and structure of language, it is a subject of interest to all of us.

CHAPTER TWO

An Initial Look

at Language

LANGUAGE ACQUISITION

Children display an amazing ability to become fluent speakers of any language consistently spoken around them. Every normal human child who is not reared in virtual isolation from language use soon comes to speak one or more languages natively.

The child's acquisition of his native language is not dependent on any special tutoring. Parents may spend many hours "reinforcing" every recognizable bit of their child's verbal activity with a smile or some other reward, or trying by means of "baby talk" to bridge the gap between their mature linguistic competence and the child's incipient one. But there is no particular reason to believe that such activity has any bearing on the child's ultimate success in becoming a native speaker of his parents' language. Children can pick up a language by playing with other children who happen to speak it just as well as they can through the concentrated efforts of doting parents. All they seem to need is sufficient exposure to the language in question.

This capacity for acquiring language is remarkable for a number of reasons. It is remarkable first because of its uniformity throughout the human race. There simply are no cases of normal human children who, given the chance, fail to acquire a native language. By way of comparison, it is not at all unusual for a child to fail to master arithmetic, reading, swimming, or gymnastics despite a considerable amount of instruction. Language acquisition, in other words, is species uniform. It is also species specific. Every normal person learns a human language, but no other animal, not even the most intelligent ape, has been shown to be capable of making the slightest progress in this direction, although some animals can learn to solve problems, use tools, and so on. Language acquisition thus appears to be different in kind from acquisition of the other skills mentioned.

The process is further remarkable for its comparative speed and perfection. When we actually attempt to take a language apart to see how it works, we find that it is extraordinarily complex and that it involves highly abstract organizational principles. Yet, within the first few years of his life, every human child has succeeded in mastering at least one such system. Furthermore, the linguistic system that the child masters is for all practical purposes identical to the one employed by the people around him. The differences are slight indeed when measured against the magnitude of the accomplishment. If the child is regularly exposed to two languages, he will very probably learn both; moreover, he will by and large succeed in keeping the two linguistic systems separate, which is a considerable achievement in itself.

It has often been observed that adults are not capable of learning a language in the natural, spontaneous way that children are. For the adult, learning a foreign language usually involves great effort and seldom results in perfect mastery of the new idiom. An American child of six who moves to Japan with his parents will be at home in Japanese in no time; his parents, however, may have to depend on the child as an interpreter. The differences between language learning in the child and in the adult may have been exaggerated, but the onset of adolescence does seem to constitute some sort of dividing line in the ability to master a new linguistic system. For example, a person past adolescence is not likely to learn to speak a foreign language without a noticeable accent, however slight.

The observation that every normal human child learns one or more languages unless he is reared in isolation from the regular use of language raises some interesting questions. What constitutes normality in this context? What happens when a child is not exposed to language during his early years?

With regard to language acquisition, normality can be interpreted very broadly. In fact, language learning is possible despite severe physical or psychological deficiencies. Neither the inability to hear nor the inability to vocalize will necessarily prevent a child from mastering a linguistic system. In the case of deaf children, some special training is of course required, since the deaf obviously cannot learn a language by hearing it. Nevertheless, deaf children can acquire a very good grasp of a language through various visual devices. Language learning is even possible when deafness is accompanied by blindness, as shown by the accomplishments of Helen Keller. It is chiefly in the domain of vocal articulation that deaf children have the greatest difficulty, as would be expected. But language is like an iceberg: its overt manifestation is only a small part of the whole. The ability of the child to master all but this one small part, despite total deafness, is remarkable indeed. Moreover, even deaf children can make significant progress toward learning to speak normally, particularly when deafness sets in some time after birth.

Children who are unable to use their vocal organs to produce speech sounds nevertheless learn a language with no particular difficulty. They are able to understand language perfectly and can learn to communicate through writing as well as anyone else can. The acquisition of language is thus in no crucial way dependent on verbalization.

Native language acquisition is much less likely to be affected by mental retardation than is the acquisition of other intellectual skills. A child who is mentally deficient to the extent that he cannot be taught arithmetic can still acquire language. Only in the most severe cases, in the lower range of idiocy, is language completely absent. Here is another indication that language learning is different in kind, in some essential way, from the attainment of other intellectual abilities.

Children can be quite inventive in regard to language. Secret languages like pig latin provide good illustrations of their linguistic flexibility and creativeness. According to specific principles of transposition, the speaker of pig latin transforms ordinary English utterances into sound sequences that prove quite baffling to the uninitiated observer: *Is-thay entence-say, or-fay example-ay, is-ay itten-wray in-ay ig-pay atin-lay.* Such languages, usually based on a standard language in a straightforward way, are not at all uncommon. Children can easily become fluent in such a language, and, since adults are usually slower in these matters, can use it as a secret code to prevent adults from monitoring their conversations.

However, a child cannot invent a language from scratch. There are a number of cases on record of children who grew up in the wilderness in isolation from human society, in some instances raised by wolves as extra cubs. None of them had invented any kind of language when found. Similarly, there are cases of children raised in human society but in isolation from language use (for instance, raised by a deaf-mute or shut off from the world except for feeding). Under such conditions, language apparently does not develop, even when two children are raised together. Exposure to language is thus a minimum requirement for language acquisition. Once brought into normal society, where language is regularly used, children who have grown up in the wilderness or in linguistic isolation can usually make some progress toward learning to use a language. If the child is found at an early enough age and is not deficient in hearing or intelligence, the effects of isolation may be largely or totally overcome. It is difficult to say anything more conclusive because of the paucity of such cases and the difficulty of interpreting them.

As we noted in Chapter One, the business of linguistics is to arrive at an understanding of language. Central to this concern is an understanding of the capacity for language acquisition, which we have seen to be noteworthy for a number of reasons. An adequate account of language acquisition is still very far from our grasp, but this goal provides a great deal of motivation for investigating the structure of languages. One reason why linguistics is worth doing, in other words, is that it can ultimately be expected to shed some light on the nature of this rather remarkable aspect of the psychological development of the human child.

ON ORIGIN AND SPECIES

We observed in the preceding section that language acquisition is species uniform and species specific. All human beings learn a language, but no other animals, not even the most intelligent ones, attain to anything comparable. These remarks deserve some amplification, since misconceptions related to this point are quite common.

People have sometimes supposed that racial differences are responsible for linguistic differences, but there is absolutely no evidence to support such a contention. Language acquisition is species uniform—any human child is capable of becoming a native speaker of any human language. Which language a child learns depends entirely on his models, those from whom he learns to talk. Consider the American Negro population, for instance. Imported originally from Africa, this population now has English for its native tongue. Thus both Negroes and whites speak English, and both English and African languages (which are unrelated to English) are spoken by Negroes; this observation is perhaps sufficient to establish that language and race are independent. We may also cite the children of American immigrants of all races and nationalities, who grow up speaking perfect American English.

American Negro speech is in general noticeably distinct from the speech of white Americans, and it might be supposed that the differences stem from racial characteristics. Differences in pronunciation might be attributed to anatomical details, such as the size of the lips, to take one conceivable hypothesis. In fact, however, the speech of many Negroes is indistinguishable from that of the white population, which rules out the possibility that race is the determining factor. No more significance is to be attached to the special character of Negro speech than, say, to the special character of New England speech. These race-correlated dialect differences are perpetuated because Negro children usually learn to talk from other Negroes.

Just as there is no inherent relation between language and race, there is none between language and culture. The Athabaskan family of American Indian languages embraces speakers of several distinct cultures. Conversely, languages of two unrelated families, Keresan and Tanoan, are represented in the Rio Grande Pueblo culture. Such examples demonstrate that neither language nor culture dictates the form the other will assume. Nevertheless, language and culture are tightly intertwined. The most obvious instance is literature, oral and written; principles of literary style, prosody, and so on that are developed in terms of one language cannot always find satisfactory equivalents in a second. Words designating concepts specific to a given culture are likely to present a serious translation problem. The adoption of a new language is often accompanied by the gradual adoption of a new culture. Language and culture are closely associated in practice, therefore, but they are basically independent from one another.

It has sometimes been maintained that primitive peoples speak primitive languages. In fact, however, there is no correlation between degree of cultural advancement and complexity of linguistic structure. The languages of primitive peoples can be every bit as complex and rich in expressive power as any European language. Anything that can be said in one language can be said in any other, though perhaps more clumsily. Claims that "primitive" languages have very small vocabularies, that they have no grammar, that most of their words are onomatopoetic, that they cannot express abstract ideas, and so on are just plain false. The Eskimos have words for specific varieties of snow but no generic, more abstract term (like our *snow*) that embraces all varieties of it. This does not mean that they are incapable of abstract thought or that their language is impoverished; it simply means that snow is more important to them than to us, so that their linguistic categorization in this area of experience is more detailed than ours.

Just as there are no primitive languages, there are no "corrupt" languages. Languages change, but they do not decay. On no rational basis is it correct to lament that language X, at some distant point in the past, was a pure and perfect vehicle to express our thoughts but that it has declined steadily to its present state of decadence. This is so much puristic nonsense. The English of today and the English of a thousand years ago are very different; by the same token, however, the English of a thousand years ago was radically different from its antecedent of a still earlier period. At any stage, a language is fully adequate to its purpose. It is the product of change and, if it continues to be spoken, will continue to undergo changes. The idea of a "pure" language is illusory.

The question of how language arose in the human species has intrigued scholars for centuries, but we really know nothing about the origin of language. As far back as we can trace any language historically, it looks like the same kind of entity as any contemporary language. The languages of two or three thousand years ago do not seem to be any simpler or any more primitive than the languages of today, or any different in kind. There must have been a time in the history of mankind when language was not fully developed, when men used some primitive forerunner of the complex linguistic systems used today. From all indications, however, this time must be so far in the past that we cannot hope to find any record of these earlier stages. With respect to the origin of human language, it is quite possible that we will always be limited to speculation.

Many theories concerning the origin of language have been advanced, but none worth taking seriously. Some people have speculated that language stems from primitive man's imitation of animal cries. Others have suggested that instinctive cries of pain or the grunts that accompany great physical exertion were the original source of speech. Neither idea has any evidence in its favor. Moreover, such vocalizations are so untypical of human language that it is hard to see why they should be postulated as the source of all language. Beyond this, no one has ever demonstrated how, in accordance with reasonable psychological principles, language in all its present complexity and abstractness could ever develop from such modest beginnings. Future alleviation of our ignorance concerning the origin of language, if it ever comes, will have to be the by-product of a great increase in our understanding of psychological structure and the principles of neural evolution. It is almost certain that man acquired language as the result of evolutionary changes in the structure of his mind. It was not a matter of someone "getting the idea" and others "catching on," which is almost equivalent to the notion that a group of primitive men sat down around a conference table and decided to invent language.

We learn nothing about the origin of language by examining the various ways in which animals communicate. Some animal communication takes place via fixed systems of signals, but there the resemblance between animal communication and human language ends.

Systems of animal communication invariably reflect one of two organizational schemes. Under one scheme, signals vary continuously along one or a small number of dimensions. Bees, for instance, are able to communicate to one another with great precision the location of a food source by means of a dance done in the hive. The distance of the source from the hive is indicated by the frequency with which the dancing bee makes a turn; the greater the distance, the less frequent the turns. The direction of the source, with respect to the position of the sun, is indicated by the angle of the straight portion of the bee's dance. Bees can therefore transmit an unlimited number of messages. They are unlimited in a rather trivial sense, however, for every message is a variant of the single message schema "There is nectar at distance X from here in direction Y." Human language has aspects similar to this, but they are rather peripheral. A parallel case would be the spectrum of our verbal responses to pain. According to the intensity of the pain, the response varies along a continuum from a mild "Ouch!" all the way up to an agonized scream.

Human languages are unlimited in a much more interesting sense than this. If you try to write down all the sentences of English, or of any other language, you will quickly come to realize the futility of the task. You could go on writing forever without exhausting the set of well-formed sentences, each of which has its own particular meaning. In this way human languages differ from systems of animal communication displaying the second type of organizational scheme, which calls for a small, finite number of discrete signals. Higher primates, such as gibbons or chimpanzees, are often credited with such a system. One type of cry may indicate impending danger, another the desire for food, and so on, up to a dozen or so separate signals. With this scheme, there is a strict numerical limitation on possible messages, something that is lacking in human language.

Human language is thus crucially different from both varieties of animal communication. A human speaker controls an unlimited set of discrete signals; animal communication systems involve either a limited set of discrete signals or a continuum of nondiscrete signals along just a few dimensions. This very fundamental difference between human language and animal communication in itself far outweighs their similarities. Several other important differences can be pointed out, however.

The most glaring difference lies in the great structural complexity of the signals of a human language. A bee's dance or a chimpanzee's cry has virtually no internal structure other than that involved in the actual physical production of the signal. Every sentence of a human language, however, displays structure on at least two levels. First, it consists of a linear string of words, each of which has a more or less definite individual meaning and each of which consists of a sequence of sounds drawn from the small inventory of sounds used systematically in the language. Second, every sentence has a complex grammatical structure. (We will examine grammatical structures in Chapter Five.) There is no counterpart to either of these levels of structure in systems of animal communication.

Another difference is that learning is much more important as a factor in human language than in animal communication. Human languages have very much in common, but they differ from one another on many specific points. When a person learns German, he must learn at least all those details that distinguish German from Burmese and every other possible human language. Regardless of how much of human language is innate, the learning task is considerable. Just mastering the collection of words to be found in a small German dictionary is a sizable task. The communicative dance of bees, by way of contrast, must be innately specified virtually in its entirety, and there is nothing to suggest that the situation is basically different with respect to other systems of animal communication.

Finally, we may observe that animal communication systems are closed, whereas human languages are open-ended. As long as bees communicate, they will only be able to exchange variants of the same message—in what direction the nectar is and how far away. Apes cannot communicate freely about anything for which they do not have a specific signal, and even in these cases the possibilities are extremely restricted. People, on the other hand, can talk about anything they can observe or imagine. Moreover, what they can say on any given topic is almost unlimited. This greater flexibility stems in large part from the complex grammatical structure of human languages. Furthermore, new items are constantly being added to the lexicon of a language. Words and fixed phrases are continually being coined and borrowed from other languages to meet the changing communicative needs of speakers. There is no counterpart to this in animal communication.

From these observations, it seems to follow that there is no reason to posit any significant relation between the communication systems of humans and other animals. They are similar only in that they allow for the transmission of information according to fixed principles, and this similarity is dwarfed by the differences.

SOUND AND MEANING

If the difference between human and animal communication had to be summarized in one word, a good choice for that word would be **novelty**.

Every time a bee communicates the location of a supply of nectar, it is repeating a variant of one basic message that has already been transmitted among bees countless times. When an animal gives a call warning others of its kind that danger is imminent, it does not make up a new one; the call is one that these animals have used many times before. There is no novelty here, only a repetition of past communicative events.

This is decidedly not the case with respect to human language. One outstanding characteristic of language use is its creativity, its freedom from control on the basis of the past linguistic activity of the user. Almost every sentence that occurs is a novel one and has never occurred before. (If you are not convinced of this, you might try to find in some other book a duplicate of any sentence on this page.) Exceptions of course have to be made for popular expressions and very short sentences—for example, **Come in!** or **Supper is ready**—as well as for instances of intentional quotation, but the point is still a valid one. A human speaker has the ability to create and understand an unlimited number of completely novel sentences. If a sentence duplicates one that has occurred previously, chances are that it was created anew the second time and that the repetition was purely coincidental. Talking does not consist of parroting sentences that have been heard and memorized.

Our ability to create and understand novel sentences cannot be accounted for by any appeal to the human capacity for analogizing. Some people have maintained that novel sentences are constructed by analogy from sentences previously experienced. Suppose, for example, that someone has heard and remembered the sentences **Peter will help with the dishes, Peter will help with the laundry**, and **Barbara will help with the dishes**. By analogizing from these three, by solving the proportion, he creates the sentence **Barbara will help with the laundry**. The latter sentence has never before occurred in his experience, but on the analogy of the other three, he is able to create or understand it, despite its novelty. This claim is simply false, for we do not go around collecting sentences to hold in memory for future use in speaking and understanding. Nor do we have to search through our personal linguistic archives and carry out the steps of solving a proportion whenever we want to say something. We create and understand sentences quite spontaneously.

Equally inadequate to account for the novel character of our linguistic creations is the view that a language is a set of verbal habits. We will not attempt to document why this view is untenable; it is so deeply embedded in the tradition of behaviorist psychology that a careful exposition of the concepts involved would take us far beyond the scope of this book. Suffice it to say that no version of the stimulus-response model of psychological organization can even begin to account for the complex structure of human language (to be examined in Part Two) and that the mechanisms of conditioning and reinforcement are in principle inadequate to explain language acquisition.

By the time a child reaches the age of five or six, he has mastered the fundamentals of his native language. He has achieved the ability to create and understand, spontaneously and effortlessly, an unlimited number of sentences that are completely novel to his experience. If we wish to understand language and language acquisition (to the extent that we can at present), we must first have some idea about the nature of the competence that is acquired when someone learns to talk. Bearing linguistic creativity in mind, let us therefore address ourselves to this question: What sort of thing is a language?

To start out in very broad terms, we may say that a language is an instrument of communication. When person A has some idea he wishes to convey to person B, he performs certain physical actions with his articulatory organs (for example, his lips, tongue, and vocal cords). These actions create sound waves which travel through the air to B. B hears the sounds and, if all goes well, B gets the message. This characterization is basically valid, even though a language may sometimes be used without communicative intent. If A stubs his toe and lets fly a volley of profanity, for instance, his verbalization is probably quite devoid of any desire to communicate.

Any given attempt to communicate by way of a language is of course subject to partial or complete failure. Speaker A may try to get an idea across to B and simply fail. Perhaps B does not speak the language A is using. Perhaps B cannot hear the utterance clearly and mistakes one word for another. Perhaps A makes a slip of the tongue and says exactly the opposite of what he wants to say. For the most part, however, our communicative attempts are reasonably successful. The idea B gets is usually the idea A wants to convey. Although there are many possible sources of error, and despite the fact that communication is never perfect, we are usually successful enough with speech to continue using it without having to worry very much about its effectiveness.

When A wishes to convey an idea to B, the signal that A produces to do so is a sequence of sounds. B cannot observe A's idea directly; he can only observe the sounds A emits. From them, he somehow deduces what he believes A's thought to be. A and B use a language to communicate, but the language is neither the sounds passing through the air nor the thought they represent. The language is the device that allows A and B to pair the two. It is some set of principles that make it possible for A to translate the idea he wants to express into an overt signal and that enable

B to reconstruct this idea from that signal. A language is a device that establishes sound–meaning correlations, pairing meanings with signals to enable people to exchange ideas via observable sequences of sounds.

Take a concrete example. A is looking out the window and sees a strange sight. To let B in on what is going on, A utters the sentence *The cat just chased a dog up a tree!* B gets the message; he understands the sentence and is now in possession of information about the essential aspects of the situation that A is reporting. A has used English to translate this information into a sound sequence, and B has used English to deduce the same or comparable information from the sound sequence. English is a device which, among other things, establishes a correlation between the sound sequence *The cat just chased a dog up a tree!* and a meaning. Part Two of this book is devoted to a detailed examination of the internal structure of a language. For the moment we will limit ourselves to a few preliminary but important observations about this structure.

It is apparent that the sentence *The cat just chased a dog up a tree!* has meaning only because the individual words of the sentence have meanings. The meaning of a sentence is determined in some way by the meanings of the words from which it is constructed. It is of course not true that the meaning of a sentence is the simple sum of the meanings of the words it contains; *The cat just chased a dog up a tree!* and *The dog just chased a cat up a tree!* contain the same words, but their meanings differ. The relationship between the meaning of a sentence and the meanings of its parts is thus more abstract than a simple additive one. It will be examined more carefully in Chapter Four.

The relation between a word and its meaning is in general quite arbitrary; it is a matter of convention. There is no inherent reason why felines should be designated by the word *cat* instead of by some other word. That the word *cat* is used in this way by English speakers is merely an accident of linguistic history. In other languages, other strings of sounds are used to designate those furry creatures with sharp claws. Moreover, it would not be at all surprising to learn that in some other language a similarly pronounced word meant something else entirely. There is no mysterious sense in which a word and the concept with which it is paired are specially suited to one another. A language would function just as well if its word–concept pairings were entirely different.

As we look at various languages, we do in fact find that they differ from one another in their word–meaning pairings (except, of course, for words that are borrowed from one language into another and for cognate forms in related languages; these will be discussed in Part Three). Occasionally there are similarities. For example, the Aztec word **huel**, pronounced like the English adverb **well**, has a similar meaning. Such similarities, however, are sporadic and stand out clearly as exceptions to the general rule. Looking beyond this isolated case, we find, for instance, that the English and Aztec forms for something that is eaten are quite different; **food** and **tlaqual** are not at all similar. Conversely, similar forms normally differ in meaning. The English word **ma** means 'mother.' There happens to be a form **ma** in Aztec, but it means 'hand,' not 'mother.' The few similar pairings that do crop up can safely be attributed to chance.

It is a generally valid principle, therefore, that the relation between a word and its meaning is arbitrary. A word designates some concept, but there is no inherent connection between the two. That they are paired is an accident of linguistic history.

One must admit a number of partial exceptions to this generally valid principle. Their importance is hard to assess with any precision, but it is certainly not major. The principle requires only qualification, not drastic amendment.

Many words are clearly **onomatopoetic**, that is, imitative of non-linguistic sounds. For these words, of course, there is a special relationship between meaning and pronunciation. The English words **bow-wow** and **moo,** for example, resemble to some degree the sounds made by dogs and cows respectively. This is not an accident. These words were most certainly coined with imitative intent, since the incidence of apparently imitative English words used to designate the sounds made by animals is much too great to attribute to chance. **Meow** does sound something like the sound made by a cat; **baa** is not a bad imitation of what sheep do; and so on. Onomatopoetic forms are not limited to this semantic domain, although the imitative character of forms cited from other semantic domains is not always so obvious. In English, a bell goes **ding-dong**; a clock goes **tick-tock**; we speak of a metallic **clang**; a bomb explodes with a **boom**; and so forth.

It is interesting to observe that even imitative words such as these are to a large degree conventionalized. The corresponding imitative words are different in different languages, despite their similarity to one another and to the sound they designate. To take some classic examples, the crowing of a rooster is represented as **cock-a-doodle-doo** in English, as **kikeriki** in German, and as **coquerico** in French. The sound of whispering is imitated

25

to a certain degree in English *whisper,* German *flüstern,* French *chuchoter,* and Spanish *susurar,* but these imitative attempts are somewhat different from one another; a speaker must learn the correct imitation for his language, and to this extent the forms are conventional. French sheep go *bê* instead of *baa,* and bells go *bim-bam* when they ring in German.

A second qualification of the principle is often proposed, the validity of which is much harder to assess. Words, generally speaking, have meaning, but the individual sounds that make them up do not. *Ma,* for instance, means something, but the vowel of *ma,* which is symbolized [a], by itself means nothing. (Linguists use square brackets to enclose phonetic symbols designating sounds; they are to be distinguished from the representations of these sounds in ordinary spelling.) It is often maintained, however, that some sounds are associated with particular ideas or give certain impressions. For example, the vowel sound of *heat,* symbolized [i], is said to be connected with the notion of lightness, brightness, or lack of substance, at least when contrasted with [a]. The latter, in relative terms, tends to give the impression of size and power. These claims cannot be dismissed entirely, but it would be easy and tempting to overestimate their importance. We will examine two more examples but reserve final judgment.

The vowel sound of *hut,* symbolized [ʌ], often occurs in English words that denote concepts involving heaviness, dullness, or filth. Among others, we find: *dull, blunder, bungle, clumsy, tub, stub, slug, plug, rut, gutter, gull, gully, gullet, gullible, bug, jug, humdrum, dumb, humbug, slum, slush, muck, mud, muddle, mug, numb, numskull, slut, mumble, grumble, grunt, disgruntled, mumps, gummy, sullen, mull, bum, plumbing, stun, slumber, flunk, bump, lump, club, rubble, rumble, hulk, rump, pudgy, sulk, pump, clump, bulk, cudgel, thump, hump, bulge, junk.* It would be easy to add more. On the basis of this list, the sound [ʌ] seems to have negative connotations for English speakers.

The vowel sound of *hit,* symbolized [ɪ], often occurs in English words whose meanings involve rapid or repetitive motion, lack of intensity, or smallness: *flip, twitter, swish, flit, titter, giggle, limp, little, fiddle, rip, tip, flimsy, sip, pimple, dimple, zip, whip, slip, pin, flicker, strip, primp, fickle, tickle, nimble, nipple, film, thimble, lick, tingle, jingle, gimmick, tint, lint, hint, slit, twig, twinkle, twinge, twit, sizzle, skim, whim, kid, wrinkle, click, fizzle, fidget, filch, pilfer, ripple, cricket, crimp, crick, crinkle, frill, fringe, pinch, nibble, whisper.* It would not be entirely unreasonable, therefore, to argue that the sound [ɪ] gives the impression of rapidity or insignificance.

We should be careful not to overestimate the importance of this kind of **sound symbolism.** It is all too easy to abuse the concept and read symbolism into all sorts of cases where it is not operative. Sound symbolism is not imaginary, but neither is it very powerful; there are many exceptions to seeming correspondences between sounds and components of meaning. While [ʌ] is often associated in English with heaviness, dullness, or filth, *cut* and *sun* are hardly characterized by these notions. Conversely, neither *heavy* nor *filth* contains the vowel [ʌ]. In any event, sound symbolism merely qualifies the arbitrary character of word–meaning pairings and in no sense prevails over it. Given the negative connotations of the sound [ʌ], it is still an almost wholly arbitrary, unpredictable fact about English that insects are designated by the word *bug.* The symbolism in no way renders nonarbitrary the choice of *bug* to designate them, out of the many possible words containing [ʌ].

Nursery words constitute another partial exception to the principle that the relation between a word and its meaning is arbitrary. Perhaps because of their ease of articulation, certain sounds are consistently among the first that a child learns to produce deliberately. These include the vowels [a] and [æ] (as in *bra* and *hat*) and consonants like [m n b d p t] (which are pronounced the way you think they are). It turns out that the words children use for 'father' and 'mother,' in languages all over the world, are very often composed of sounds drawn from this list. In English, for example, we have the words *mama, papa, mom, mommy, dada, daddy, dad, ma, pa,* and *pop.* Compare the words designating the father in a number of other languages: Spanish *papá,* Russian *papa,* German **Papa,** Swahili *baba,* Turkish *baba,* Hungarian *apa,* Takelma *ma,* Aztec *ta,* and Diegueño *ntat.* (Takelma, Aztec, and Diegueño are three unrelated American Indian languages.) Forms designating the mother include French *maman,* Russian *mama,* Swahili *mama,* Turkish *ana,* Hungarian *anya,* Takelma *ni,* Aztec *nan,* Diegueño *ntal,* and Chinese *ma.* These similarities are not too surprising, since the sounds in these words are among those acquired early and since the child's parents are virtually the first entities he has occasion to name. Another contributing factor, no doubt, is the eagerness of the parents to recognize references to themselves in the child's vocalizations.

To summarize, a language can be viewed as an instrument of communication. It serves to establish sound–meaning correlations, so that messages can be sent by the exchange of overt acoustic signals. The meaning of a sentence is determined by the meanings of the words from which it is constructed, and the basis for the sound–meaning correlations established by a language is thus to be found in the relations between individual words and their meanings. The bond between a word and its meaning is for the most part arbitrary, or conventional, with only marginal qualifications.

LINGUISTIC SUBSYSTEMS

As speakers of a language, we are capable of stringing words together to form novel sentences that express our thoughts. In learning a language, then, one thing that we have to learn is a set of words, each of which pairs a meaning and a pronunciation. In addition, we must learn some set of principles that tell us how individual words may be combined to form sentences. For purposes of discussion, we can therefore isolate three aspects of linguistic structure; to describe a language, we have to talk about the meanings of words, about the sound sequences that are paired with these meanings, and about the ways in which words combine with one another to form sentences. Accordingly, we will speak of a language as involving a **semantic system**, a **phonological system**, and a **syntactic system**.

In speaking of the semantic system of a language, we are referring not only to the fact that the words of the language have meanings but also to the way in which they divide the range of our conceptual experience into categories. In English, for example, we make a linguistic distinction between the colors designated by the words **blue** and **green**. There is no psychological necessity to this distinction; in many languages, a single term covers the entire portion of the color spectrum that includes blue and green. In Hopi (an American Indian language), different words are used for water in its free states and water held in a container. There is no corresponding lexical distinction in English, since we use **water** for both. No two languages match exactly with respect to how experience is categorized.

Although the choice of a sound sequence to designate a given concept is essentially arbitrary, the sequence that is chosen must fall within certain limits imposed by the structure of the language. A language is characterized by a phonological system, and every native word of the language is represented by a sound sequence that meets the restrictions of this system.

Listen to someone speaking English and compare this with someone speaking, say, French. The auditory effect is very different; English and French just do not sound alike. They have different phonological systems, different sets of principles determining the pronunciation of sentences. Phonological systems will be discussed more fully in Chapter Six, so we will be content here with some general observations. At least three main facets of phonological structure can be discerned: inventories of sound types, effects of neighboring sounds on one another, and permissible sound sequences. The fact that languages invariably differ from one another in these three areas accounts in part for their different auditory effects.

A language is characterized by an inventory of sound types, and every native word of the language is composed of a sequence of sounds drawn from this inventory. Among the sounds characteristic of English, we have already used [a æ i ɪ ʌ m n b d p t] in examples, and there are quite a few more. Other languages use other sounds. English has the sounds [č ǰ] (the initial sounds of *char* and *jar*), but French has neither; German has the sound [x] (the last sound of *Bach*), but neither English nor French has; and so on. Moreover, sounds that we would be inclined to call "the same" in two languages are not necessarily identical in phonetic detail. Both English and French have a [t] sound, but the two sounds differ noticeably in their phonetic properties, at least to a trained observer.

Neighboring sounds in an utterance tend to affect one another, in ways that differ somewhat from language to language. A sound may be pronounced in one way when uttered in isolation but in a slightly different way when placed in a given phonological environment. For instance, the [n] of *ten* is pronounced with the front part of the tongue touching the ridge just behind the upper teeth. However, if the *-th* suffix is added to *ten* to form the word *tenth*, the [n] sound is pronounced differently, with the tongue touching the teeth. This phonological alternation is not peculiar to the word *ten*. The same alternation can be observed by pronouncing *eleven* and *eleventh*, or by comparing the articulation of *ant* and *anthem*.

The phonological system of a language imposes restrictions on combinations of sounds permitted in words. Taking English as an example, we find that some sound sequences are possible English forms and others are not. *Slim* is an English word. *Slin* is not an English word, but it could be. English words may begin with [slɪ] (*slim*); end with [ɪn] (*tin*); have [ɪn]

29

after [l] (*lint*); or have [sl] before [ɪ] (*slit*). The fact that *slin* is not an English word is not due to any constraint on sound sequences imposed by the phonological system of English; it is just an accident of linguistic history. On the other hand, *slih* is not an English word and could not be one. No English word can end in [h], the initial sound of *hat*. (Here we are of course speaking of sounds, not of orthography. Many words, for instance *English*, are spelled with a final *h*, but none ends with the sound [h].) No English word can begin with [tl]. No English word consists entirely of consonants, or has fourteen consecutive vowels, and so on. These constraints hold across the board for all English words. They specify a range of phonological possibilities within which any form must fall for it to be a word of our language. *Stug* is a possible English word that does not happen to occur; *bnug* could not occur as an English form.

Just as there are constraints on the ways in which sounds can be combined to form words, so there are constraints on the ways in which words can be combined to form sentences. Not every string of English words constitutes a grammatical English sentence. The string *Helen picked a flower yesterday* does, but the strings *Snow are white* and *Tree cat dog chased just a up a the* do not. As part of the process of learning a language, a person must master some set of principles that allow him to string words together to form acceptable sentences and to avoid forming unacceptable ones. The syntactic system, or syntax, of a language consists of these principles.

Consider the set of all English words. This set contains many elements, thousands in fact, but it is clearly finite. An exhaustive list of them can be drawn up, as in an unabridged dictionary. It is true that new words are being added to the English lexicon all the time, with others falling into oblivion, and the compilers of dictionaries no doubt overlook some words. Nevertheless, the point remains valid. If one were to list all the words of a language, or all the words familiar to a given speaker, the list could in principle be finite and exhaustive. Things are entirely different with regard to sentences. It is in principle impossible to list all the sentences of a language. A simple observation is enough to establish this: There is no sentence to which we can point and say "Aha! This is the longest sentence of language X." Given any sentence of English (or any other language), it is easy to find a longer sentence, no matter how long the original is. If S is a declarative sentence of English, *I know that S* is also an English sentence. Therefore, since *Booze is expensive* is a grammatical sentence of English, so is *I know that booze is expensive*. Since the latter is, so is the still longer string *I know that I know that booze is expensive*. This entails that *I know that I know that I know that booze is expensive* is also a grammatical sentence. Obviously, we could continue without limit and construct a well-formed sentence of any desired length.

The example is a trivial one, but the point is not. The set of well-formed sentences of English is infinite, and the same is true of every other language. Just as there is no greatest number, so there is no longest sentence of a language. It is in principle impossible to list all the sentences of a language, just as it is in principle impossible to list all the natural numbers. When a person learns a language, he obtains some grasp of an infinite set of sentences. He cannot learn these sentences as a list; rather, he must master some finite set of principles in accordance with which words can be combined to form sentences. These principles are such that they allow for the construction of any one of an unbounded set of possible sentences. Some analogies may prove helpful.

Learning to count involves mastering a small, finite set of principles. We can conceive of these principles as a set of instructions a person learns to carry out. They are such that he can give you the immediate successor of any positive integer you may present him with. Presented with the integer 3749, he can give back 3750. Starting from 1 and applying these principles, a person who has learned to count can continue to count indefinitely. From 1, he arrives at 2; from 2, he arrives at 3; and so on. At no point does he reach a number to which the instructions fail to assign an immediate successor. There is no upper bound beyond which the instructions fail to apply. Clearly, learning to count does not involve simply memorizing pairs of numbers, the second of which is the immediate successor of the first. For one thing, the burden placed on memory would be prohibitive. Moreover, a person who has learned to count can correctly give the successor of a number that he has never before encountered. If someone presents you with the number 459,768,312, you have no particular difficulty arriving at its successor, 459,768,313, and you do not do so by consulting your memory and asking yourself, "Let's see, what number was 459,768,312 paired with?"

Similarly, what a person does when he learns to multiply is master some finite set of principles that are applicable to an unbounded set of pairs of numbers and that yield the correct product for each pair. Once learned, these principles enable him to multiply any two numbers, even if

31

he has never encountered either previously. By mastering a finite set of principles, or instructions, for multiplying, a person obtains a grasp of infinitely many sets of numbers x-y-z such that x times y equals z. In some sense, he "knows" that 13,479 times 231,641 equals 3,122,289,039; he has probably never reflected on this particular fact, but it is within his competence to discover or verify it should he have occasion to. His competence is finite (it must be, since the human organism is finite), but it projects to an infinity of cases.

In just this sense the fluent speaker of a language controls an unbounded set of grammatical sentences. He has mastered a finite set of principles specifying how words can be combined to form sentences, and these principles project to an infinite set of grammatical sentences of the language. Most of these sentences will never actually occur in his linguistic experience, yet they fall within the range of syntactic possibilities specified by the structural principles he has mastered. By mastering them, he has in effect learned the distinction between strings of words that constitute grammatical sentences and strings of words that do not. If English is the language he has mastered, he has learned the distinction between grammatical strings like *Snow is white* and *The cat just chased a dog up a tree* on the one hand, and on the other hand ungrammatical strings such as *Snow are white* and *Tree cat dog chased just a up a the*. The principles of sentence construction that he has internalized yield all of the former but fail to specify any of the latter. We will discuss syntactic systems extensively in Chapter Five.

GRAMMATICALNESS

A few words are perhaps in order about the notion of "grammatical sentence," since this notion has played an important role in our discussion. The linguist's use of the grammatical-ungrammatical distinction has generated a great deal of animosity, most of it based on simple misunderstanding. Let us make clear from the start just what is meant.

It is the task of linguists to describe languages, but it is not their task or prerogative to prescribe. Linguists want to say what languages are like, but they have no right to say what languages should be like or to dictate how people should talk. It is sometimes charged that linguists are violating this canon and being prescriptive when they distinguish between grammatical and ungrammatical sentences. But this is not the case. What is being claimed by the linguist, when he distinguishes between well-formed sentences and ill-formed ones, is that the speaker whose language is being described makes such a distinction himself. The linguist is simply describing in a straightforward way what he finds; he is not imposing a false dichotomy on anyone.

Any fluent speaker of English can recognize that the sentence **Helen picked a flower yesterday** is well formed in a sense in which **Flower Helen yesterday a picked** is not. He can recognize that **Bill and Patricia kissed** is structurally correct in a sense in which **Kissed Patricia Bill and** is not. He may never have occasion to reflect on these differences, but at the same time he could hardly fail to perceive them should they be called to his attention. There are infinitely many sentences that are clearly well formed in English, without any doubt. Likewise, there are infinitely many sentences that can be excluded, without any doubt, from the class of grammatical English sentences. Linguists claim nothing more. There may be cases that are not so clear, sentences about which a given speaker might have difficulty making up his mind. No one denies this, but neither is it a crucial point. The syntactic principles of a language may well be blurred around the edges. However, this in no way casts doubt on the existence of a set of principles of sentence construction that a person masters when he learns a language—principles that specify certain sequences of words as being grammatical sentences of the language and exclude others. To abandon the distinction because of some borderline cases would be to distort our picture of language far more than it is distorted by the idealizing assumption that a decision can be made for every sentence.

"Why so much emphasis on sentences?" it is sometimes asked. "People do not always use full sentences. In many situations, the production of a full sentence would be very much out of place. A word or a short phrase is often all that is necessary or expected." Very true, but no one has ever denied this, least of all the linguists who distinguish between grammatical and ungrammatical sentences.

Conversations abound with exclamations—**Heavens!, Damn!, Hell!**— and fragments of sentences—**Hardly, Can he really?, Could be, But Marvin does, True.** They belong to a language just as much as full sentences do, and therefore would have to be described in any full linguistic description; no one proposes to leave them out. There are a number of reasons, however, for placing a great deal of emphasis on full sentences and comparatively little emphasis on shorter expressions.

Exclamations such as **Heavens!** and **Damn!** are to be found in all languages; every speaker has an inventory of them that he draws upon when he has occasion to. This inventory, unlike the inventory of sentences of a language, is clearly finite and can be listed exhaustively. These exclamations are used over and over again and are anything but novel. There is really nothing more to say about them, so far as the structure of the language is concerned; writing down an exhaustive list of standard exclamations is only a matter of patience.

Sentence fragments are just what the name implies. They can be recognized as elliptical versions of more complete sentences, though it is not always obvious what particular sentence a given fragment abbreviates. **Can he really?** is to be understood as **Can he really do that?**, **Can he really be so cruel?**, or whatever other sentence happens to be appropriate for the occasion. Behind **True** lurk fuller sentences such as **What you say is true**. In these observations we find the reason for placing primary emphasis on full sentences and only secondary emphasis on sentence fragments: Sentence fragments can be understood and described in terms of full sentences, but the opposite does not hold true. By describing full sentences, we are going a long way toward the description of sentence fragments. If, on the other hand, we were to focus all our attention on fragmentary expressions like **True** and **Could be**, we would learn little or nothing about the syntactic principles that account for full sentences and hence for linguistic creativity. (Notice, by the way, that sentence fragments are not necessarily ungrammatical. Fragments can be either grammatical or ungrammatical, just as full sentences can. **Could be**, for instance, is a grammatical fragment, but **Be could** is not.)

People frequently make errors when they talk. They put words in the wrong places, talk themselves into syntactic corners from which no grammatical escape is possible, neglect to make the verb agree with the subject, and commit all sorts of other syntactic sins. Are we therefore justified in claiming that people can recognize the difference between well-formed and ill-formed sentences?

The answer is that we are. In saying that a person has mastered a set of principles for constructing sentences, we in no way imply that he cannot make mistakes in applying these principles. Similarly, the claim that a person is capable of multiplying 13,479 and 231,641 does not mean that he will necessarily come out with the right answer on a given attempt. People can make mistakes even in working problems they are competent to solve, and talking is no different from other kinds of problem-solving in this respect. If anything, there are more possible sources of error in speaking than in other domains. A person may commit an error in uttering a sentence because he is too tired to pay attention to what he is saying, because something distracts him in the middle of it, because he changes his mind about what he wants to say while he is saying it, because he attempts to perform a sentence so long that near the end he forgets how he began, and so on. That he controls the boundless class of grammatical sentences of his language does not mean that he will always employ this linguistic competence flawlessly in speaking or hearing.

This point is a very important one. It is essential to distinguish between the structure of a language and the way in which this structure is used. With respect to a speaker, we may refer to the distinction between his linguistic **competence** and his linguistic **performance**.

A language is a set of principles establishing correlations between meanings and sound sequences. These principles underlie and make possible communication by means of overt verbal behavior, but they cannot be equated with this behavior. A language is a set of principles that a speaker masters; it is not anything a speaker does. The same kind of distinction can be made between a symphony and the performance of it. No matter how poorly it is performed, the symphony remains unaffected. It is an abstract musical system that underlies the activity of musicians but cannot be equated with their activity. In the same sense, a linguistic system underlies the verbal activity of its speakers. A language is an abstract set of psychological principles that constitute a person's competence as a speaker. These principles make available to him an unbounded class of sentences that he can draw upon in concrete situations. They are a crucial ingredient of linguistic creativity.

It is this abstract linguistic system that linguists seek to describe. They are at most secondarily concerned with actual verbal behavior, which is only an indirect manifestation of the psychological principles that make human language unique. The structure of a language is not affected when its speakers make mistakes in talking any more than a symphony is affected when it is poorly performed. A speaker possesses a set of principles that specify some sentences as being well formed and exclude others, but this does not mean that every string of words he utters will be grammatical.

Linguists intend no such claim when they distinguish between grammatical and ungrammatical sentences.

There is a related point that requires comment because it is so often misunderstood. When linguists describe the structure of a language, in no sense are they describing what people do when they create or understand sentences. The grammar of a language is not a recipe that can be followed in diagnosing the communicative needs of the situation, deciding what has to be said, selecting a sentence to say it, and translating this sentence into action. Nor is it a recipe for the hearer to follow when he monitors an utterance and figures out what is being said. It is a description of the principles that specify what strings of words are well-formed sentences of the language, a description of the intrinsic structure of the linguistic system. How this structure is translated into verbal behavior is another question entirely.

The grammatical description of a language is like the written score of a symphony in this respect. The notes of the score do not describe step by step the precise motions that the conductor makes with his arms, nor do they say what the violinist does with his fingers to produce the right sounds on his instrument. Rather, they symbolize the intrinsic structure of the musical work. What physical motions the members of the orchestra must carry out in order to manifest this work in observable form are far beyond the domain of the score. The grammar of a language is a symbolic representation of the abstract linguistic system in the same way that the musical score represents the abstract musical system. In describing the structure of a language, the linguist does not aim to say what physical and mental motions speakers of a language perform when they produce sentences. He attempts to characterize the abstract linguistic system that speakers draw upon when they talk and understand but not to give a step-by-step account of verbal behavior. In other words, he attempts to describe linguistic competence rather than linguistic performance.

It is not that linguistic performance is devoid of interest. On the contrary, the linguist would like very much to learn just what people do, step by step, when they speak and listen. The reason for his concern with linguistic competence is, quite simply, that a description of linguistic competence is logically prior to a description of linguistic performance. The principles that specify the well-formed sentences of a language constitute one essential component of the psychological apparatus involved in speaking and understanding; we draw upon these principles when we produce and comprehend sentences. Any adequate account of linguistic performance therefore presupposes an adequate account of the abstract linguistic system, but the opposite is not true. We must know what sort of thing a language is before we can hope to understand how the speaker and the hearer use it in practice.

LANGUAGE AND THOUGHT

The fact that language can be used to express our thoughts gives rise to some interesting questions. How are language and thought related? Can we think without language? Is our thinking molded by the structure of our language? These are very difficult questions, questions that we cannot hope to answer definitively without a much better understanding of human psychological structure than we presently have. Conflicting opinions have been advanced. The following observations carry no guarantee that all linguists or psychologists would agree with them.

If we define thought as conscious mental activity, we can observe first that thought, or at least certain kinds of thought, can take place completely independently of language. The simplest example is that of music. We have all had the experience of being absorbed in listening to an instrumental work or mentally running through a familiar tune. Language is simply not involved. (The existence of music with lyrics is of course beside the point.) Musical composition is in no way dependent on language, so far as the actual process of creation is concerned, and the same would seem to be true of various other forms of creative or problem-solving activity. The sculptor at work is in no significant sense guided by language. He may, of course, receive much of his instruction through language, talk about his creations, and even entertain himself with an internal verbal soliloquy as he chips away with hammer and chisel. But such verbalization does not appear to be instrumental in his creative activity. There may be many stretches of time during which he is so busy conceptualizing forms and techniques that words disappear entirely from his thoughts. Much the same is true of a person engrossed in solving a jigsaw puzzle. Suddenly perceiving that two independently completed sections belong together is in no way a linguistic accomplishment, although one may subsequently exclaim "Aha! This must go over here!" It is thus hard to understand why some people have maintained that thought without language is impossible. They have probably been construing thought quite narrowly to mean something like propositional thought. If thought is construed too narrowly, the claim becomes a tautology; it is not very informative to learn that thought which involves language is impossible without language.

A further argument for the existence of thought without language is the common experience of wishing to express some idea but being unable to find a satisfactory way to put it into words. If thought were impossible without language, this problem would never arise.

Nevertheless, much of our thought clearly does involve language, some of it in an essential way. The problem of assessing the influence of language on thought, however, deserves to be treated with great caution. It is all too easy to lament the tyranny of language and to claim that the world view of a person or community is shaped by the language used. Certainly people have sometimes been misled by a blind reliance on words, but we can recognize such cases and set the record straight; if language were all that tyrannical, we would be unable to perceive that it sometimes leads us into error when we are not being careful. Furthermore, we must entertain the possibility that much of what passes for linguistically conditioned thought is not molded by language at all; there may be a more general human cognitive capacity at play, for which language merely serves as a medium, just as music serves as a medium for the composer's creative powers.

Scholars generally agree that words greatly facilitate certain kinds of thinking by serving as counters, or symbols, that can easily be manipulated. We all have a fairly good idea of what arithmetic is; we know how to add, subtract, multiply, and divide. We also know the word *arithmetic*, which serves as a label for this conceptual complex. When we think about arithmetic (how it fits into the rest of mathematics, how it is taught in our schools, whether our children are good at it, whether we like it, how hard it is), we can use the word *arithmetic* as a symbol in our thought processes. It is much easier to manipulate the word *arithmetic* in our thoughts than to operate with the entire conceptual complex that this word symbolizes. The use of verbal symbols thus makes thought easier in many cases. One might even argue that some kinds of thinking would be impossible without the existence of these convenient counters to operate with.

Verbal labels are particularly important in the realm of abstract ideas. *Justice, democracy, liberty, communism,* and *education* are familiar terms, yet it would be very hard to pin down their meaning precisely. *Justice* does not evoke a concrete image in the way *table* does. We can usually agree on whether or not something is a table, but how sure can we ever be about justice? When is something correctly labeled **obscene**? Does the word *liberty* have any real significance? We certainly have at least a vague idea of what is meant by these terms, but their meanings tend to be quite elusive and to vary considerably from person to person. These concepts probably would not exist at all if there were no words for them, serving to gather and hold together a number of vague, not too coherent notions. Because they are abstract, words like these are quite loosely tied to reality. In a sense, they are almost empty. If one is not careful, they can become emotionally charged labels functioning only to brand someone or something as good or bad. It is unfortunately very easy to call someone a ***communist*** or to do something *in the name of liberty*, and it is very easy to be misled by the empty use of words.

What is the relation between our thought processes and the structure of our language? Is language a tyrannical master, relentlessly forcing our thinking to follow certain well-worn paths, blinding us to all other possibilities? Is our conception of the world crucially conditioned by the language we speak, as some people have claimed? These questions can be posed with respect both to words and to grammatical structures.

We have seen that a word can be helpful in forming, retaining, or operating with the concept it designates. We have also seen that no two languages match precisely in the way in which they break up conceptual space and assign the pieces to words as meanings; recall that English distinguishes between *green* and *blue* while other languages use a single word to designate this entire range of the spectrum, and that the Eskimos use a number of words to designate different kinds of snow where English has the single word *snow*. Differences like these extend throughout the vocabulary and will be found no matter what two languages are compared. Our question, then, is to what extent these differences in the linguistic categorization of experience are responsible for corresponding differences in thought.

There is little doubt that lexical differences have some effect on thought, at least in the sense that it is easier to think about things we have words for. We are accustomed to labeling some colors with the term *red* and others with the term *blue*. When presented with a typically red or blue object, we can quickly name its color; the terms *red* and *blue* are readily available to us, for we have had lifelong experience in calling some things red and others blue. We will have little trouble remembering the color of a red or blue object. Suppose, however, that you are presented with an object that is an extremely dark shade of brown, so dark that it is almost black. There is no common term in English for this particular color. Most likely you will hesitate to call it either **brown** or **black**, because it is not typical of the colors usually called **brown** or **black**. Eventually you may resort to a phrase like **very dark brown** or **brownish black**, but such a phrase will probably not come to mind as quickly and readily as **red** or **blue**. We are not so accustomed to distinguishing shades of brown from one another as we are to distinguishing red from blue. It will prove harder to remember a particular shade of brown (as opposed to other shades of brown) than to remember the color of a typically red object. If our language, on the other hand, had a separate word for this very dark shade of brown and if we were accustomed to categorizing objects of this color by describing them with this word, there would be no such difficulties.

Our thinking is thus conditioned by the linguistic categorization of experience in that it is easier to operate with concepts coded by single words than with concepts for which no single term is available. The way in which one's language breaks up conceptual space thus has at least a minimal effect on thought. But there is absolutely no evidence to suggest that this influence is in any significant way a tyrannical or even a powerful one. We are perfectly capable of forming and mentally manipulating concepts for which no word is available. We can make up imaginary entities at will and, if we so choose, proceed to name them. For example, imagine a unicorn with a flower growing out of each nostril. No word exists for such an entity, but it is easy to think about it nevertheless. We could dream up a name for it, but we do not have to.

What about the grammatical structures of a language? Do they force our thinking into certain customary grooves to the exclusion of other possibilities? Do they determine our way of viewing the world, as many scholars have maintained?

Overtly, languages sometimes display very striking differences in grammatical structure. (We will see later, however, that upon deeper examination languages appear to be very similar to one another grammatically.) For example, what we express in English with adjectives is expressed in some other languages with the equivalent of intransitive verbs. The word-for-word translation of the sentence meaning 'The tree is tall' would thus be *The tree talls*. To say that the river is deep, one would say literally *The river deeps*. Much more commonly, languages differ in the grammatical categories that are obligatorily represented in sentences. One such category is gender. In French, for instance, every noun is classified as either masculine or feminine, and in the singular the article meaning 'the' appears as *le* if its noun is masculine but as *la* if its noun is feminine. Whereas in English we say *the cheese* and *the meat*, in French one makes a distinction and says *le fromage* but *la viande*. In German, there is a three-way distinction. *Der Käse* 'the cheese' is masculine; *die Kartoffel* 'the potato' is feminine; and *das Fleisch* 'the meat' is neuter. In other languages, there are even more gender categories requiring agreement. (These distinctions, by the way, are grammatical ones; they have nothing very directly to do with sex.)

Gender is of course only one example. Number, case, tense, and aspect are other categories often found in familiar European languages. And many languages mark categories that seem more exotic to speakers of English. It is not unusual for the plural to be marked differently depending on whether the objects involved are close together or scattered about. Certain Navaho verbs of handling, meaning such things as 'drop' or 'pick up,' vary in form depending on the shape of the thing that is handled. Thus one form will be used if the object is round or amorphous in shape, another form will be used if it is long, slender, and rigid, and so on. Sentences in the Siouan languages contain markers indicating the speaker's estimation of the veracity of what is expressed.

No one denies that these overt grammatical differences exist. If two languages are different enough in structure, a literal, item-by-item translation of a sentence from one language into the other can seem most bizarre to speakers of the second language. It is quite another thing, however, to claim that these differences in grammatical structure entail significant differences in the thought processes of the speakers. No evidence has ever been presented to support this claim. Grandiose assumptions about one's world view being determined by the structure of one's language have never been shown to be anchored in fact. There is absolutely no reason to believe that the grammatical structure of our language holds our thoughts in a tyrannical, vise-like grip.

It is not really surprising that no such evidence has been found. The claims are based on really very superficial aspects of linguistic structure. If French nouns are divided into two gender classes while English nouns are not, so what? No valid psychological conclusions follow from this arbitrary, rather uninteresting grammatical fact. If, in your native language, you were brought up to say the equivalent of *The flower reds, The tree talls,* and *The river deeps,* it would not follow that you lived in an especially exciting mental world where colors were actions on the part of objects, where trees continually participated in the activity of tallness, where rivers stretched themselves vertically while flowing horizontally. These ways of expressing yourself, being customary, would not strike you as poetic, as they strike a speaker of English. You would live in the same world you live in now.

CHAPTER THREE

Language

in Society

LINGUISTIC DIVERSITY

It is believed that some three to five thousand languages are spoken in the world today. It is difficult to be precise about the number, however, for at least two reasons. For one thing, we do not have the voluminous, detailed information from all parts of the world that we need in order to make an accurate estimate. The second reason involves the very concept of a language. While we have a rough, intuitive idea of what we mean by the term **language**, the facts of language use are such that it is often extremely hard in practice to decide when this term is properly applied.

At first glance there might seem to be no problem. English is a language, as are French and Dutch. English is the language spoken in the United States, England, Canada, and a few other places; French is the language spoken in France, parts of Canada, and so on; Dutch is the language spoken in the Netherlands. But things are really not this simple.

When we try to determine language boundaries, we find that they cannot be marked on a map in the straightforward way in which national boundaries can, at least not without gross oversimplification.

To understand the problems, let us postulate a situation in which language areas could easily be marked on a map, just as countries are marked. Thus Figure 3.1 might be a linguistic map of some geographical area. A map such as this one has two implications. First, it implies that there is linguistic uniformity within each subarea marked off by the boundary lines. For instance, everyone living in the region marked "Language A" is said to speak the same language. Second, the map implies that there are clear enough linguistic differences between any two regions that one is justified in drawing a line between them. Thus, according to Figure 3.1, language B and language C are easily distinguished, so that a single line of demarcation can realistically be drawn between them.

In fact, however, neither of these implications holds true. In the first place, language areas in general display a surprising amount of internal diversity. Moreover, they very often merge gradually with one another, so that any dividing line on a map has to be drawn more or less arbitrarily. Linguistic situations like that in Figure 3.1 are therefore never found in reality. Actual situations approach it in varying degrees, but never very closely.

Consider first the arbitrariness of any dividing line. In some cases, a reasonable dividing line can be drawn without much distortion of the facts. The border between Mexico and the United States, for instance, will serve fairly well as a line of demarcation between English and Spanish. But even here some important qualifications must be added. Many people living near the border on the American side speak Spanish better than English, and many speak only Spanish. Furthermore, many people on the Mexican side know English. Between the area where English is spoken to the virtual exclusion of Spanish and the area where the opposite situation obtains, there is a sizable region where both are used, where English words creep into Spanish conversations, and so on. Even here, any sharp line of demarcation represents an oversimplification.

In other cases, the difficulties involved in drawing a dividing line are much greater. We can illustrate this with the boundary, or lack of one, between French and Italian. We are accustomed to thinking of French and Italian as two distinct languages. Indeed, the French spoken in Paris and the Italian spoken in Naples are mutually unintelligible. Nevertheless,

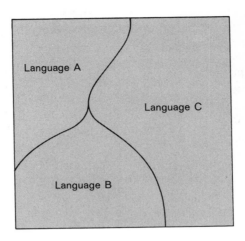

FIGURE 3.1

we cannot simply point to a spot on a map and say "Here is where French stops and Italian begins." The transition from clearly French-speaking areas to clearly Italian-speaking areas is a gradual one. Going from town to town between Paris and Naples, one would seldom if ever be conscious of leaving one language area and entering another, because the linguistic differences from one town to the next are relatively minor. It would never be clearly reasonable to say "Aha! I've just left French behind; now I'm in the territory where they speak Italian." In situations such as this one, we may not even be justified in speaking of two separate languages, since there is essentially a continuum. Yet, if we just looked at the speech of Paris and Naples, we would no doubt conclude that two separate languages were involved.

It is evident, then, that any lines like those in Figure 3.1 are bound to be artificial to some degree, since the geographical boundary between two languages is never sharp. The transition may be relatively abrupt (like that from English to Spanish along the Mexican border), very gradual (like that from French to Italian), or anywhere in between. This qualification does not mean that we cannot speak of separate languages, but it does mean that in so speaking we are abstracting to a greater or lesser degree from reality.

The other implication of Figure 3.1 is that there is linguistic uniformity within each subarea marked off by the boundary lines. Even in the United States, where there is comparatively little linguistic diversity, we find that this implication does not hold true, even if we leave aside such obvious exceptions as the people who speak more than one language and the areas (mainly in large cities) where Spanish, Chinese, Italian, or other foreign languages are spoken. The speech of Texas is not the same as the speech of New England; Midwesterners do not talk the same way as Southerners. We are all aware of these surface differences to a certain extent, even having some fun occasionally at the expense of other dialects.

The differences are of various sorts. Most familiar, perhaps, are the variations in pronunciation discerned between virtually any two speakers of the same language. Some people pronounce *roof* and *root* to rhyme with *goof* and *shoot*, while others pronounce them with the vowel sound of *put*. The word *greasy* is generally pronounced to rhyme with *fleecy* in the northern parts of the country; in the South, it rhymes with *easy*. In many parts of the East and South, *r* is not pronounced at the end of a word or before a consonant, while it is in the West and Midwest. In many dialects where it is not, for instance, *par* rhymes with *pa*, and *startle* with *throttle*. Examples of this sort could easily be multiplied. There are also many variations in vocabulary and syntax. In some parts of the country the term *hot cakes* is preferred for what are called *pancakes* or *griddle cakes* in other areas. Some people *stand in line* and others *stand on line* (while in England they *queue up*). In western Pennsylvania, people can say things like *This blouse needs pressed;* in most dialects, one would say instead *This blouse needs to be pressed* or *This blouse needs pressing*.

These are only a few examples of the thousands of details on which Americans differ in their speech. In the strictest possible sense, then, it cannot be maintained that the area where American English is spoken is characterized by linguistic uniformity. And in many other parts of the world, areas we would be inclined to mark off on a map as areas in which a single language is spoken display even more internal linguistic diversity than our country does. Thus we must complicate our picture of language areas to accommodate the reality of linguistic variation.

Dialects

One obvious way to make the picture more realistic is to subdivide a language area into dialect areas; within the geographical domain

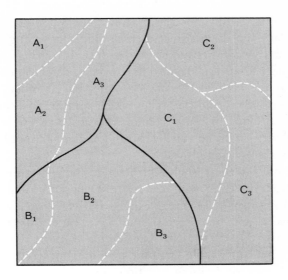

Figure 3.2

Figure 3.2

of American English, for instance, we might want to mark off a Southern dialect, a New England dialect, a Midwestern dialect, and others. This slightly more realistic picture, where dialect divisions within a language are indicated, is schematized in Figure 3.2. Language A is here divided into dialects A_1, A_2, and A_3, and languages B and C are similarly divided. Naturally, the lines indicating dialect boundaries deserve to be treated with as much caution as the lines indicating language boundaries. Seldom if ever can we point to a line on a map and say with accuracy that one dialect abruptly ends at that location and another begins.

The basis for distinguishing various dialects of a language is that the linguistic system used by speakers of one dialect differs in certain respects from that used by speakers of the others. To take a hypothetical example, dialect B_1 of Figure 3.2 might be considered a distinct variety of language B because of these differences and a number of comparable ones: (1) the speakers of B_1 use the sound [u] (as in *shoot*) in words that other speakers of B pronounce with [ʊ] (the vowel of *put*); (2) [i] is used in words where other dialects have [ɪ] (this is the difference between *beet* and *bit*); and (3) the word *tawpa* is used to designate a certain kind of bird, whereas speakers of B_2 and B_3 use the word *kenso*.

47

Matters are not really this simple, however. When one tries to draw dialect boundaries on the basis of points of difference in linguistic systems, one gets different results depending on which traits of the linguistic system are used as criteria in establishing the lines of demarcation. If we had looked, not at the particular examples above, but at other traits of pronunciation, vocabulary, and syntax on which speakers of B vary, B might have been partitioned in quite a different manner. Moreover, the alternative boundaries would be equally as valid as the first, both having been established on similar grounds.

Linguists use the term **isogloss** to refer to the geographical boundary of a linguistic trait. Even within a relatively homogeneous speech area, quite a large number of isoglosses can be traced. There is no necessary relation between any one isogloss and any other; they crisscross and diverge and often present a rather bewildering picture.

Figure 3.3 is a conceivable linguistic map on which three isoglosses are marked. The linguistic traits in question are lexical ones. Some speakers call a certain sparrow-like bird found in the region *finu*; others use the word *tawen* to designate this kind of bird. The isogloss running vertically demarcates roughly the subareas characterized by these alternate lexical items—speakers to the left of this line in general use *finu*, while those to the right use *tawen*. Similarly, the *stanu/lufa* and the *sen/iktaw* isoglosses indicate the extensions of the use of alternate lexical items.

The three isoglosses divide the region represented in Figure 3.3 into six subregions, each of which is distinct from the other five. In one subregion, speakers use *finu, stanu,* and *sen*; in another they use *tawen, stanu,* and *sen*. Where, then, is there a dialect boundary? There is really no satisfactory answer to this question. Dialect boundaries are established on the basis of different linguistic traits, but the three linguistic traits indicated in Figure 3.3 contradict one another as to where a dialect boundary lies. The dividing line will be drawn in one place if the criterion is the *finu/tawen* distinction, in another if it is the *stanu/lufa* alternation, and in still another if it is the *sen/iktaw* distinction. If we added more isoglosses to Figure 3.3, the situation would be worse yet.

One way out of the difficulty is to say that six dialect areas are represented in Figure 3.3, not two. In other words, we can define a dialect in such a way that two people speak different dialects if their linguistic systems differ with respect to at least one trait. Thus a person from the *finu/lufa/sen* area speaks a different dialect from the one spoken by a

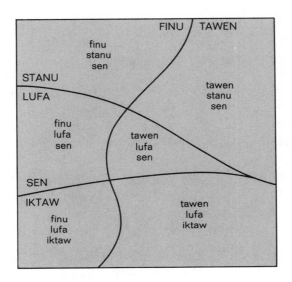

FIGURE 3.3

person from the *tawen/lufa/sen* area, since one person uses *finu* while the other uses *tawen*.

The problem with this definition is that no two people have absolutely identical linguistic systems. Any given pair of speakers will differ with respect to some points of syntax, phonology, and vocabulary, whether or not they are normally conscious of these differences. It is probably true, for instance, that no two speakers of English know exactly the same set of words. One speaker will invariably happen to have learned some word that the other has not. Therefore, if we follow to its logical conclusion the proposition that a single trait is sufficient to establish a dialect boundary, we end up claiming that every speaker has his own dialect, one that no other speaker shares.

Thus we arrive at a definition of **dialect** that, while perfectly reasonable, is extremely narrow. It does not permit us to speak of the New England dialect of American English, for example, because no two New Englanders possess exactly the same linguistic system. But obviously it is often useful to be able to speak of dialects in the broader sense, in which the term is not restricted to the linguistic system of just one person. The term **idiolect** is therefore commonly used to designate the dialect of one person, and the term **dialect** is defined more loosely, so that it is proper to speak of a New England dialect. Some other rationale must then be found for carving up a language area into dialect areas.

We implicitly used such a rationale earlier in discussing Figure 3.2. We justified demarcating region B_1 as a separate dialect area of language B because the speakers in area B_1 shared, not one, but a large number of linguistic traits not characteristic of other dialects of language B. In other words, the line dividing B_1 and B_2 represents a whole bundle of isoglosses that roughly coincide. Along or near the line dividing B_1 and B_2 are the [u]/[ʊ] isogloss, the [i]/[ɪ] isogloss, the *tawpa*/*kenso* isogloss, and various other isoglosses as well. The speakers of B_1 retain many individual differences, but they cohere as a group at least in the sense that they have in common many linguistic traits that set them apart from other speakers of the same language.

Defining dialect boundaries in terms of bundles of isoglosses rather than single isoglosses leads, therefore, to fairly reasonable results. However, a dialect map like Figure 3.2 still represents a considerable abstraction from reality, just as Figure 3.1 does. It is a gross oversimplification to draw dialect boundaries that exhaustively partition a language area into non-overlapping subareas. Consider Figure 3.4, in which each of the numbered lines represents an isogloss. Isoglosses 7, 8, 9, 10, and 11 run together roughly as a bundle. We are thus justified to some extent in speaking of a major dialect boundary between the areas on either side of this bundle. At the same time, however, isoglosses 3, 4, 5, and 6 form a bundle that is equally suitable as the basis for establishing a basic dialect division. If we insist on dialect areas that do not overlap, we are faced with an arbitrary decision about which isogloss bundle or bundles to choose as the criteria. If all of them are defined as criteria simultaneously, they will intersect to yield very many small dialect areas. In any case, the picture is always quite complex, and the linguistic facts of a region usually do not lend themselves to a natural division of the region into dialect areas. Whatever choice we make will be somewhat arbitrary and will leave some facts out of consideration. There will always be stray isoglosses like 1 and 2 to complicate the situation. Dialects, then, are more a product of our conceptualization and desire for simplification than a natural linguistic phenomenon.

Linguistic diversity cannot be discussed fully in geographical terms; it has at least two other dimensions. One is the dimension of social groups and classes. Within a given geographical area, particularly an urban one,

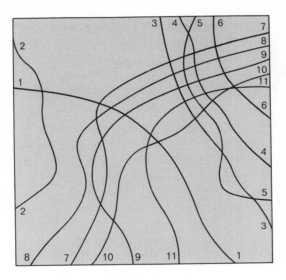

FIGURE 3.4

there are speech differences correlated with social structure. Denizens of high society and workers of the lower economic classes commonly differ quite noticeably in their speech. In university towns, the members of the academic community (most of whom come from other areas) can be quite distinct linguistically from the townspeople native to the region. People who work together or who have a common occupation or hobby often share many specialized vocabulary items not known by the community as a whole. Policemen, for example, have a professional jargon, as do baseball fans and members of the underworld.

The other dimension of linguistic diversity is to be found within individual speakers. Not only does a single speaker possess his own unique linguistic system; he has different **styles** of speech that he employs in different circumstances. The style he uses when being interviewed for a job differs considerably from the style he uses in conversation among close friends, for instance. We are attuned to differences in style, even if they seldom come to our conscious attention. Witness the mildly humorous effect of mixing styles: ***It is incumbent upon me to humbly submit to your attention the request that you get the hell outta here.*** Thus we encounter linguistic diversity even when we restrict ourselves to considering only one speaker and ignore the fact that a person's linguistic system undergoes at least minor changes throughout his lifetime.

We have stressed linguistic diversity to the point of calling into question the validity of the very notions of **language** and **dialect**. Strictly speaking, no two linguistic systems are identical, so that any description of a linguistic system has to be a description of the linguistic system of a single individual. And even here there are qualifications. We must not conclude from all this, however, that there is nothing uniting all the varieties of speech that we call English or Japanese. Linguistic diversity will naturally seem extremely important when we examine it alone, without attempting to ferret out features on which all or most of the idiolects of a language are in agreement. The more deeply we pry into the structure of a language, though, the less impressive idiolectal differences appear to be. Speakers of English have vastly more linguistic traits in common than traits in which they differ. The differences, moreover, tend to be of a rather peripheral nature. It is important to have some appreciation of the complexities of language use, but at the same time we must not concentrate on differences to the point where we are blind to similarities.

STANDARDIZING TENDENCIES

Linguistic diversity exists because languages are learned and used and because language learning and use are creative processes involving an extremely complex system. When a child learns to talk, the linguistic system he masters is virtually identical to the one used around him. Inevitably, however, there will be some differences between the linguistic system the child assimilates and the ones his models use. In the first place, the child cannot observe the systems of his models directly; he can only observe their linguistic performance, and on the basis of this rather indirect evidence he must proceed (subconsciously, of course) to formulate a linguistic system that reproduces their linguistic competence. Given the vast amount of detail that a language comprises, minor discrepancies will inevitably arise. Moreover, we have seen that no two people possess precisely the same linguistic system, and the child usually learns to talk from more than one person. On the points where his models diverge, he must make some decision as to which model to follow. The child's idiolect, therefore, will normally represent a mixture of the idiolects of the various people most influential in his learning to talk, not a carbon copy of any single idiolect.

Every act of speech is to some extent a creative one. A language is an instrument of communication, but a language itself does not communicate. To express an idea, a speaker must assess the situation and use the linguistic system at his command to encode the idea in a signal from which the hearer will be able to reconstruct at least approximately the idea that prompted the utterance. The communicative potential of the language must somehow be exploited in a manner appropriate to the context. In arriving at an utterance that will do what he wants it to do, the speaker has to make his language fit the situation, no matter how unusual; to construct a phrase or a sentence to express what no single word is available to express; and sometimes even to innovate, to alter the linguistic system to make it more nearly adequate to present needs. The seeds of linguistic diversity are thus to be found in the application of the abstract linguistic system to concrete situations for specific communicative purposes. If the word a speaker needs is not available, he may coin a suitable one; a listener watching someone scraping paint off a table will probably understand you if you say that the table is being *depainted*. People often resort to metaphorical expressions to get their ideas across, and some of these stick as part of the innovator's idiolect or even spread to other speakers. Languages are full of expressions of metaphorical origin, such as *the heart of the matter, bridge the gap, the apple of his eye*, and *stir up trouble*. Quirks of pronunciation are sometimes adopted for their stylistic or expressive value.

The tendency of linguistic diversity to grow is checked by several forces, however. Since a language is used primarily for communication, a speaker is not free to innovate without limit; his linguistic system must remain similar enough to the systems of the people around him to enable them to understand him. Besides this essentially negative factor, a speaker is subjected to certain positive forces tending toward standardization.

Whatever the psychological motivations may be, people commonly model their speech after the speech of the people they communicate with. They may sometimes do so simply out of a desire for change. A more important motivation, no doubt, is the desire to fit in well with a social group, to be one of the gang linguistically as well as in other ways. This tendency toward linguistic uniformity within a group is probably for the most part unconscious, and it is certainly not without exceptions. One member of a group, for example, may try to enhance his group standing by deliberately adopting unorthodox modes of speech.

The prestige motive is perhaps the most potent of all. A person will imitate someone he admires and would like to resemble, in speech as in other ways. He is not likely to imitate someone who stands low in his estimation. The speech of prominent or admired people is often adopted as a standard or model, although there is no reason to think that any dialect of a language has intrinsic merit over the others. Sometimes the dialect of a certain region or social class takes on special prestige for the community or nation as a whole. Parisian French, for example, has more prestige throughout France than the other local dialects. To a somewhat lesser extent, British English enjoys special favor in the eyes of many Americans. Boston English is considered by many people to be more prestigious than Southern speech or Brooklynese.

When a dialect comes to be accorded special prestige by the community as a whole, that dialect can serve as a standardizing influence. Parisian French is a good example. It was originally just a local dialect, like many other local dialects spoken in what is now France. They were all continuations of spoken Latin, and there is no particular reason to claim that any one was intrinsically more adequate, logical, or pleasing than any other. Paris, however, gradually became a social, economic, and political center of great importance. Moreover, the Parisian dialect was written and served as the medium for a flourishing literary tradition. Parisian French, in short, came to be held in high regard in France, but for purely external reasons; it is not inherently better than any other local *patois* and it has no claim to historical priority. For most Frenchmen, though, this dialect is *the* dialect, the one to be emulated. The other, equally legitimate dialects are looked down upon as provincial and inferior, or even as corrupt versions of the standard language (which they are not at all).

Whatever its precise causes may be, the high prestige of the Parisian dialect is a powerful factor in the linguistic attitudes and practices of French society. One is not likely to rise to national prominence in France without speaking the dialect of Paris, and an individual may even be hampered by a provincial accent, despite an otherwise perfect command of this dialect. A writer cannot hope for wide fame if he writes in one of the *patois*. Furthermore, Parisian French has been institutionalized as a standard language. It is the language authorized by the Académie Française, taught in schools, used on formal occasions, and (quite importantly in our age) projected throughout France by radio, television, and the press. Under the strong influence of the standard language, the local *patois* are gradually dying out; everyone is exposed to standard French, if only through the schools, and there are strong practical and social reasons for learning it. When so many factors combine to favor one particular dialect, its influence may be enough to override the tendency toward linguistic diversity and effect a trend toward linguistic uniformity, particularly in our age of mass communication, when spoken and written messages in the standard language reach millions of people.

A dialect that is accorded special prestige frequently comes to be regarded as more correct, more adequate, or purer than less prestigious dialects. It should be clear by now that these attitudes will not stand up to objective critical scrutiny. There is a sense in which it is proper to speak of correctness in language. A speaker often makes mistakes in speaking; if these really are mistakes (that is, distortions of his linguistic system as this system is reflected in performance), he will be able to recognize them as such if they are called to his attention and to correct them. But this is true of all dialects and constitutes no basis for setting one dialect apart from the others as being the most correct. Every dialect is adequate to its job; if it were not, its users would modify it until it were. The process of keeping a dialect in tune with communicative needs goes on continually, in fact. We adopt new words and phrases throughout our lives. Thus one dialect could hardly be more adequate than another. Nor is any dialect a corrupt form of another, purer dialect. Languages change; they do not degenerate (or we would have abandoned speech long ago in favor of grunts). Southern American English, for instance, is not a degenerate version of any other variety of American English, but is on a par with the others in all respects.

The idea that there are correct and incorrect varieties of a language is fostered to a considerable degree by pedagogical practice. American school children, for instance, are told not to say *ain't*, to avoid double negatives, to distinguish between *shall* and *will* in a fairly complicated way, and so on. There are practical reasons for getting school children to modify their speech in some of these ways—a person could well be handicapped socially and professionally by speech traits that run counter to those accepted as "correct" by people he will have to deal with. However, the child who drills and drills to add to his linguistic system a *who/whom* distinction that was not there in the first place is likely, unless he is otherwise informed, to come to the erroneous conclusion that one version of a language is intrinsically more correct than any other, including his own.

It is doubtful that fine grammatical points of English like the distinctions between *shall* and *will, who* and *whom,* or *like* and *as* would have survived (to the slight extent that they have survived) if speakers had been left to their own devices. Despite grammatical instruction, many speakers of English are not at all sure when to use *who* and when to use *whom.* When attempting to speak "very properly," for example, a speaker may use *whom* where *who* is required, since *whom* sounds more formal and hence seems, fallaciously, more correct. This phenomenon of a speaker going astray by trying too hard to conform to the requirements of a dialect more prestigious than his own is called **hypercorrection** and is not at all unusual where linguistic norms are taken seriously.

To what extent linguistic practice can be legislated, by teachers or by governments, is an open question. The very fact that people still worry about *who* and *whom* and try to avoid split infinitives is evidence that such attempts are not wholly without success. On the other hand, the pronouncements of prescriptively oriented teachers and grammarians are quite without effect on the vast majority of spontaneous conversation; in general, people are content to communicate successfully, regardless of whether or not they do so "correctly." Nothing is really changed when a grammarian breaks down and allows *like* to be used to introduce an adverbial clause instead of insisting on *as*—most English speakers are way ahead of him, since they have been using it that way all their lives.

The matter is much more serious when language reform is adopted as governmental policy. The lack of a common linguistic medium can be a serious bar to national unity, or even to efficient administration. French, Italian, and Swiss German coexist harmoniously as "official" languages in Switzerland, but there only three main languages are involved. The bewildering array of languages in widespread use in India, by way of contrast, constitutes a serious obstacle to national progress. What can a government do in such a case? With a strong educational system that provides effective language instruction over a long period of time, there is at least hope that one or a small number of languages will become sufficiently well established on a large scale to be functional as genuine national languages. The prospect is at best doubtful, though, even if we disregard the understandable hostility of people who are disappointed that their language was not chosen for a national language. Formal instruction is seldom able to compete effectively with the constant influence of spontaneous language use. We have seen, however, that a tendency toward linguistic uniformity can arise naturally from the dynamics of social intercourse; one might hope to channel this tendency in some way. In any event, linguistic practice is much more likely to follow its own course than the dictates of those who would presume to direct it.

Although we draw isoglosses on a map and talk of languages and dialects shared by thousands or millions of people, the real story of trends toward linguistic diversity and uniformity is to be found at the level of individual speakers. The innovation of a linguistic trait presupposes a speaker who makes that innovation. If an innovation spreads, it does so because people with whom the innovator communicates, and subsequently people who communicate with them, adopt the new trait and incorporate it into their personal linguistic systems. If no one chooses to adopt it, the innovation will die out or be restricted to its originator. When an innovation catches on, its isogloss tends to spread out in a gradually widening circle from the innovator, who occupies the center of the circle. The precise shape of the isogloss will depend on the form of the network of channels of communication linking the speakers involved, on the density of communication along the various channels, on the relative prestige of the speakers, and so forth.

This process occurs not just with new linguistic creations, but with all linguistic traits on which speakers vary. Where there is communication via language, there is a tendency for features of one idiolect to creep into the speech of people exposed to it. Isoglosses are therefore by no means static. Over a period of years, the position of an isogloss on a map can shift noticeably. As one might expect, isoglosses tend to spread outward from a high-prestige dialect, even forming concentric circles around the area where this dialect is spoken. If two or more prestige dialects are influential in a region, the isoglosses emanating from them will flow together and intersect, like ripples on a pond when a handful of pebbles are tossed into the water. Hence the proneness of dialect areas to intersect and overlap, as in Figure 3.4.

The diffusion of linguistic traits depends ultimately on communication and on the willingness of people to change their speech patterns after the example of others. Where little or no communication takes place, there can be little in the way of a trend toward linguistic uniformity. Geographical obstacles, such as mountains, can therefore be quite effective in preserving dialect differences. Isoglosses cannot cross a mountain unless people or their messages do so with some regularity, and the same is true of political or social boundaries. Isoglosses will thus tend to pile up in bundles along gaps in the network of communication channels. This tendency will emerge as an important factor in our later discussion of linguistic relatedness.

WRITING

Most languages have existed as purely oral forms of communication. People had been talking successfully for thousands of years before writing was invented, and millions of people today get along fine with their language even though it has no written form. Written languages like English are the exception, not the rule.

Language is speech and the linguistic competence underlying speech. Writing is no more than a secondary, graphic representation of language, but one with certain advantages. A written message is relatively permanent, whereas speech is quite ephemeral. Once emitted, a speech signal is gone forever (although electronic recording techniques are changing that to a certain extent); a written message can be kept and consulted at any future time. Facts and ideas committed to writing can be preserved without being a burden on memory. Moreover, written messages can be read by any number of people at different times and places. It is much easier to distribute pieces of paper than to train messengers to memorize long messages and to travel about presenting them orally.

The debt of modern society to writing is enormous. Writing is not just a convenience; our highly integrated, technologically oriented civilization could hardly exist in anything like its present form without the ability to record and preserve linguistic messages. To realize this, it is perhaps sufficient to try to imagine the chaotic state of affairs that would result if all written representations of language were to disappear permanently. The mail system that ties society together would be nonexistent. There would be no newspapers or magazines to tell us of current events. The vast store of knowledge and culture that is preserved in writing would be wiped out. One could not go to a library to read and do research but would have to resort to personal interviews. We could not organize our thoughts and render them coherent by committing them to writing; everything would have to be worked out in our heads. All written records would disappear. Bureaucratic machinery would come to a halt. One could not even post a FOR SALE sign. Electronic communication devices could take up some of the slack, but this is really beside the point. It is safe to say that the technology responsible for them could never have been developed if man had not first learned the art of writing, which made possible the accumulation of a large body of scientific and technical knowledge.

Granted the practical importance of writing, it does not follow that written messages deserve to be treated with more reverence than oral ones. Oral communication is even more important than writing, which is still only a secondary representation of language. Nevertheless, the written word is commonly regarded with great, perhaps excessive, respect. The written form of language even exerts some influence on its spoken form, notably in the phenomenon of **spelling pronunciation**. The word *often,* to take just one example, is pronounced by most people without a [t] sound, but because of the way it is spelled some people have introduced a [t] in their pronunciation of this word. Also noteworthy is the popular practice of forming a new word by pronouncing as a word the sequence of letters used to abbreviate a longer title. In this way the word **NATO** was obtained from the cumbersome **North Atlantic Treaty Organization. SEATO, UNESCO, HUAC**, and many more have been formed in similar fashion. An even more common variant of this practice is simply to pronounce the sequence of letters one at a time, as in **F.B.I., C.I.A., U.N., U.S.A., G.I., D.A.R., U.C.L.A.**, and countless others.

People sometimes regard the written word with special reverence, even going so far as to believe that something must be true if it occurs in print. Since most people do not write books or articles that get printed, there is perhaps a natural tendency to regard printed words with wonder or admiration and to forget that they carry no guarantee of truth or quality. False or stupid things can be, and often are, printed as easily as anything else. A more common instance of our reverence for the written word is the concern, so prevalent in our society today, over correct spelling. There is really no good reason why a word has to have a unique spelling; we could get along perfectly well if everyone spelled words as he thought they should be spelled. That was the practice in earlier centuries, and it led to no particular difficulties. Why, then, do we spend so much time and effort trying (and failing) to teach people to spell correctly? Why these endless pilgrimages to the dictionary?

Whatever the explanation, this attitude is no doubt connected with the more general idea, discussed earlier, that some versions of a language are more correct or proper than others. Correct spelling is regarded as an integral facet of the correct use of language, and the written dialect, as manifested in books, magazines, and newspapers, is the dialect to be emulated. This dialect is the one described in grammar books, and its words are neatly listed in compendious dictionaries complete with their pronunciations, spellings, definitions, syllabifications, and even etymologies. We consult these dictionaries when in doubt as to how to use or spell a word, or where to hyphenate it at the end of a line. We stand corrected if the dictionary says that a word means something other than what we have always thought it meant or is pronounced in a way we would never have dreamed of pronouncing it. This attitude is not necessarily bad, but it is not the only possible one, nor even the most rational. When in conflict with a dictionary, we always have the alternative of claiming that the dictionary does not accurately reflect our dialect.

Writing can be an important factor in establishing or maintaining a dialect as a standard one. A written language has great prestige, as we have seen. When represented in writing, a language or dialect is better able to serve as a model, since it has greater permanence. People who compile dictionaries and grammar books prefer to work from written documents, and their descriptions are in practice interpreted as prescriptions to be observed in speaking and writing correctly.

A dialect thus established tends to take on an existence of its own, one maintained independently of developments in the spoken language. Languages, especially in their primary (spoken) form, are continually changing. Written languages are for the most part more conservative than their spoken progenitors, for a number of reasons. People usually write with more care and formality than they speak, so that innovations are slower to appear in writing. The tradition of correctness in spelling keeps changes in pronunciation from being reflected in written messages. Because writing is relatively permanent, writings from the past (unlike past speech) continue to remind people of the way things used to be done and thus act as a restraining influence. People concerned with the correctness or purity of language will regard developments in the spoken language as evidence of linguistic corruption and resist their incorporation into writing.

As a result, the written language and its spoken counterparts sometimes drift quite far apart. It even happens that few if any people speak as their native dialect the spoken analog of the literary language; the literary language sustains itself solely through formal instruction in such cases. The spoken and the literary tongues are noticeably different in French; there is quite a jump from the standards of speech and writing taught in the schools and adopted for formal occasions to the informal conversational idiom. The formal Latin of Cicero differs considerably from the spoken Latin of the time, as reflected in the works of Plautus, who used the vernacular, and in casual scribblings that have been preserved. The spoken and literary languages may even diverge so far as to be mutually incomprehensible.

The isolation of liturgical languages from their spoken origins is a similar phenomenon. There is, of course, even greater resistance to change in a language used as the vehicle of religious doctrine and devotion than in a literary language. Moreover, the religious significance is sometimes sufficient to preserve a liturgical language long after its spoken counterpart has ceased to exist in other domains. Latin, as the language of Roman Catholicism, has been preserved in something like its classical form, though Latin as a spoken language has evolved into the modern Romance languages, which are quite different. Sanskrit is no longer spoken as a vernacular, but it remains as a language of religion and scholarship. Hebrew is being established as a spoken language in Israel, but for many centuries it survived only as a liturgical language.

Types of Writing Systems

The technique of writing grew out of the more general institution of pictorial art. The crucial difference between a pictorial representation of a situation and a written representation is that a pictorial representation is direct, whereas writing represents a situation through the mediation of language. We can describe a situation by drawing a picture or by talking about it, and writing combines aspects of each, being a graphic representation of a spoken message.

A picture may be worth a thousand words, but drawing pictures is not a very practical means of graphic communication. Besides being cumbersome, a pictorial system is inadequate to deal with many messages. For instance, how would you draw a picture to convey to someone the information represented in the sentence *Harvey's father-in-law's second wife will not be able to sympathize with the anti-war demonstrators until the views they sometimes advocate become more respectable in the eyes of those with firm commitments to morality and the future welfare of the nation?* Perhaps it could be done. It is much easier to write it, though, and the possibility of misinterpretation is much reduced when words are used instead of pictures.

The transition from direct representation to language-mediated representation came about when certain conventional pictures, or signs, were understood as designating words instead of things or ideas. Rather than drawing a picture of a man plowing a field, for instance, one would simply write in linear order the stylized signs normally used to designate a man, a plow, and a field. In this case it is not the event that is directly depicted; if it were, the man would be shown in the field with the plow. Instead, the three symbols are strung out in linear order corresponding to the words in the sentence describing the situation. The graphic signs now represent parts of the sentence, which in turn describes the event.

In all writing systems, symbols designate linguistic units rather than ideas or things. The distinct advantage of such an arrangement is that anything that can be said can be written (if the writing system is adequate). There are limitations, of course. Most writing systems lack any satisfactory way of indicating intonation, for instance. Gestures cannot be represented. On the whole, however, these minor deficiencies do not bother us.

Writing systems differ in two fundamental ways. First, they differ in their choice of symbols. The English, Greek, and Russian alphabets, for example, have radically different inventories of symbols, although there is some overlap among them. This difference is actually a superficial one, however; the three systems are of basically the same character, where one letter stands for one sound type. A more important difference in writing systems involves the kinds of units their symbols designate. On the basis of this distinction, three kinds of writing systems can be differentiated, although any one writing system will to some extent represent a mixture of two or more of these types.

Chinese orthography is the usual example of a **logographic**, or word-writing, system. Essentially, each symbol or character stands for a word; it has no phonetic value except by virtue of the fact that the word it stands for has a characteristic pronunciation. A word-writing system is advantageous in one way. Written Chinese can be understood over a wide area, even though the spoken dialects in this area are not all mutually intelligible, because differences in pronunciation are not reflected in the orthography, the symbols of which indicate words and not specific sounds. Although a given word may sound quite different in two dialects, the corresponding written character will be the same. But word-writing systems also have many disadvantages, mainly because so many symbols—literally thousands—are required. Learning to read and write involves much more time and effort than with other kinds of writing systems; for each word that is to be used and comprehended in writing, a separate symbol has to be memorized. One cannot figure out how to write a word, or what a character stands for, by means of any fixed relationship between symbols and sounds. The difficulties that the thousands of characters of a word-writing system present for purposes of printing are obvious.

Many writing systems are **syllabic,** or syllable-writing, systems: each symbol represents a single syllable or syllable type. If English were written syllabically, for instance, the word *macaroni* would be written with four symbols, one each for *ma, ca, ro,* and *ni.* Each symbol in a syllable-writing system has a particular phonetic value, and it is used in any word that contains the phonetic sequence it stands for. Thus it is possible to figure out how a word is pronounced from the way it is written, and vice versa. The signs of a syllabic system will be counted in the dozens, not in the thousands, which makes such a system much less cumbersome than a word-writing system. Japanese is a well-known example of a language written syllabically.

Most familiar to us are **alphabetic** writing systems. Basically, each symbol in an alphabetic system represents, not a whole syllable, but a single sound segment. The English word *cat,* for instance, contains three letters, one each for the sound segments [k], [æ], and [t]. Since only a relatively small number of sound types are systematically distinguished in a language, the number of symbols required in an alphabetic writing system is comparatively small; we get along with twenty-six letters for English.

The above characterizations of the three main types of writing systems are idealized and oversimplified in various ways. For example, some of the characters of Chinese resemble syllabic signs rather than word signs. Thus the same character is used for both 'wheat' and 'come,' since both are pronounced *lai.* Most Japanese writing is not purely syllabic but involves a mixture of syllabic signs and word signs (of Chinese origin). We even

63

use word signs in English; $ is a word sign for the same word that can be written *dollars* using alphabetic symbols. Numerals, such as 3 and 7, are also word signs.

Furthermore, writing systems are seldom as rational as the descriptions might lead one to expect. English is often cited as a language whose orthography is plagued with irrationality and irregularity. One letter may stand for a sequence of sounds (x = [ks]), and a sequence of letters may stand for one sound (*th* for the initial sound in *thing* or *thin*). A single letter or sequence of letters can have many different phonetic values (*ough* is very different in *through, rough, cough, bought, hiccough, dough,* and *bough*). Conversely, the same sound sequence can be represented in many different ways (*cite, site, sight*). In no strict sense, then, does English orthography manifest a simple, regular pairing of one symbol with one sound type. On the other hand, it would be misleading to point out these irregularities of English orthography without at the same time mentioning the regularities; we can only speak of irregularity in the context of a coherent, basically regular system.

A great many letters used in English orthography have constant phonetic value. For example, the letters *m, f, v, z, b, d, r,* and *l* almost always stand respectively for the sounds [m f v z b d r l]; most of the exceptions are cases of a letter not being pronounced, like the first *m* in *mnemonic*. Observe that even the deviations from the one sound/one symbol pairing tend to fall into standard patterns. Consider *thing, philosophy,* and *shell,* for instance. The initial sound of each of these words is represented by two letters (*th* = [θ], *ph* = [f], and *sh* = [š]). But these three sounds are very similar (linguists call them **fricatives**—compare them with [a] or [t]), and at the same time their orthographic representations are similar, each consisting of two letters the second of which is *h*. The fact that *c* stands for [s] in *cite* but for [k] in *care* is not wholly idiosyncratic; the use of *c* is quite regular. Leaving aside the special sequence *ch*, we can observe the following: *c* always represents [s] before the letters *i, e,* and *y* (*medicine, city, cent, notice, cycle,* and *juicy*); elsewhere it represents [k] (*car, coil, cut, electric, act, success,* and *acrid*). As a subregularity, notice that the pronunciation of *c* is modified from [s] to [š] when *ci* or *ce* is immediately followed by a vowel, as in *facial, special, vicious,* and *ocean*; this does not happen, though, when the first vowel after *c* is accented (thus we have *sócial,* with [š], but *society, scíon,* and *scíence* with [s]). There are very few exceptions.

The orthographic representation of English vowels is also full of regularities, although it has often been criticized as irregular. Upon encountering the nonsense words *vack* and *vake*, for example, you will probably have no trouble deciding how to pronounce them. If English vowel orthography were not highly systematic, you would have no basis for this knowledge. But you do, since *-ack* and *-ake* are systematically used with constant phonetic values. Compare *vack* with *back, lack, rack, whack,* and *stack;* and *vake* with *wake, cake, lake, take, rake, stake,* and *flake.* It should also prove instructive to examine the pairs *rack/rake, man/mane, fat/fate, pal/pale, Sam/same, tap/tape,* and *mad/made.* On the whole, then, English spelling is quite reasonable and we have no real cause for complaint.

A Brief History of Writing

The art of writing first developed in the Middle East, sometime around 3000 B.C. The Sumerians were apparently the first to use a writing system, and the practice soon spread. It is quite possible that all writing systems stem ultimately from the Sumerian achievement, but we cannot conclude this with certainty.

The Egyptian writing system developed under Sumerian influence. It was a mixed system, part word-writing and part syllable-writing. Although the natural evolution seems to be from word-writing systems to syllable-writing systems, probably no system has ever been purely logographic. Right from the start, word signs come to be used as syllabic signs by means of the rebus principle. For example, suppose word signs were available for *ray* and *sing*, but not for *racing*. The natural thing to do when the word *racing* was needed in a written message would be to represent it by combining the signs for *ray* and *sing*. When this system is followed consistently, the signs involved lose their status as word signs and take on purely phonetic significance. In this way a basically syllabic system can develop from a basically logographic one.

Out of the Egyptian writing system grew various syllabic ones used by West Semitic peoples from the second millennium B.C. Hebrew, Aramaic, and Phoenician, among other languages, were written with these syllabic systems. The writing practices of the Semites in turn spread to the Greeks, apparently through the Phoenicians. It is to the ancient Greeks that we owe the principle of alphabetic writing.

65

What the Greeks did was to systematize a device often used to render syllable-writing more precise. Syllabic signs were sometimes ambiguous; for instance, the same sign could designate *ta, ti, te,* and *to*. Vowel signs were therefore added to the ambiguous syllabic signs to avoid confusion. Thus, if the sign for *ta* could also be used for *ti, te,* and *to,* one would add to it a sign for *a* to indicate that *ta* was meant. In effect, then, *ta* was written *ta-a, ti* was written *ti-i,* and so on. When this device was used systematically, the original ambiguous syllabic signs came to be reinterpreted as signs for single consonants. The sign for *ta,* when accompanied consistently by the *a* sign, was interpreted as standing for the single segment *t*.

Alphabetic writing in various forms has spread throughout the world, although other kinds of writing systems are also in use. The Latin alphabet developed on the Greek model; modified in only minor ways through the centuries, it has been adopted throughout Western Europe and the New World. All other alphabetic writing systems can be traced back to the Greek invention in one way or another. Its success has been phenomenal.

Writing has become an indispensable component of modern society, and in all probability we will rely on it even more heavily in the future than we have in the past. As civilization becomes more complex and greater quantities of information have to be stored and transmitted, the written word will become even more indispensable than it already is. Language will continue to be a basically oral competence whose written representation is only secondary, but even now the development of languages is often influenced by their written representations. We must expect the connection between speech and writing to become even more intimate.

PART TWO

Language

Structure

CHAPTER
FOUR

The Organization
of Grammar

SIMPLE LEXICAL ITEMS

The Discreteness of Linguistic Units

A language can be conceived of as an infinite set of sentences, each of which pairs a meaning with a sound sequence. A sentence consists of a string of words. The meaning of a sentence depends on the meanings of the words it contains, just as the pronunciation of a sentence depends on the pronunciation of its words.

In characterizing a sentence in this way, we are making the assumption that linguistic units are basically discrete, that it is possible and correct to divide a sentence into word-like units, each of which is further divided into a linear string of individual sound segments. The discrete character of linguistic units may seem obvious, but an acoustic examination of a speech signal would not in itself lead one to this conclusion. In purely physical terms, there is for the most part no clear break between adjacent words in an utterance or between the sound segments of a single word. A speech signal is more nearly like a continuous stream than like a string of beads, none of which merges with any other. It is true that we can pause between words in uttering a sentence, or even in the middle of a word, but for the most part we do not.

Yet we feel intuitively that a sentence can be broken up into words and that words can be broken up into individual sounds. Our writing system reflects such an assumption of discreteness, for in general we leave spaces between words and represent each sound of a word with a separate symbol. There can be no real doubt that linguistic units are in fact basically discrete, despite the testimony of the speech signal itself. A language, remember, is not sound waves in the air; a language is the competence, the set of principles mastered by a speaker in which resides his grasp of an infinite set of sentences. On the basis of this competence, a speaker somehow constructs sentences and pronounces them, thereby producing the physical speech signal. Thus there is no conflict in claiming that linguistic units are discrete although the speech signal is continuous. The claim of discreteness is made for the units of linguistic competence, for the psychological representation of linguistic structure that underlies verbal behavior. Let us now proceed to examine these units.

Words and Morphemes

Up to now we have been using the common term **word** to designate an intermediate unit of structure smaller than a whole sentence yet larger than a single sound segment. Words seem to have psychological validity; we might misspell *antipathy*, but we would probably not do so by leaving a space before *thy* to indicate a word boundary: *antipa thy*. Moreover, when we pause in uttering a sentence, there are some places where it is more natural to pause than others. The sentence *Frederick is very antipathetic toward communists* could be interrupted naturally after every orthographically marked word, but hardly after *Freder*.

In studying the structure of a language, however, we readily recognize the existence of units of grammatical structure smaller than words. The word *gardens*, for instance, divides naturally into the components *garden* and *s*. *Garden* can appear by itself as an individual word, as well as in the words *gardening, gardener*, and so on. The plural *s* of *gardens* also appears in *cars, furs, telephones, ideas*, and many other nouns. The *tele* of *tele-*

phones shows up in *telegraph, television, teletype,* and *telescope.* The word *unfaithfulness* decomposes into *unfaithful* and *ness. Unfaithful* decomposes into *un* and *faithful,* which in turn consists of *faith* and *ful.* Each of the four components—*un, faith, ful,* and *ness*—appears in other words or can stand alone as an independent word (as in *unprepared, faith, careful, stubbornness*).

Minimal units of grammatical structure, such as the four components of *unfaithfulness,* are called **morphemes.** *Telephones* thus has three morphemes, while *telephone* contains two and *phone* just one. A morpheme usually has a fairly clear and constant meaning in all its uses, although it is easy to find exceptions. *Un* has negative force in *unfaithful, unemployed, unenthusiastic, unremorseful, unable, unerring,* and many other words. *Er* has a constant meaning in *painter, teacher, fighter, beholder, writer, passer, protester,* and *speaker.* On the other hand, it would be hard to pin down any constant meaning for *spect* in *respect, inspect, circumspect,* and *spectacle,* or for *pro* in *protest, prospective, profess, protract, progress, process,* and *proceed. To* really has no meaning in sentences like *I want to go,* although it must be present for such sentences to be grammatical. *Do* in *Why do they grow beards and demonstrate so often?* and *it* and *that* in *I dislike it that Harvey refuses to burn his draft card* are similarly without meaning.

Morphemes sometimes vary in their phonetic manifestations. *Pro,* for instance, is pronounced differently in *profess* and the noun *progress.* The plural morpheme is pronounced [s] in words like *lamps, ropes, births, puffs, nuts, racks,* and *fights.* In words like *ideas, bras, cards, pencils, dams, cans, bibs,* and *pills,* however, it is pronounced [z], and it is pronounced a third way in *churches, judges, juices, roses, flashes,* and *rouges.* The plural morpheme has no phonetic form at all with some nouns; consider, for example, *I stole a lot of sheep* and *I caught four fish.* Then there are completely idiosyncratic forms such as *oxen, children,* and *brethren.* It is not always obvious whether or not a given sound sequence should be considered a morpheme. For instance, should *animal* be said to consist of two morphemes, *anim(a)* and *(a)l,* or just one? (Consider *animate, nature/ natural.*) Is *woman* to be broken up into *wo* plus *man*? In any case, a sound sequence that is a morpheme in some words does not necessarily constitute a morpheme wherever it appears. *Un* is clearly a morpheme in *unremorseful* and *unfaithful,* but it is not a morpheme in *under* or *sun.*

Types of Morphemes

Linguists sometimes distinguish between **full** and **empty** morphemes, between **free** and **bound** morphemes, and between **roots** and **affixes**. Although these distinctions are rather superficial, they are worth discussing if only to illustrate the various ways in which morphemes differ from one another in their behavior.

Consider the string *Man chop wood axe*. This string is not a grammatical sentence of English, although it consists of English morphemes. On the other hand, it is fairly easy to grasp the general import of this ungrammatical string. With no difficulty we can picture to ourselves a man holding an axe and using it to chop some wood. This ungrammatical sentence is more or less meaningful—it is somewhat vague, but to a large extent we can reconstruct the conceptual situation the sentence portrays.

To make *Man chop wood axe* into a grammatical sentence, we could add the morphemes *the*, **PAST** (indicating the tense of the verb), *some*, *with*, and *a*, giving us *The man chopped some wood with an axe*. The sentence is now well formed and quite a bit more precise, but the added morphemes do not introduce a great deal of semantic content. They bring the conceptual situation portrayed by the sentence into sharper focus, but the meaning they contribute somehow seems secondary. The essential components of meaning were provided by the morphemes *man*, *chop*, *wood*, and *axe*.

Full morphemes are forms like *man, chop, wood,* and *axe*; **empty** morphemes are forms like *the, some, with, a,* and the past tense morpheme. Full morphemes are nouns, verbs, adjectives, and adverbs. They have more or less independent meaning, so that one or a series of full forms in isolation can be fairly meaningful. *Axe* suggests something pretty definite to us, as does *Man chop wood axe*. *With, a,* or *The some with a* by itself leaves us in the dark. Classes of full morphemes contain hundreds or thousands of members. There are thousands of nouns in English, for example, and it is very common for new ones to be added to the lexicon of a language. Empty morphemes are things like prepositions, articles, conjunctions, forms indicating number, gender, or tense, and so on. Such classes contain relatively few members, and new members are added to a language rather infrequently.

The distinction between full and empty morphemes is handy and correct up to a point, but it should not be pushed too far. It is somewhat artificial, for there is really a continuum without any sharp break stretching from morphemes with semantic content, like *wood*, to morphemes devoid of semantic content, such as *it* in *I dislike it that Harvey refuses to burn his draft card*. Prepositions are classed as empty morphemes, yet they are not all empty of semantic content. The sentence *The coins are on the desk*, for instance, is changed significantly in meaning when *on* is replaced by *under, over, by, near, in, off, around*, or *for*. Empty morphemes such as the *ly* of *rapidly*, the *un* of *unable*, and the *er* of *gardener* have definite semantic content. *And, or,* and *but* are by no means synonymous. On the other hand, not all full morphemes have independent meaning. What is the meaning of *stand* in *understand*, for example? The numerical differences are not very clear-cut either. English prepositions are fairly numerous, at least when compared with the single-morpheme adverbs of place, such as *here* and *there*, or with the single-morpheme adverbs of time, such as *now, then,* and *soon*.

Free morphemes are those that can stand alone as independent words; all others are said to be **bound** morphemes. *Dog, sad, rapid, berry,* and *able* are thus examples of free morphemes, while the plural morpheme *s* of *dogs*, the *ness* of *sadness*, the *ly* of *rapidly*, and the *un* of *unable* exemplify bound morphemes. Most full morphemes are free (at least in English), and many empty morphemes are bound, as the above examples show. But the two distinctions do not coincide; there are exceptions in both directions. *And, or,* and *but* are empty morphemes, yet they constitute independent words. *Cran* and *boisen* would be considered full morphemes, but they are bound to *berry* and do not occur alone.

A great many words are constructed by the addition of one or a succession of empty morphemes to a full morpheme. We saw that *ful* is added to *faith* to give *faithful*, which can subsequently be expanded to *unfaithful* and then to *unfaithfulness*. To the full morpheme *quick* we can add the empty morpheme *ly* to obtain the word *quickly*. *S* is added to *dog* to give *dogs*. The Aztec word *nitetlazotla* means 'I love' or 'I love someone.' *Tlazotla* is a full form, the verb 'love.' *Ni* and *te* are empty forms. *Ni* indicates that the subject of the verb is 'I.' *Te* indicates that the object of the verb is human but specified no further. The Aztec word *tlamatini* means 'wise man' or 'knower.' The verb *mati* means 'know.' The empty morphemes *tla* and *ni* are added to this to form *tlamatini*.

Tla is similar to *te*; it indicates that the object of the verb *mati* is not specified and also that it is nonhuman. *Ni* is added to the end of the verb form *tlamati* and contributes agentive meaning in the same way that the *er* of *gardener* does. Notice, incidentally, that the *ni* of *nitetlazotla* and the *ni* of *tlamatini* are not the same morpheme, despite the fact that they have the same phonological shape. Similarly, the *er* of *gardener* and the *er* of *stronger* are different morphemes; apart from pronunciation, they have radically different properties.

The full morpheme that constitutes the core of such words is called a **root,** while the empty morphemes that are added to a root to form larger units are called **affixes.** Thus, *faith* is the root to which are added the affixes *ful, un,* and *ness* to form *unfaithfulness.* In *quickly, quick* is a root and *ly* an affix. The affixes *tla* and *ni* flank the root *mati* in *tlamatini.* Affixes which precede the root, *tla* for example, are called **prefixes;** *ly,* which follows the root *quick,* is a **suffix.** In some languages, such as Arabic, affixes can be inserted inside a root; such affixes, called **infixes,** are much less common than prefixes and suffixes.

Inflection and Derivation

Affixes have varying effects when they are added to roots. When *s* is added to *dog* to form *dogs,* the effect is to further specify *dog* with respect to the number of animals being referred to. Both *dog* and *dogs* are nouns; adding the plural morpheme does not change the grammatical class (or, to use an older term, does not change the part of speech) of the word. Similarly, suffixing the past tense morpheme to the verb *chop* gives us another verb, *chopped.* On the other hand, *quick* and *quickly* belong to different grammatical classes; *quick* is an adjective, but *quickly* is an adverb. *Tlamati* is a verb form meaning 'know something'; the addition of the suffix *ni* gives us *tlamatini* 'wise man, knower,' which is not a verb but a noun. By the addition of the proper affix, an adverb can be derived from an adjective, or a noun from a verb. Other affixes relate still other grammatical classes.

Accordingly, linguists often distinguish between **inflectional** and **derivational** affixes. *Boy* and *boys,* to speak in loose, rather intuitive terms, are alternate forms of the same entity, as are *chop* and *chopped,* or Latin *laudō* 'I praise,' *laudās* 'you praise,' *laudat* 'he praises,' *laudāmus* 'we praise,' *laudātis* 'you (plural) praise,' and *laudant* 'they praise.' The endings added to *boy, chop,* and *laud* in the above forms are inflectional affixes. English nouns like *boy* can be inflected for number. *Chopped* contains an inflectional ending to indicate past tense. Latin verbs are inflected to agree with the subject in person ('I' versus 'you' versus 'he') and in number (singular versus plural). The Spanish adjective *hermosas* 'beautiful' contains two inflectional suffixes. It agrees with the noun it modifies in number and gender; *a* indicates that the noun is feminine and *s* that it is plural.

The relation between *quick* and *quickly* is of a different kind. When *ly* is added to *quick,* it does not serve to mark agreement with some other element of the sentence or to qualify the root with respect to number, tense, or anything comparable. It does not simply give us another version of the same entity; rather it derives from it an entity that is quite distinct. *Ly* is thus referred to as a derivational affix. The Aztec suffix *ni* is a derivational suffix that forms a noun from a verb, as in *tlamatini.*

The processes of word formation in English exploit the device of derivational affixes quite heavily. Consider, for instance, some of the affixes that can be used to derive nouns from verbs. *Ing* is very productive, giving us *hunting, dating, dancing, singing,* and many others. *Ment* yields *argument, placement,* and *establishment* from the corresponding verbs. The agentive *er* suffix yields *gardener, singer, swimmer, robber,* and countless others. Verb/noun pairs that illustrate other affixes of this type include *refuse/refusal, illustrate/illustration, criticize/criticism,* and *impose/imposition.*

Derivational affixes do not always effect a change in grammatical class. The derivational prefix *de,* for example, relates *populate* and *depopulate,* yet both are verbs. Also compare *apply/reapply, imaginative/unimaginative,* and *possible/impossible.* Nor is a shift in grammatical class always signalled by an overt marker. *Star* and *face* are basically nouns, but they can also be used as verbs, with no affix: *The governor will star in a new movie; Some people can never face reality.* The adjectives *major* and *minor* can similarly function as verbs. One can *major* in linguistics and *minor* in physics.

COMPLEX LEXICAL ITEMS

Affixation

The **lexicon** of a language is its inventory of morphemes, together with information about how these morphemes can be combined to form more complex lexical items, such as words. In some cases, the combination of morphemes into complex lexical units is very regular. The past tense morpheme, for instance, can be added to virtually any English verb. Thus we have *chop/chopped, slice/sliced, see/saw, buy/bought, can/could, am/was, bite/bit, raise/raised*, and so on. (One exception is *beware*, which can only be used in the present tense as an imperative.) The phonetic effect of putting a verb into the past tense varies from verb to verb. For some verbs, the addition of the past tense morpheme has no phonetic effect at all—*cut*, for example. Compare *I cut meat every day* and *I cut meat yesterday*. The point to note, however, is that there is almost always some way to do it. In general, the formation of words through the addition of inflectional morphemes is quite regular.

The combination of roots with derivational affixes tends to be less regular. One can *untie* a knot or *unhand* a maiden, but not *unclose* a door. A person can be *impish, boyish, foolish, childish,* or *waspish*, but not *geniusish, enemyish,* or *antish*. Something can be *reapplied, reassembled, reheated,* or *reapportioned*, but hardly *resaid, rereceived, reseen,* or *rebitten*. One who dances is a *dancer*; one who golfs is a *golfer*; but one who exists is not an *exister*. Derivational processes, as opposed to inflectional ones, range from fairly regular to highly idiosyncratic and irregular.

The distinction between essentially regular linguistic phenomena and essentially irregular or idiosyncratic ones is quite significant, as we will see in our examination of syntactic and phonological systems. It bears directly on the question of the nature of language and language acquisition.

Suppose a friend of yours reports that he has discovered a hitherto unknown plant in the wilderness of New Guinea, and that he has decided to call it a *dack*. Now you know a new noun morpheme, *dack*. Without being told, you know that to speak of more than one *dack* the proper word is *dacks*. Plural formation in English is not an idiosyncratic property of individual nouns; it is governed by regular, general principles that you have mastered in becoming an English speaker. In learning English, you did not learn individually for thousands of nouns that *pencil* has a plural that *apple* has a plural, that *box* has a plural, and so forth. You internalized the general structural principle that any common noun referring to a concrete, individual object has a plural. (*John, evaporation,* and *butter* are instances of nouns that normally do not have plurals. *John* is a proper noun or name, not a common noun; *evaporation* is not a concrete object; *butter* is not an individual object.) It is the possession of this general principle that tells you that *dack* has a plural. This principle projects to new cases, to new lexical items that you have never encountered before. What a speaker has to learn is simply the set of nouns of this type and the single principle that all such nouns can be combined with the plural morpheme.

On the other hand, the addition of the derivational affix *un*, meaning 'not,' to adjectives in English is not completely regular. Clearly, the same process of word formation is responsible for *untrue, unhappy, unintelligent,* and so on. The construction of these words is governed by a fairly general principle of English. Individual adjectives, however, behave idiosyncratically with respect to this process of word formation. There would seem to be no principle by which we say *untrue* but not *unfalse*; *undivided* but not *unsplit*; *unhappy* but not *unsad*; *unintelligent* but not *unbright* or *unsmart*; *unattractive* but not *unpretty* or *unugly*. It is not enough, in learning English, just to learn the inventory of English adjectives and the principle of derivation whereby *un* can be attached to an adjective. It is also necessary to learn, along with each individual adjective, whether or not it can undergo this principle of derivation. What cannot be predicted by general linguistic principles must be learned separately for each lexical item.

Compounds

The addition of affixes to full morphemes is one way of constructing complex lexical items from simple ones. There are various other ways of forming complex lexical units, and for the most part they are less regular than affixation.

Affixation, as we have seen, involves adding an empty morpheme to a full morpheme or to a larger unit containing a full morpheme. Some words, by way of contrast, are formed by combining two or more empty morphemes. By combining two prepositions, we obtain the English word *into* or *upon*. The French word *des*, if it is considered a separate word, represents the fusion of three empty morphemes. *Les* is *le* or *la* (the definite article 'the') plus the plural morpheme. *De* 'of' plus *les* is manifested as *des*. *Des* thus means 'of the (plural).'

More common, probably, are lexical units known as **compounds**. A compound is a lexical unit consisting of two or more full morphemes. Although languages differ greatly in the number of compounds in the lexicon, English is very rich in them. To name just a few, we may cite *textbook, wasteland, grandstand, longbow, whitecap, bloomer girl, bedside, homing pigeon, blowtorch, sunburn, suction pump, gas mask, water tower, fingerprint*, and *dishwater*. Notice that in some cases an empty morpheme is attached to one of the full morphemes entering into the compound, for example in *homing pigeon* or *catcher's mitt*. In English, but not necessarily in other languages, compounds are characterized by a special stress pattern: the first full morpheme is pronounced with much greater emphasis than the second. Thus we distinguish by means of stress the adjective–noun sequence *red skin*, skin which is red, and the compound *redskin*, where *red*, not *skin*, is pronounced with greater emphasis. Note also that the orthographic treatment of compounds is by no means consistent. Some are written as one word, while others are written as two. This is perhaps to be expected, since compounds have something of an intermediate status. On the one hand they are single complex units, but at the same time they differ from other words, and resemble word sequences, in that they contain more than one full morpheme.

Compounding is extremely prevalent in Aztec. Let us take just two examples, *tizanamacac* and *apannemini*. *Tizanamacac* means 'chalk seller.' It consists of *tiza* 'chalk' plus *namacac* 'seller,' which is in turn derived from the verb *namaca* 'sell.' *Apannemini* is even more complex. The two full morphemes are *a* 'water' and *nemi* 'live.' *Pan* is an empty morpheme meaning 'on,' and *ni* is the agentive affix we have already encountered in *tlamatini* 'wise man, knower.' The entire compound thus means 'water-on-live-er,' or 'one who lives on (the) water.'

Although a number of regularities can be observed, compound formation tends to be idiosyncratic. Consider English compounds consisting of an adjective and a noun, for instance. The following seem quite regular: *longbow, madman, Frenchman, wildflower, dirty work, deaf mute*, and *white man*. They can all be paraphrased by an expression of the form *noun that is adjective*. Thus a *longbow* is a *bow that is long*; a *madman* is a *man that is mad*; and so on. This is a recurrent pattern of compound formation in English; in other words, an adjective-noun compound can be formed given the existence of a corresponding expression of the form *noun that is adjective*.

A person learning English must learn more than just this principle of compound formation, however. He must at the same time learn a wealth of unpredictable, arbitrary facts about compounds of this type. It is just an arbitrary fact that *dirty work* is an English compound, but not *clean work, dry work*, or *wet work*. Why do we have *madman* but not *sadman, saneman, shyman*, or *dumbman*? Further, many compounds that are superficially of this type do not mean what we would predict on the basis of the regular pattern. A *redskin* is not a skin that is red but an Indian. A *bigwig* is not the same thing as a *big wig*. Other examples of this kind are *greenhorn, tenderfoot, dumbbell, redcoat, yellowjacket, sourpuss*, and *paleface*. Similar observations could be made for compounds other than those consisting of an adjective and a noun.

Idioms

Another kind of complex lexical item is the **idiom**. An idiom is a phrase whose meaning cannot be predicted from the individual meanings of the morphemes it comprises. If you *beat a dead horse*, you do not necessarily strike a carcass. A person can *die with his boots on* with his boots off. A *red herring* is not necessarily a fish. Nor is a pail always involved when someone *kicks the bucket*. Languages are full of idioms. Some others from English are *hit the sack, bury the hatchet, come up smelling like a rose, stick to the straight and narrow, hit the nail right on the head*, and *sing a different tune*. Almost by definition, idioms are idiosyncratic rather than regular in their formation.

Because they are constructed from morphemes that are also used non-idiomatically, most idioms can also be interpreted literally. If someone *beats a dead horse*, for instance, he may in fact be engaged in striking the carcass of a certain kind of animal. *Beat a dead horse*, in other words, is ambiguous between this literal interpretation and the figurative interpretation of harping on an issue that has long since been decided. It is interesting to observe that idioms are not just semantically different from the corresponding string of morphemes taken in the literal sense; the semantic peculiarity of idioms is often accompanied by special syntactic properties.

79

In the literal sense, to take an example, **Penelope kicked the bucket** has the passive variant **The bucket was kicked by Penelope**. When **kicked the bucket** means 'died,' it is incorrect to resort to this passive locution.

Idioms are in many cases similar to standardized metaphors, such as **stir up trouble** or **the heart of the matter**. In fact, the metaphorical origin of many idioms is quite apparent, and there is no reason to try to draw a dividing line. But not all idioms begin as metaphors. If **kick the bucket** had a metaphorical origin, the nature of the metaphor is no longer apparent to English speakers. Other idioms result, not from metaphor, but from ellipsis. The Spanish **No hay de qué**, literally 'There is not for what,' means 'You're welcome' or 'Don't mention it.' This expression is puzzling until one realizes that the full expression would translate literally as 'There is not anything for which to thank me' or something similar. The French **Il n'y a pas de quoi** is exactly parallel.

Idioms and standard metaphors (not to mention other complex lexical items) are clearly hammered out on the anvil of language use. Metaphorical expressions, if well suited to the occasion, are more colorful and effective than straightforward, prosaic statements. Successful metaphors are picked up and reapplied, so that they eventually become well established in the language. We use hundreds of them daily without even noticing them. The high redundancy of most common communication situations, coupled with the natural desire for brevity and the path of least resistance, renders very understandable indeed the tendency toward ellipsis that results in such expressions as **No hay de qué**. We can see perhaps the same tendency at work in the adoption of compounds; it is much simpler to say **suction pump** than **pump that works by suction**.

Words that are constantly associated in usage sometimes begin to cohere as lexical units. **Bread and butter** is such a common expression that it is somewhat odd to hear **butter and bread**. **Ham and eggs** is another example; **eggs and ham** just isn't the way to say it. Other examples are **bread and wine** and **bread and water**. **The stars and stripes** refers to more than just any aggregation of stars and stripes; **stripes and stars** does not have this special significance. The same can be said of **hammer and sickle**. The morphemes **in, so,** and **far** are used together so often that they have virtually fused into one word. We can write either **in so far as** or **insofar as**. **Nevertheless** has a similar origin. Those who know French will recognize **cependant** 'however' and **parce que** 'because' as fused forms of the same type.

PHONOLOGICAL, SEMANTIC, AND SYNTACTIC REPRESENTATIONS

When a person learns a morpheme, what he does, essentially, is tie together three kinds of information: phonological, semantic, and syntactic.

Suppose, for example, that he masters the English morpheme *cat*. In so doing, he must master a certain amount of phonological information, the information that the pronunciation of this morpheme is *cat* ([kæt]), and not *filk, liberty, dog, act, tack,* or anything else. More precisely, he has to learn that this morpheme consists phonologically of three sound segments (not two or four or seven); that these are [k], [æ], and [t] (not [s], [æ], and [t] or any other combination); and that these are ordered [k]–[æ]–[t] (not [æ]–[k]–[t], [t]–[æ]–[k], or any other way). We can say that, as part of the process of learning a morpheme, a person learns a **phonological representation** for that morpheme. The phonological representation of *cat* includes at least the information given above.

We have seen that some morphemes are semantically empty; *to*, for instance, has no meaning in *I want to go*. Most morphemes do have meaning, however, and this meaning must be learned as part of the process of learning a morpheme. We do not at present know how to characterize the **semantic representation** of a morpheme, to say what kind of information must be associated with a morpheme for it to have a certain meaning as opposed to all other possible meanings. It is clear, however, that morphemes do have semantic representations of some kind and that the pairing of a semantic representation and a phonological representation in a morpheme is in most cases fully arbitrary or conventional. English would work just as well if the semantic representation of *cat* were associated with some other phonological entity.

A morpheme is not fully defined by its semantic and phonological properties alone. A morpheme also has syntactic properties, some **syntactic representation** that determines how it functions with respect to the grammatical processes of the language. *Cat*, for example, can function only as a noun, and never, say, as an adjective. Thus the sentence *That fat cat spat at flat black mats* is grammatical, but the sentence *It is very cat* is not. Consequently, morphemes can be viewed as bundles of semantic, phonological, and syntactic properties.

The picture is not really this simple, however. *Route*, for example, has two alternate pronunciations, sometimes even within the same idiolect; it can be pronounced to rhyme with either *shout* or *shoot*. *Economics* can start with the vowel of either *peck* or *peek*, and some people use the two variants interchangeably. *Light* can be the semantic opposite of either *dark* or *heavy*, not to mention *filling* (*Ice cream is light, but pie is very filling*). *Square* can function syntactically as a noun, verb, or adjective (*Mark an X in the proper square; It is useless to try to square the circle; The table is square*). It is the exception for a common full morpheme to have a single phonological representation, a single semantic representation, and a single syntactic representation, as a glance at any page in a dictionary will show. In describing the lexicon of a language, we must somehow make provision for these alternate possibilities.

The question naturally arises as to how these entities that seem to be variants of the same morpheme are related to one another. For cases like *route* and *economics*, there is not much to be said. The morpheme *route*, for some speakers, has two alternate vowels in its phonological representation; the speaker has a choice whenever he goes about pronouncing this form. Much more interesting are the cases where the same phonological representation is associated with different semantic or syntactic representations.

We can observe first that there are many forms with identical phonological shape that have little or nothing further in common. In these instances, we are justified in saying that the forms are different morphemes. The two *ni* morphemes of Aztec are a good example. One indicates that the subject is 'I,' the other is an agentive suffix, and they have nothing in common except pronunciation. The two *er* suffixes of English (in *stronger* and *dancer*) are another example. *Read* and *reed*, both pronounced [rid], clearly have no special affinity, and neither do *ant* and *aunt*, both pronounced [ænt] in some dialects. The existence of such phonologically identical sets of morphemes in a language can be considered purely coincidental.

In other cases, though, the similarities are such as to suggest, with varying degrees of force, some special relationship between identically pronounced forms. Consider, for example, the phrases *sharp razor, sharp mind, sharp focus*, and *sharp outfit*. In the strict sense, these four instances of *sharp* are semantically different; they might be paraphrased respectively as 'having an edge that cuts well,' 'quick, intelligent,' 'not blurry,' and 'stylish, smart.' But in a broader sense these four versions of *sharp* display a special semantic relationship that justifies treating them as variants of a single morpheme. On purely intuitive grounds, one could maintain that *sharp* in the sense of 'having an edge that cuts well' is somehow basic and that the other versions of *sharp* are secondary, being derived from it as essentially metaphorical creations. A mind is sharp in that it cuts with ease through difficult problems; a picture is in sharp focus when the lines are thin and well defined, like the blade of a keen knife; a sharp outfit is one that stands out in sharp focus against the background of mediocrity.

Examples of such metaphorical extensions are legion. Compare *clear water, clear issue, clear presentation,* and *clear weather*; or *I bumped my head, head of a pin,* and *head of a department*; or *The car struck a pole, Harvey struck his mother, The clock struck twelve, Strike that from the record, strike a match, strike out,* and *strike oil.* Even restricting ourselves to simple lexical units consisting of a single morpheme, we encounter the widely pervasive influence of metaphor. However, the relationship between two senses of the same morpheme is not always one of basic meaning and metaphorical extension. The *drive* of *drive a car* and the *drive* of *drive a golf ball* are to a certain extent similar in meaning (they both involve imparting motion to the thing driven), but neither seems to be a metaphorical extension of the other.

Most difficult and intriguing of all are those variants of what seems to be the same morpheme that differ semantically according to syntactic use. There is an evident relationship between the noun *circle* in *He drew a circle in the sand* and the verb *circle* in *The Indians circled the cabin,* or between the noun *fire* (*I will light a fire*) and the homonymous verb (*fire the pottery*). It would be tempting to suppose that the difference in meaning is attributable directly to the difference in syntactic use: to say, for instance, that the two versions of *circle* have the same semantic representation and that the difference between *circle* as a geometrical figure and as movement in a path resembling that geometrical figure resides solely in the difference between nouns and verbs. This may be part of the truth, but it cannot be the whole truth. It is sufficient to observe that no constant semantic effect is associated with the functioning of a morpheme as a noun, as a verb, or as any other part of speech. The semantic difference between *circle* as a noun and as a verb is one of movement. Whatever the precise difference between *fire* as a noun and as a verb may be, it is not one of lack of movement versus movement. The semantic distinction between the noun *skin* (*My skin is soft*) and the verb *skin* (*I skinned my*

83

knee) is of another sort entirely. Squaring a circle and circling a circle are very different enterprises.

MEANING AND ITS MANIFESTATION

In coming to grips with linguistic structure, we have so far mainly directed our efforts at dissecting language to see what kinds of parts it has. We have seen that sentences are divisible into lexical items of various sorts, some of which can be further divided into smaller lexical units. We have seen that a linguistic system as a whole can, at least for convenience of discussion, be broken up into semantic, syntactic, and phonological subsystems. A lexical item can be analyzed for its semantic, syntactic, and phonological representations, each of which corresponds to one of these subsystems. It is time that we shifted the emphasis from dissection to anatomy and physiology in order to get some kind of overview of how the components of a language are organized in a coherent system and how they interact. Semantic considerations must play a prominent part in this discussion. In Chapters Five and Six we will examine in more detail the nature of syntactic and phonological systems.

Let us return to our original conception of a language as a device for pairing meanings and sound sequences. It is the possession of such a device that enables a speaker to translate his thoughts into sequences of sounds for communication to others and to understand the sound signals emitted by other speakers, to reconstruct (at least approximately) the thoughts that prompted the emission of these signals. This device for linking meanings and sound sequences consists in a set of conventions and principles. By using these conventions and principles in some complex way that is not at all understood, a person manages to create and understand utterances. Our immediate concern is not with how these conventions and principles are used in practice, but rather with their intrinsic character. In other words, our task is to understand linguistic competence as best we can; little is known about linguistic performance, and in any case it is beyond the scope of this book. The following paragraphs, then, will not outline step by step what a speaker does when he produces or perceives an utterance, but rather will sketch the organization of the system that underlies his performance, that enables him to function in the dual capacity of speaker and hearer.

Figure 4.1

Consider the sentence *The cat scratched the dog*. It has both a meaning and a pronunciation. The problem is to state how, by what organizational scheme, this meaning and this pronunciation (and all similar pairs) are connected. If we depict the situation as in Figure 4.1, the problem is that of characterizing the relationship symbolized by the arrow. The relationship is complex, even for the simplest of sentences, so we will examine it a little bit at a time.

The Role of Phonological Rules

We will start from the phonological end. *The cat scratched the dog* consists of a string of morphemes. Letting **PAST** symbolize the past tense morpheme, and putting a plus sign between successive morphemes of the string, this sentence can be represented as *the+cat+scratch+PAST +the+dog*. Each of these morphemes has some phonological representation, as we have seen. The morpheme *cat*, for instance, is defined in part by the information that it consists of three sound segments, [k], [æ], and [t], arranged in that order.

The phonological representations of these individual morphemes do not themselves specify fully the pronunciation of the sentence in all its phonetic detail. A language, remember, is characterized by a phonological system, by general phonological principles that do not pertain to individual morphemes but hold across the board for all morphemes of the language. These principles combine and interact with the phonological representations of individual morphemes in determining the full, detailed pronunciation of a sentence. A sound segment has different pronunciations, for example, depending on what sound segments are adjacent to it in the string. English [n] is not phonetically the same in *tenth*, where it occurs before [θ], and in *ten*, where it does not. The English [k] is pronounced differently at the beginning of a word (where a slight puff of air

85

is released as it is articulated) and after [s] (where the puff of air is much weaker or is missing altogether). General phonological principles such as these combine with the special phonological properties of individual morphemes in determining precisely how a sentence is pronounced.

Retaining *The cat scratched the dog* as our example, we can modify the above diagram to the one shown in Figure 4.2. The phonological system of the language is responsible for determining the full pronunciation of this sentence on the basis of the phonological representations of its individual morphemes. The principles of the phonological system do such things as specify that the (word-initial) [k] of *cat* is pronounced with a slight puff of air and that the [k] of *scratch* (which occurs after [s]) is not. These principles are called **phonological rules**. (**Rule** is simply a less cumbersome term than **principle**—it implies nothing more or less than the latter.) The nature of phonological rules and representations will be discussed more fully in Chapter Six.

Conceptual and Surface Structures

Given the representation of a sentence as a string of morphemes, then, each with some phonological representation, the phonological rules of the language determine its detailed phonetic form, or pronunciation. The next point we must examine is the relationship between a thought that a speaker wants to express (or that a hearer reconstructs) and the string of morphemes that corresponds to it. How are meanings and strings of morphemes connected? This is, to say the least, a difficult question. In fact, it is the crucial question that linguists are faced with today in their investigation of linguistic organization. Answering it involves clarifying the relation between **syntax** (the set of principles or rules specifying the set of grammatical sentences of a language and their structures) and **semantics** (the study of meaning). The difficulty is rendered even more acute by the close connection between semantics and human psychology in general; to describe meaning, or even to say what sort of thing meaning is, we are forced to talk about the structure of thought and cognition. Very little of substance is known about the principles of psychological organization, however. It is fairly easy to observe the motions of our speech organs to see how sounds are produced, but it is not so easy to observe and charac-

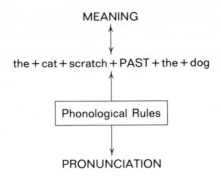

MEANING

the + cat + scratch + PAST + the + dog

Phonological Rules

PRONUNCIATION

FIGURE 4.2

terize the operation of the mind. While we can with some assurance say quite a bit about the relation between meaning and strings of morphemes, there are many large and serious gaps in our knowledge.

What is the relation between the string *the+cat+scratch+PAST+the+ dog* and the meaning of this sentence? The first thing to notice is that both entities are highly structured. *The+cat+scratch+PAST+the+dog* is not just a jumble of morphemes randomly thrown together; it is a group of morphemes arranged in a very particular way. For one thing, these morphemes are arranged in a specific linear order, one after another. Changing this linear order gives either an ungrammatical string or another sentence. Moreover, certain adjacent morphemes of the string cohere in some sense to form distinct substrings. *The+cat* seems to be some sort of special group; this substring functions as a unit in a way in which *PAST+the*, for example, does not. Similarly, *scratch+PAST+the+dog* is some sort of unit (with subgroups *scratch+PAST* and *the+dog*), while *cat+scratch+PAST+the* is not. We are dealing, therefore, with a rather abstract structure, of which the linear sequence of morphemes is only one facet. This structure will be called the **surface structure** of the sentence.

It is equally clear that the meaning of the sentence *The cat scratched the dog* is structured, but it is not so easy to say just how. What does the meaning of a sentence look like, anyway? This is a fair question, but one to which we cannot at present give a very satisfying answer.

As organisms with complex central nervous systems, we possess vast stores of conceptual knowledge, knowledge that is highly organized and integrated. Thinking is the manipulation of concepts, the activation of subparts of our total conceptual apparatus. A sentence is meaningful, if at all, just because it relates to aspects of our psychological structure, because it is capable of evoking or being evoked by some conception of a situation.

We use sentences to talk about conceived situations, which arise in various ways. The situations we conceive of may be based squarely on immediate perceptions. If A is giving to B a play-by-play account of a fight between a cat and a dog, he may have occasion to use the sentence *The cat scratched the dog* by way of reporting on something he has seen happen only seconds before. In this case, A's conceptualization of this situation results directly from sensory experience. He is thinking of a cat and dog because he is watching an event in which they are participating, and he thinks of them as having engaged in the act of scratching because he has just watched such an action unfold. B thinks of an act of scratching because A says to him *The cat scratched the dog*. On the basis of the sentence he perceives, he constructs some conceptual picture of the happening. If the act of communication is successful, B's conceptual picture will have much in common with the one that prompted A to make the report; they will differ in fine detail, no doubt, but not in fundamentals.

The conceptualization of a situation may arise without being evoked by immediate perceptions at all, linguistic or nonlinguistic. A person may conceive of a situation from memory and proceed to report on the remembered state of affairs. Or he may manipulate his store of concepts so as to conceive of something he has never witnessed at all; our mental processes have a considerable degree of freedom from sensory control. If you know what cats and dogs are, and what it is for something to scratch something, you are capable of conceiving of a cat scratching a dog, even if no such event has ever occurred in your experience or been reported to you via language. By rearranging and restructuring familiar conceptual entities, we can make up new ones that have hitherto never occupied our consciousness. Such is the origin of unicorns (with or without flowers growing from their nostrils) and of all products of human creativity.

The meaning of a sentence is thus a conceptual situation, and it is structured. The meaning of *The cat scratched the dog* is not the precise mental picture that A had last Tuesday when he uttered the sentence for B, nor is it the precise mental picture that B constructed when he heard it. Maybe A was thinking of a Siamese cat and a collie when he produced the sentence, and he was interested in the fact that the Siamese used its left front paw to do the scratching, but these details are clearly not part of the meaning of the sentence itself; if B had no information other than the sentence to go on, he could not deduce these details from it. To the extent that *The cat scratched the dog* has a definite meaning at all, it has one because the particular conceptual situations that it evokes or that evoke it have certain fundamental properties in common. If we could extract all the irrelevant frills and complications involved in any actual conceptualization underlying a sentence, the conceptual picture that would be left could reasonably be called the meaning of that sentence.

Conceptual pictures are highly structured. The conceptual situation represented by *The cat scratched the dog* is far from being just a random arrangement of ideas. It consists of parts arranged in a very specific way. One component of this complex thought is the conception of a cat; another is the conception of a dog. These components are combined as participants in the envisaged act of scratching. The activity is conceived of as being located in time prior to the present. If these components were combined differently, a different thought would result. For example, the same components structured in another manner would constitute the conceptual situation represented by *The dog scratched the cat* or by *In the presence of the dog, the cat scratched itself*. Similarly, our conception of a bicycle does not consist simply in the association of the concepts wheel, pedal, handlebar, frame, seat, and so on, but rather in the arrangement of these in a coherent, familiar structure. Without the configuration, we have nothing but a pile of junk.

Both the string of morphemes constituting a sentence and the conceptual situation underlying it, therefore, are structured entities. We have called the former the surface structure of the sentence. Let us adopt the term **conceptual structure** to designate the latter. The semantic and syntactic systems of a language comprise the principles that relate conceptual structures and surface structures. For every sentence of a language, these principles specify the relationship between its form as a string of morphemes and its conceptual import. We can now revise our diagram (Figure 4.2) of the way in which the components of a language interact to pair meanings and pronunciations in the form of sentences. The result is Figure 4.3, in which the terms **meaning** and **pronunciation** have been replaced by slightly more descriptive ones; we can say that a sentence represents a **conceptual structure** and has a **phonetic manifestation**.

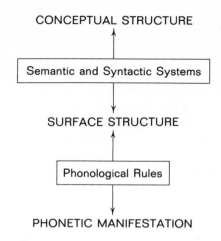

CONCEPTUAL STRUCTURE

Semantic and Syntactic Systems

SURFACE STRUCTURE

Phonological Rules

PHONETIC MANIFESTATION

FIGURE 4.3

Lexical Choices and Syntactic Rules

In Chapter Two, we took a brief look at semantic and syntactic systems. We saw that lexical items have meaning, or conceptual import, and that the meaning of a sentence depends ultimately on the meanings of its lexical items. This aspect of a language was said to be its semantic system. The syntactic system of a language was characterized simply as the set of principles or rules specifying which strings of lexical items, out of all possible ones, are grammatical sentences. The syntax of a language can be viewed, in other words, as a system of rules for constructing the infinite set of strings that are grammatical in the language. We can now describe more precisely how these systems function to link conceptual structures with surface structures.

A sentence can be used to talk about some conception of a situation because the morphemes that make it up have individual conceptual import, or semantic representations. Morphemes can thus be used to designate components of a complex thought or aspects of its configuration.

Suppose, once again, that A is reporting to B on a battle between a cat and a dog. A sees the cat scratch the dog, and a moment later he goes about reporting this to B. As the result of recent sensory experience, A has conceived of a rather complex situation. He has conceived of an event involving two participants with certain characteristics. In order to translate this complex notion into linguistic form, he chooses morphemes to designate subparts of it. The conceptual import of the morpheme *cat* matches one component of the conceptual situation; that of *dog* another; and that of *scratch* a third. Furthermore, A conceives of the event as having taken place prior to the present moment. He can therefore choose the morpheme *PAST* to indicate the temporal location of the event. Estimating that B's attention has already been focused on a particular dog and a particular cat, he chooses the definite article *the* to precede *dog* and *cat* (as opposed to *some, a,* or some specification as to which dog and cat are involved).

The assignment of lexical items to represent parts of a conceptual structure is of course only one facet of the relationship between the conceptual structure of a sentence and its surface structure, which phonological rules connect with a phonetic manifestation. Conceptual and surface structures are by no means identical, and consequently there must be some set of principles that relate them. These principles are the syntactic rules of the language, its syntactic system.

A few examples will demonstrate that the conceptual and surface structures of sentences are not identical. In some cases, components that are present in a conceptual structure are simply not present in the corresponding surface structure. English imperative sentences are a good example. *Come here!* does not display overtly any noun designating the person or thing that is to come. Yet the conceptual import of this sentence most certainly includes some entity that is being ordered to change location with respect to the speaker. Conversely, there are sentences that contain in their surface structure elements that have no place in the conceptual structure. The *to* in *I want to go* is an example; it is quite devoid of meaning. *Harvey broke the window* and *The window was broken by Harvey* have different surface structures, but they obviously have the same meaning, the same conceptual structure. *Biting dogs can be bothersome* can result from either of two radically different conceptual structures (do the dogs bite or get bitten?), but the surface structure is the same or very similar under either interpretation. The surface and conceptual structures of sentences therefore cannot be identical.

We have now arrived at the scheme of linguistic organization depicted in Figure 4.4. In learning a language, a person must learn a set of lexical items, a set of syntactic rules, and a set of phonological rules. Each lexical item involves a semantic representation, a phonological representation, and a syntactic representation. A conceptual structure is connected with a

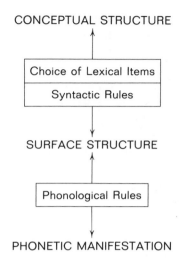

FIGURE 4.4

surface structure by the choice of lexical items, whose semantic representations make them suitable to designate parts of the conceptual structure,
and by syntactic rules. Phonological rules connect the surface structure of
a sentence with its phonetic manifestation on the basis of the phonological
representations of its lexical items.

LINGUISTIC AND PSYCHOLOGICAL CONSTRAINTS

To complete this outline of the organization of linguistic systems,
let us return to the notion that the syntax of a language is a set of rules
specifying an infinite set of grammatical sentences, differentiating those
strings of morphemes that are well-formed sentences from those that are not.

The sentences of a language form an infinite set because there is, in
principle, no limit to their length; just as there is no highest number,
there is no longest sentence. As languages are organized, then, sentences
of any desired degree of complexity can be constructed. The source of this
property of human language is twofold. First, the human mind is in principle capable of conceiving thoughts of any desired degree of complexity.

Second, the syntactic rules of a language are capable of connecting conceptual structures, regardless of their complexity, with surface structures. This feature of syntactic rules will be examined in some detail in the next chapter. The first point should be clarified before we go any further.

Our psychological mechanisms are such that conceptual situations of unlimited complexity can, in principle, arise. A person can conceive of a cat having scratched a dog. He can also conceive of someone believing that some state of affairs obtains. These two conceptions can in turn serve as components of a more complex thought, the thought of person A believing that the cat scratched the dog. This thought in turn can be a subpart of a still more complex conceptualization, in which person B hopes that A believes that the cat scratched the dog; and so on. It is easy to see that these conceptual situations are structured, that the component ideas are not just randomly piled together. For B to hope that A believes that the cat scratched the dog is not at all the same as for A to hope that B believes that the cat scratched the dog or for the cat to believe that A hopes that the dog scratched B. It should also be apparent that there is no *intrinsic* limit to the possible complexity of such conceptual situations.

To say that there is no intrinsic limit is not to say that human conceptual powers have no bounds. Obviously, they are highly constrained in many ways, although no one knows precisely what these constraints are. Try to visualize something that is round and square simultaneously, for instance. It cannot be done. It is possible to visualize something that is simultaneously round and red, say, but not round and square. It is only possible to visualize a round figure, or a square one, or to switch rapidly back and forth between a round and a square figure, or to visualize a square figure superimposed on a round one. There must be many similar constraints. Moreover, there are bounds on cognitive performance, just as there are bounds on linguistic performance. In trying to conceive of a very complicated situation, we are likely to get confused, to put the components together in the wrong way, and so forth. We can handle ideas of only so much complexity before we start to make mistakes. There are definite limits on the amount of information we can hold in mind and operate with at one time.

Consequently, some thoughts are just too complicated to handle all at once. In playing chess, for example, it is easy to think of the next move, and it is not too hard to think two moves ahead. When we try to conceptualize all the possibilities and their consequences for three, four, or five moves in advance, however, we quickly lose track and have to start over again, taking it one step at a time. Some thoughts, therefore, are just too complex for us to entertain, even though they are possible thoughts, just as some grammatical sentences are too complex for us to produce. This constraint is radically different in kind from the one that precludes our visualizing square circles. The possibility of visualizing square circles is flatly ruled out by the principles of human psychological organization. It has nothing to do with complexity or memory limitations. But none of the components of the complex conceptualization involved in planning eleven moves ahead in chess is ruled out by psychological constraints, and neither is their arrangement; there are simply too many for us to remember simultaneously.

With this distinction in mind, let us return to the notion of grammaticalness. Some sentences are likely never to occur simply because of performance limitations of the kind just discussed. No sentence three billion words long has any real chance of ever being uttered, although such a sentence could, in principle, be constructed; we simply could not handle a sentence that long. Even sentences of reasonable length can be so involved that we cannot easily operate with them. *That Josephine came is annoying* should bother no one; *That that Josephine came is annoying is surprising* is much less likely to be understood the first time around; *That that that Josephine came is annoying is surprising is obvious* is too involved for most people to grasp immediately, although they can probably figure it out if it is written down and they have enough time. All three sentences are equally grammatical and meaningful. It is important not to confuse ungrammaticalness with excessive complexity that makes a sentence difficult or impossible to use. By virtue of speaking a language, we have a grasp of infinitely many well-formed sentences that are too complicated for us to handle with ease, just as we are capable of multiplying any two numbers even though there are many multiplications that are too difficult for us to carry out in our heads. This is one of the reasons for distinguishing between competence and performance.

Deviant or ungrammatical sentences are those which violate some constraint; whether or not they are too complex to be used readily is irrelevant in this regard. We may distinguish between ungrammaticalness in a narrow and in a broad sense.

In the narrow sense, a sentence is ungrammatical if it violates some syntactic rule of the language. For example, *The boys am stupid* is ungrammatical in this narrow sense. It is a syntactic principle of English that the verb of a sentence agrees with the subject in number and person. The subject of *The boys am stupid* is third person plural, but the verb form *am* is a form taken only by a first person singular subject (*I*). Another syntactic principle of English is that a simple adjective, such as *stupid*, must precede the noun it modifies, not follow it. *The stupid boys* is thus a well-formed expression, but *the boys stupid* is ungrammatical.

Other sentences are deviant in some sense, but not because they violate any syntactic rule. In this broader sense, sentences like the following are ungrammatical: *That circle is square; Harvey rode the fragrance around the room; I heard a purple symphony.* These sentences violate psychological constraints of some kind, not syntactic ones. That is, the conceptual structures that would have to underlie these sentences are simply not possible thoughts. We cannot conceptualize something that is both round and square at the same time (although there are various ways to cheat and make it seem that we can, say by switching back and forth rapidly between the conception of a circle and that of a square). The only way we can conceive of a person riding on a fragrance is by mentally turning a fragrance into something concrete, like a ribbon of smoke, and to imagine this as having enough body to support a rider as it floats around the room serving as a magic carpet. A symphony can be purple only if one performs a similar mental transformation. When we turn a fragrance or a symphony into something concrete, we are, of course, no longer conceiving of a fragrance or a symphony; we have used our conceptual powers to dream up some new kind of physical object. *The brick elapsed* is deviant in the same way. No possible conceptual situation qualifies as the conceptual structure underlying this sentence, and in this case it is even difficult to dream up a metaphorical kind of brick that would be the sort of thing that could elapse. We can interpret these sentences if we try hard enough, but only in a secondary or metaphorical sense. It is necessary to modify the conceptual import of one of the lexical items just for the sake of making the conceptual structure a psychologically possible one.

A sentence will be said to be **ungrammatical** only when it is syntactically deviant, that is, when it violates some syntactic rule. Sentences like *I heard a purple symphony* are more naturally said to be semantically deviant or to violate psychological constraints. It may not always be clear whether a sentence is syntactically or semantically deviant, if only because there is much concerning syntactic rules and psychological processes that is still unknown. The distinction seems to be a reasonable one, however. Some sentences, of course, are syntactically and semantically deviant simultaneously, for example *I are listening to a purple symphony*. Others deviate so far from the syntactic patterns of a language, or from possible manifestations of conceptual structures, that one would hesitate even to call them sentences. *And but though chocolate or thrice willow noose abstract square square asunder Harvey* is an English sentence only in the sense that it is a string of English words. It would be completely arbitrary to single out any particular syntactic or psychological constraints as those violated by this string.

CHAPTER FIVE

Syntactic Systems

SURFACE STRUCTURES

The function of syntactic rules is to link conceptual structures with surface structures. We know very little about conceptual structures, since we know so little about human cognition in general. In comparison, the nature of surface structures is relatively easy to ascertain, and our examination of syntactic systems will consequently start with them. Although we will concentrate on English, much of the following discussion will prove valid for all languages.

A sentence, as we have seen, can be segmented into a series of morphemes. *The cat scratched the dog* can be represented as *the+cat+scratch +PAST+the+dog*. *An old man gave the airplane to Helen* consists of the morpheme sequence *an+old+man+give+PAST+the+air+plane+to+ Helen*. The morphemes of a sentence are not randomly arranged but are combined in a very specific way to form a surface structure. We can note three aspects of the configuration of surface structures: their linear arrangement, their hierarchical arrangement, and the types of units they contain.

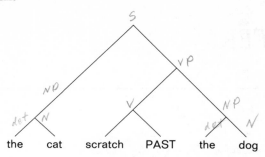

FIGURE 5.1

Linear and Hierarchical Arrangement

The linear ordering of the morphemes of a sentence is self-evident. In the first string above, *the* precedes *cat* precedes *scratch* precedes *PAST,* and so on. Changing the order of the morphemes in a sentence results either in an ungrammatical string or in another sentence. *Cat the dog the scratched,* for instance, is an ungrammatical string. *The dog scratched the cat* is grammatical, but it is simply not the same sentence as *The cat scratched the dog.*

The morphemes of a sentence are also arranged hierarchically. We observed earlier that the morphemes of *The cat scratched the dog* cohere to form larger units. *The* and *cat* function as a group in some sense, whereas *PAST* and *the* in no way stand apart from the rest of the string as a unit. A string of morphemes that constitutes such a unit is called a constituent. *The+cat* is thus a constituent of *The cat scratched the dog,* but *PAST+the* is not.

The entire string *the+cat+scratch+PAST+the+dog* can be considered a constituent, since it constitutes a special kind of unit, a sentence. This string can be broken down into two smaller constituents, *the+cat* and *scratch+PAST+the+dog,* and the latter has the subconstituents *scratch+ PAST* and *the+dog.* Finally, each individual morpheme is a constituent. The hierarchical grouping of the morphemes of a sentence can be illustrated in a diagram such as Figure 5.1. In this **tree structure,** *the+cat,* *scratch+PAST,* and *the+dog* are shown to be units, since the members of each pair are attached to intersecting **branches.** By the same token, *scratch+PAST+the+dog* is shown to be a unit, and the entire sentence is a higher-level unit composed of the subparts *the+cat* and *scratch+PAST +the+dog.* *PAST+the,* on the other hand, does not form a unit; the

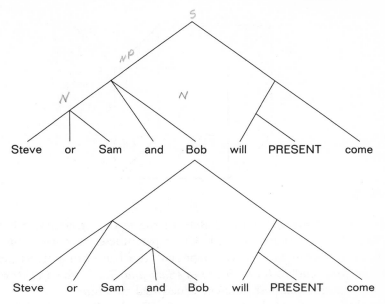

FIGURE 5.2

branch leading from **PAST** and the one leading from *the* do not intersect. Similarly, *the+cat+scratch* is shown not to be a constituent, since the branch leading from *the+cat* fails to intersect with the branch leading from *scratch*.

The ambiguity of certain sentences can be explained with reference to their tree structure. Consider, for example, the sentence **Steve or Sam and Bob will come**. This sentence can be interpreted in either of two ways. It can mean that Bob will come and that either Steve or Sam will come too; or it can mean that either Steve will come or Sam and Bob will. This difference in interpretation corresponds directly to a difference in tree structure. The first interpretation corresponds to the first structure of Figure 5.2, while the second interpretation corresponds to the second structure. (In both structures, **PRESENT** stands for the present tense morpheme, which determines that the modal verb is manifested as *will*, instead of as the past tense form *would*.)

The morpheme sequence **Steve+or+Sam+and+Bob+will+PRESENT +come** thus represents either of two surface structures. These surface structures differ, not in the identity or order of morphemes but rather in tree structure. In the first structure of Figure 5.2, **Steve or Sam** is a sub-

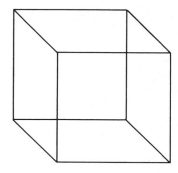

Figure 5.3

constituent of *Steve or Sam and Bob*. In the second structure, it is *Sam and Bob* that is a subconstituent. Using parentheses to enclose the elements of a constituent, we can represent the contrasting structures as *(Steve or Sam) and Bob* and *Steve or (Sam and Bob)*. These contrasting surface structures manifest different conceptual structures.

Another example of this type of structural ambiguity is *little girl's bike*. As *(little girl's) bike*, it is the bike of a little girl. As *little (girl's bike)*, it is a girl's bike that is little. Or consider *The policeman killed the woman with a gun*, which is also structurally ambiguous. *The policeman killed (the woman with a gun)* means that the woman was armed, while *The policeman killed (the woman) (with a gun)* has another interpretation. This structural ambiguity is exactly parallel to that of certain geometrical figures. Figure 5.3, for instance, can be viewed in either of two ways, just as *little girl's bike* can.

Constituent Types

We have not said everything there is to say about a surface structure when we have described the linear ordering of its morphemes and their hierarchical arrangement. Consider Figures 5.1 and 5.2 once more. The tree diagrams indicate that certain morpheme sequences belong together as constituents and that others do not, but they do not show what type of constituent a given sequence is. For instance, they do not indicate that *the cat* and *the dog* are constituents of the same kind, as opposed to, say, *scratched* or *will come*. Nothing shows that *Steve or Sam and Bob, an old man,* and *the dog* are similar, that *will come, gave the*

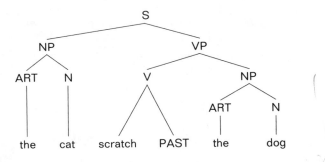

FIGURE 5.4

airplane to Helen, and *scratched the dog* are similar, but that *an old man* and *scratched the dog* are constituents of different types.

To supply this information, we can simply label the constituents, giving constituents of the same type the same label. In Figure 5.4, the labels identify the constituents of *The cat scratched the dog.* Some of the labels are obvious. S stands for sentence, N for noun, V for verb, and ART for article. NP stands for noun phrase, a constituent whose main member is a noun. By the same token, VP labels a verb phrase, a constituent built around a verb. *The cat* and *the dog* are shown to be constituents of the same type, since both are labeled as noun phrases. *The cat* and *scratched,* on the other hand, are shown to be different types of constituents.

Figure 5.5 represents the surface structure of *An old man gave the airplane to Helen.* ADJ stands for adjective, and P for preposition. We will use the term prepositional phrase (PP) to designate a constituent consisting of a preposition plus a noun phrase. *Helen* of course is a noun, as the label N indicates, but notice that it is also labeled as a noun phrase. Since *Helen* is a constituent whose main member is a noun, it meets the definition of a noun phrase given above.

We see, then, that a single-word noun like *Helen* can function as a noun phrase as well as more complex structures such as *an old man* or *Steve or Sam and Bob.* Similarly, a verb phrase may consist of just a verb, like *exists,* or it may be more complex, like *gave the airplane to Helen.* The reason why such diverse structures as *Helen, an old man,* and *Steve or Sam and Bob* are labeled as the same type of constituent is that they behave alike with respect to syntactic rules. To take just one example, consider the rule for forming questions in English. In a question, the first verb word precedes the noun-phrase subject; this contrasts with the usual word order, in which the verb follows the subject. The question form of

101

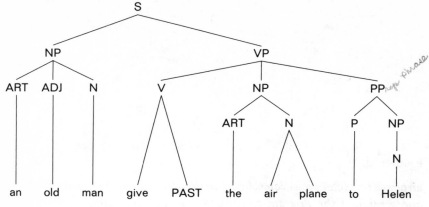

FIGURE 5.5

Helen will come, therefore, is **Will Helen come?,** the order of **Helen** and *will* being the opposite of their noninterrogative order. In the same way, the question form of **An old man will come** is **Will an old man come?,** and that of **Steve or Sam and Bob will come** is **Will Steve or Sam and Bob come?** In each case, the question differs from the noninterrogative sentence only in the relative order of *will* and the string of morphemes said to be a noun phrase. Since **Helen, an old man,** and **Steve or Sam and Bob** function alike with respect to the rule of question formation, and with respect to many other syntactic rules of English besides, we are justified in treating them as constituents of the same type.

One should not conclude that surface structures are fully understood or that it is always an easy matter to ascertain the precise tree structure to be associated with a given string of morphemes. Even at this relatively overt level of syntax, much remains to be worked out, and various details are bones of contention. Nevertheless, some things are fairly clear: the morphemes of a sentence are arranged in a hierarchical structure of some kind, the major outlines of which can be sketched with reasonable assurance, and we must identify types of constituents by labeling or by some comparable device.

COMPLEX SENTENCES

The grammatical sentences of a language form an infinite set because, in principle, there is no limit to their length. The powers of

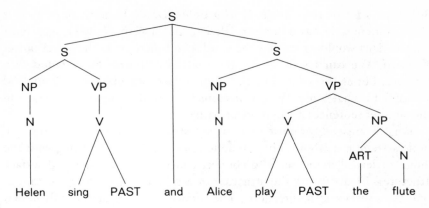

FIGURE 5.6

human conceptualization are such that thoughts of any desired degree of complexity can, again in principle, be formed. Moreover, the syntactic rules of a language connect infinitely many conceptual structures, regardless of their complexity, with surface structures. In this section, we will examine more closely those aspects of syntactic systems which project our linguistic competence to cover an infinite set of sentences.

Complex Conceptual Structures

Consider the sentence *Helen sang and Alice played the flute*. This sentence has two main constituents, *Helen sang* and *Alice played the flute*. The two are connected by the morpheme *and*. The question that immediately arises is, what kind of constituent should we call *Helen sang* and *Alice played the flute*? The only reasonable answer would seem to be that they are sentences, just as the whole string is. The structure of *Helen sang and Alice played the flute* is given in Figure 5.6. From this we see that some sentences are complex, in the sense that they contain simpler sentences as component parts.

Actually, this is something of an oversimplification. Take the sentence *Harvey married the woman who Peter hated*. *The woman who Peter hated* is clearly a constituent—a noun phrase, in fact. Moreover, *who Peter hated* is also a constituent, one component of this noun phrase.

But what kind of constituent is **who Peter hated**? In most respects it is like a sentence. It has a subject (**Peter**) and a verb (**hated**), and most grammarians would agree that the word **who** functions as the direct object of **hated**. We can hardly ignore the similarity of **who Peter hated** to a sentence, but at the same time this string of morphemes is ungrammatical by itself. In what sense, then, is it correct to say that some sentences contain simpler sentences as component parts?

For the answer, we must view surface structures in relation to the syntactic system as a whole. The syntactic rules of a language, along with the choice of lexical items, serve to connect conceptual structures and surface structures. In discussing the structure of a sentence, therefore, we cannot look at its surface structure alone. The surface structure can be fully understood only in relation to the underlying conceptual structure and to the syntactic rules linking the two.

Let us go back to **Helen sang and Alice played the flute**. The conceptual structure underlying this sentence is complex. It involves the conception of a past activity on the part of Helen and the conception of a different past activity on the part of Alice. In other words, this conceptual situation has two distinct components. Each component can stand by itself as a conceptual situation; for instance, we can conceive of Helen having sung without thinking about Alice at all. Furthermore, each component can serve as a conceptual structure that can be linked with a surface structure. If one were to think about Helen having sung, without thinking about Alice at all, this simple conceptual structure could be manifested as the surface string **Helen sang** by virtue of syntactic rules and the choice of appropriate morphemes. From the other component of the conceptual situation, one could obtain the surface string **Alice played the flute**. There is no necessary connection between the two components, but neither is there anything to prevent them from coexisting as parts of a more complex thought.

Some syntactic rules of a language serve to connect simple conceptual structures with simple sentences. In English, these rules will connect the conception of Helen having sung with **Helen sang**; they will connect the conception of Alice having performed on a certain instrument with **Alice played the flute**; and so on. (In this context, simplicity is a relative thing—sentences like **Helen sang** are much more complex than they appear to be on the surface. They are simple, however, in comparison with sentences that contain them as component parts.)

Other syntactic rules are called into play when a conceptual structure is more complex. It is a syntactic principle of English, for example, that two or more simple conceptual structures, each of which is capable of underlying a simple sentence, can be combined in a complex sentence structure by stringing them together and connecting them with the morpheme *and*. A person who conceives of the activities of Helen and Alice simultaneously, then, can arrive at the complex surface structure of Figure 5.6 in accordance with this syntactic principle. Suppose the conceived situation is more complicated still, perhaps because it involves the remembrance that George showed off his ability as a hoofer. Then this principle, in combination with the ones responsible for simple sentences, yields the still more complex sentence **Helen sang and Alice played the flute and George danced**. Another syntactic rule of English, which allows the omission of all but the last of a series of *and* morphemes, accounts for the variant **Helen sang, Alice played the flute, and George danced**.

We are now in a better position to appreciate the nature of **who Peter hated** in the sentence **Harvey married the woman who Peter hated**. The conceptual structure that underlies this sentence is complex in the same way as the one underlying **Helen sang and Alice played the flute**. The two components of this complex conceptual structure are each capable of underlying a simple sentence. One underlies the sentence **Harvey married the woman**, and the other underlies **Peter hated the woman**. It would be perfectly possible, according to the syntactic rules of English, for this conceptual structure to be manifested as the sentence **Harvey married the woman and Peter hated the woman**. Or, if the syntactic rules for forming pronouns were also to apply, it could instead be manifested as **Harvey married the woman and Peter hated her**. Notice that these two sentences mean the same; they come from the same conceptual structure. Which one results from this conceptual structure depends on which syntactic rules are followed in translating it into a surface structure.

A sentence is complex, then, if it results from a complex conceptual structure; a complex conceptual structure is one which contains components that can themselves underlie sentences. By this criterion, **Helen sang and Alice played the flute** is complex, since the two major components of its conceptual structure can each result in a sentence. The sentences are **Helen sang** and **Alice played the flute**. **Harvey married the woman who Peter hated** is also complex. One component of its conceptual

105

structure underlies *Harvey married the woman*. The other major component corresponds to the sentence *Peter hated the woman*.

The latter component can therefore be manifested either as *Peter hated the woman* or as *who Peter hated*. *Peter hated the woman* results when the component occurs in isolation as the entire conceptual structure. *Who Peter hated* results only when this component is part of a larger conceptual structure underlying a complex sentence. As a constituent of a larger sentence, the structure that would in isolation come out *Peter hated the woman* is modified by certain syntactic rules to yield instead *who Peter hated*. The surface structure of the larger sentence is given in Figure 5.7. (Notice that *the woman* itself constitutes a noun phrase, as does the larger structure *the woman who Peter hated*.)

Thus, the surface structure of any sentence-like part of a complex sentence is not necessarily the same as it would appear in isolation. Complex sentences often involve syntactic rules that are not operative in simple sentences. A simple conceptual structure, in other words, may be manifested differently in surface structure depending on whether or not it functions as a component of a more complex conceptual structure.

The syntactic rules involved are not themselves our immediate concern. The important concept under consideration in this section is that most sentences, and all sentences of any great length, are complex in the sense described above. The conceptual structures underlying them can be decomposed into substructures, each of which can itself be manifested as a simple sentence. In some cases, the corresponding part of the surface structure is identical to the surface structure of the simple sentence as it occurs in isolation. *Helen sang*, for instance, looks just the same in isolation or as a constituent of the complex sentence *Helen sang and Alice played the flute*. In other cases this is not so. *Peter hated the woman* and *who Peter hated* are only partially similar on the surface.

Conjoining and Embedding

Compare Figures 5.6 and 5.7. In both structures, two simpler sentence-like structures can be discerned, but the simple component sentences are combined in radically different ways. In Figure 5.6, *Helen sang* and *Alice played the flute* are strung together in parallel; neither is a constituent of the other. In Figure 5.7, on the other hand, one simple sen-

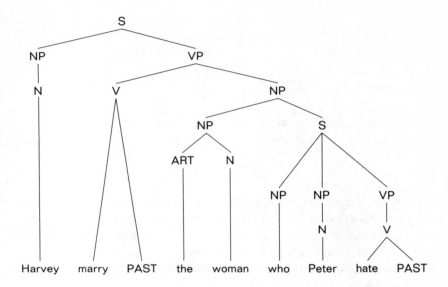

FIGURE 5.7

tence functions as a constituent of the other. The two substructures of Figure 5.6 are on a par with one another, but in Figure 5.7, *who Peter hated* is subordinate to *Harvey married the woman*. To use some traditional terms, the simple sentences of Figure 5.6 are in a relation of **coordination**, while those of Figure 5.7 are in a relation of **subordination**. To use two other very common terms, *Helen sang* and *Alice played the flute* are **conjoined** structures, whereas *who Peter hated* is **embedded** as a constituent in the structure *Harvey married the woman*.

So far we have only examined one kind of structure involving conjoining, one in which the conjoined constituents were sentences and the morpheme *and* was used to connect them. Other constituents can be conjoined, and other morphemes can be used to connect conjoined constituents. The sentence *The cruiser and the old battleship will be used for target practice* contains conjoined noun phrases. *The cruiser* is itself a noun phrase, as is *the old battleship*. In the above sentence, they are conjoined with *and* to form a complex noun phrase that functions as the subject; this structure is given in Figure 5.8. *The cruiser and the old battleship* is seen to be a noun phrase by the way it behaves with respect to syn-

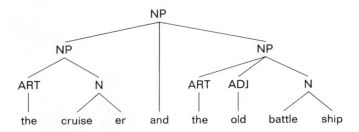

FIGURE 5.8

tactic rules. Notice, for example, that the question form *Will the cruiser and the old battleship be used for target practice?* bears the same relationship to the above sentence that *Will your father give us some money?* bears to *Your father will give us some money. The cruiser and the old battleship* and the noun phrase *your father* therefore function alike with regard to the formation of questions.

Various other constituents can be conjoined as well. For instance, *The barn is old and dingy* contains conjoined adjectives. *The waitress spilled the soup and dropped my steak on the floor* has a complex verb phrase formed by conjoining the simple verb phrases *spilled the soup* and *dropped my steak on the floor. I cleaned and cooked the fish* contains conjoined verbs. In *The old man seems tired but happy, but* is used instead of *and* to connect the conjoined constituents. *Or* (sometimes combined with *either*) is another common coordinating morpheme of English, as in *(Either) I will send you a letter or Helen will telephone.*

Likewise, we find a variety of ways in which one sentence structure can be embedded in another. Sometimes an embedded structure is identical on the surface to its manifestation in isolation. *Roger is a fink*, for instance, matches exactly the embedded sentence constituent in *I believe Roger is a fink*. In other cases, the embedded structure appears as some reduced version of the corresponding independent sentence. Thus, in *Harvey married the woman who Peter hated*, the embedded sentence structure *who Peter hated* corresponds to *Peter hated the woman*; the relative pronoun *who* is all that is left of the structure otherwise manifested as the noun phrase *the woman*. The structure underlying *I hurt myself* is reduced when embedded after *want* as a constituent in *I don't want to hurt myself*. The underlying subject of *hurt* is *I* (as the reflexive form *myself* demonstrates),

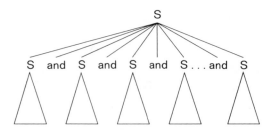

FIGURE 5.9

but it is not manifested overtly at all. Compare *I don't want to hurt my-self* with *I don't want you to hurt yourself*, in which *you*, the subject of *hurt*, shows up on the surface.

There is no inherent limit to the number of elements that can be strung together in a conjoined structure (at least with *and* and *or*). To *Helen sang and Alice played the flute*, we can add another conjoined sentence to give *Helen sang and Alice played the flute and George danced*. To this we can add still another to form *Helen sang and Alice played the flute and George danced and Harvey's mother did barnyard imitations*. Obviously, there is no point at which we can draw a line and say that the addition of another conjoined element would make the sentence ungrammatical. We have the situation of Figure 5.9, where the dots indicate that the number of sentences strung together in parallel could be extended indefinitely.

Each addition of a conjoined constituent increases the length of the sentence. Since as many elements can be conjoined as desired, there is no longest sentence that can be formed by means of this syntactic mechanism. To any given string of conjoined elements, another can be added to form a grammatical string of even greater length. Therefore, the mechanism of conjoining is itself sufficient to project the grammatical sentences of a language to an infinite set.

The various devices for embedding one sentence structure within another serve in similar fashion to project the sentences of a language to an unbounded set. Take the simple sentences *I believe it* and *Roger is a fink*. The structure underlying the latter can be embedded as a constituent in the former, the result being manifested as *I believe Roger is a fink*. This

109

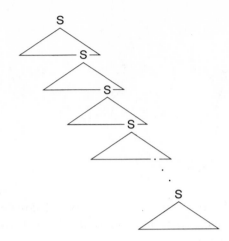

Figure 5.10

complex structure is itself eligible to be embedded as a constituent of another sentence structure, say that of *Harry knows it*, which yields the surface structure *Harry knows I believe Roger is a fink*. There is no inherent limit to the number of simple sentence structures that can be successively combined in this manner. To continue just a little further, we can easily obtain *The girl believes Harry knows I believe Roger is a fink*; and then *I know the girl believes Harry knows I believe Roger is a fink*; and so on. The structure of these sentences is depicted schematically in Figure 5.10 (in which the dots again indicate that the embedding could be extended indefinitely).

For another example, consider the sentence *I found the knight who rescued the maiden who was chased by the dragon that ravaged the village that contains the hovel in which I mixed the potion*. The conceptual structure underlying this sentence is complex; it is composed of the component structures that, taken in isolation, would be manifested as these simple sentences: *I found the knight; The knight rescued the maiden; The maiden was chased by the dragon; The dragon ravaged the village; The village contains the hovel; I mixed the potion in the hovel*. Each of these simple structures is embedded as a constituent of the preceding one, so that the sentence has a structure like that of Figure 5.10. It would, of

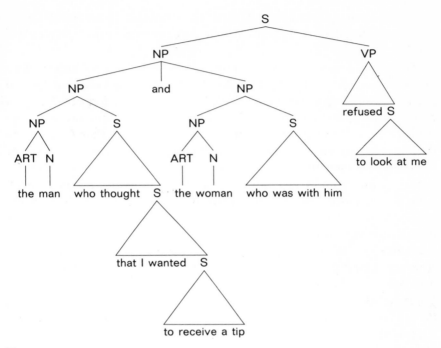

FIGURE 5.11

course, be possible to make the string still longer by adding another embedded structure. For instance, by adding the structure that would otherwise underlie *The potion will cure baldness*, the noun phrase *the potion* could be expanded to *the potion that will cure baldness*.

The structures of Figures 5.9 and 5.10 are rather monotonous. They are designed to show that the mechanism of conjoining alone, or a single repeatable mechanism of embedding alone, suffices to extend the grammatical sentences of a language to an infinite set. When taken in combination, however, the various devices of embedding and conjoining allow a much greater variety of sentence structures.

Consider this sentence, which involves both conjoining and embedding: *The man who thought that I wanted to receive a tip and the woman who was with him refused to look at me*. The surface structure of this sentence is shown in skeletal form in Figure 5.11. For the sake of simplicity, the internal structure of various constituents is not filled in; we are more interested at present in their arrangement with respect to one another.

Both the subject and the predicate of this sentence are complex. Two noun phrases, *the man who thought that I wanted to receive a tip* and *the woman who was with him,* are conjoined by *and* to form the complex noun phrase that functions as the subject. The first contains as a constituent the embedded sentence structure *who thought that I wanted to receive a tip,* which would in isolation be manifested as the independent sentence *The man thought that I wanted to receive a tip.* This constituent in turn contains an embedded sentence structure, the one underlying the sentence *I wanted to receive a tip,* in which is embedded the same structure that underlies *I receive a tip.* The other conjoined noun phrase, *the woman who was with him,* is also complex, since *the woman* is modified by the embedded clause *who was with him;* in isolation, this structure would be manifested instead as the sentence *The woman was with him.* (A sentence constituent modifying a noun in this way is called a **relative clause.** *Who was with him* is thus a relative clause modifying *the woman,* and *who thought that I wanted to receive a tip* is a complex relative clause modifying *the man.*) The verb phrase *refused to look at me* has as a constituent the sentence structure *to look at me,* in which the subject is not manifested overtly. The underlying subject of *look* is the same as the subject of the entire sentence.

Figure 5.12 shows the surface structure of **A woman that I met there caught a fish that weighed five pounds and cooked it and I caught a small bass.** This sentence is complex, consisting of the conjoined sentence structures **A woman that I met there caught a fish that weighed five pounds and cooked it** and **I caught a small bass.** The first of these **conjuncts** is complex, while the second, **I caught a small bass,** is simple (but only on the surface—it comes from the same structure that underlies the overtly complex sentence *I caught a bass that was small*). The subject of the first conjunct, the noun phrase *a woman that I met there,* contains the relative clause *that I met there.* The predicate is complex, consisting of the conjoined verb phrases *caught a fish that weighed five pounds* and *cooked it.* In the first of these, the direct object of *caught* is the noun phrase *a fish that weighed five pounds,* which contains as a constituent the embedded sentence structure *that weighed five pounds.*

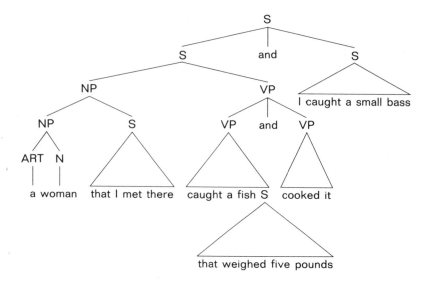

FIGURE 5.12

These are only some representative examples. It should be apparent that the syntactic principles of a language allow an endless variety of complex structures to be constructed from simpler ones.

THE RELATIONSHIP BETWEEN CONCEPTUAL AND SURFACE STRUCTURES

Derivations

Up to this point, we have concentrated on surface structures, but the surface structure of a sentence represents only one facet of its syntactic organization. Every surface structure manifests an underlying conceptual structure from which it is derived by syntactic rules and the choice of lexical items. To give a full account of how a sentence is put together, one

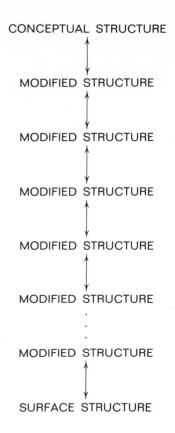

CONCEPTUAL STRUCTURE

MODIFIED STRUCTURE

MODIFIED STRUCTURE

MODIFIED STRUCTURE

MODIFIED STRUCTURE

MODIFIED STRUCTURE

MODIFIED STRUCTURE

SURFACE STRUCTURE

FIGURE 5.13

would have to describe not only its surface structure but also its conceptual structure and the step-by-step **derivation** of the former from the latter. We do not as yet know enough about human cognition to be able to describe conceptual structures, but it is clear that the relationship between conceptual and surface structures is very indirect and abstract. The translation of a conceptual structure into its surface manifestation involves, in addition to the substitution of lexical items for conceptual components, the application of a long series of syntactic rules. The derivation of a sentence is schematized in Figure 5.13.

Each lexical selection and rule application modifies the abstract underlying structure in some way, making it less abstract and more like its

114

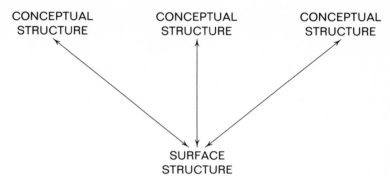

CONCEPTUAL STRUCTURE   CONCEPTUAL STRUCTURE   CONCEPTUAL STRUCTURE

SURFACE STRUCTURE

FIGURE 5.14

ultimate surface form. The difference between the conceptual and surface structure of a sentence is thus the cumulative result of a great many small modifications effected by syntactic rules and lexical choices. Each of these modifications connects an underlying structure with one that is slightly less abstract.

Ambiguous Sentences

Because the relationship between conceptual and surface structures is very distant, the differences between two or more conceptual structures will not always be evident in their surface structures. The application of syntactic rules and the choice of lexical items may obliterate the underlying differences so that a number of distinct conceptual structures have the same surface manifestation, as shown in Figure 5.14. When a sentence can represent either of two conceptual structures, we recognize it as being ambiguous, as having alternate semantic interpretations.

The quarrelsome Arabs want another war is an interesting example. This sentence is ambiguous, but under either interpretation it consists of the same string of morphemes and has the same surface tree structure. *The quarrelsome Arabs want another war* may mean that all Arabs are quarrelsome and want another war; under this interpretation, it is related to *The Arabs want another war and they are quarrelsome* and to *The Arabs, who are quarrelsome, want another war*, which come from the same

115

underlying structure. On the other hand, **The quarrelsome Arabs want another war** may imply only that those Arabs who are quarrelsome wish to fight again. Under this second interpretation, it manifests the same conceptual structure as **The Arabs who are quarrelsome want another war**.

Not every ambiguous sentence has precisely the same surface structure under its alternate interpretations, as **The quarrelsome Arabs want another war** does. Consider **I'm standing near the bank**, for instance. This sentence is ambiguous because **bank** can represent either of two noun morphemes; one **bank** designates the land along a river, and the other designates a financial institution or the building housing it. Phonologically, the sentence is the same under either interpretation, since the two nouns **bank** are pronounced alike. The two surface structures of **I'm standing near the bank** are slightly different, however, since a surface structure is a structured string of morphemes and the two nouns **bank** are different morphemes. Similar examples of lexical ambiguity are legion.

Ambiguous sentences may also differ in surface tree structure under their alternate interpretations, as some previous examples show. For instance, the sentence **Steve or Sam and Bob will come** consists of the same string of morphemes under either of its interpretations, but the syntactic rules responsible for merging the two distinct underlying structures into the same morpheme string do not obliterate entirely the corresponding differences in tree structure. The two surface tree structures of **Steve or Sam and Bob will come** were illustrated in Figure 5.2.

Here are some other examples of ambiguity that may prove amusing or instructive: **The man decided on the train; I had a car stolen; Biting dogs can be bothersome; They are flying planes; I dislike fat men and women; It's too hot to eat; I demanded what he had stolen; The chauffeur will dust or wash and polish the car; The missionaries are ready to serve; Rodney broke the barn windows with his little sister; They fed her dog biscuits; I gave John what I wanted; It's the man that stole the candy.**

Synonymous Sentences

Syntactic rules and lexical choices do not always have the effect of neutralizing underlying differences to produce relative surface uniform-

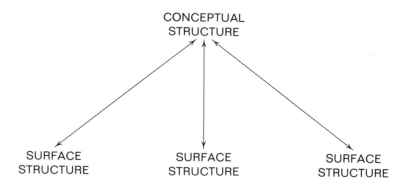

CONCEPTUAL
STRUCTURE

SURFACE
STRUCTURE

SURFACE
STRUCTURE

SURFACE
STRUCTURE

FIGURE 5.15

ity. The opposite happens as well, so that a single conceptual structure often has divergent surface manifestations, as illustrated in Figure 5.15. In such cases, the surface diversity that is introduced by syntactic rules and lexical choices conceals underlying uniformity.

The surface difference between **My uncle sweats profusely** and **My uncle perspires profusely** is introduced by the choice of different lexical items, **sweat** and **perspire**, to represent the same conceptual component. The two can be used interchangeably, since they have the same syntactic function and the same conceptual import. The two sentences thus manifest the same conceptual structure, although they consist of different strings of morphemes.

The surface differences that result from alternate lexical choices to represent identical conceptual components are sometimes more extensive. Consider, for instance, the idea of dividing something into two parts. The word **bisect** has this conceptual import, but so does the phrase **divide into two parts**. Consequently, the same conceptual structure that underlies **The East Germans bisected Berlin with a wall** has an alternate manifestation as **The East Germans divided Berlin into two parts with a wall**. No single lexical item in the second sentence has the same conceptual import as **bisect**. Instead, a number of lexical items are combined syntactically to achieve the same semantic effect. The sentences **Harvey is a bachelor** and **Harvey is a man who has never married** constitute a more extreme example. The conceptual import of **man who has never married**, which consists of the noun **man** and a sentence structure embedded after it

117

as a relative clause, is represented by the single lexical item *bachelor* in the first sentence. The effect of alternate lexical choices in determining the surface manifestation of a conceptual structure can, therefore, be quite extensive.

The surface differences introduced by syntactic rules can also be quite extensive, as we will see later in some detail. For the moment, we will content ourselves with a single example. Consider the sentences **A detective hunted down the killer, The policeman looked over the situation,** and **The robber tied up the manager of the bank.** Each of these sentences contains a two-part verb constituent that consists of a verb and a preposition-like **particle.** *Hunted down, looked over,* and *tied up* are the verb constituents, and *down, over,* and *up* are their particles.

Each of these three sentences can be matched with another that manifests the same conceptual structure and contains the same lexical items. The matching sentences are, respectively, **A detective hunted the killer down, The policeman looked the situation over,** and **The robber tied the manager of the bank up.** A syntactic rule that we will call the Particle Shift rule accounts for the differences between these sentence pairs. This rule separates a verb and a particle by placing the particle after the following direct object noun phrase. Applied to the structure underlying **A detective hunted down the killer,** the Particle Shift rule produces the structure underlying **A detective hunted the killer down** by permuting the particle *down* with the noun phrase *the killer.* Similarly, this rule changes (*looked over) (the situation)* to (*looked) (the situation) (over)* and (*tied up) (the manager of the bank)* to (*tied) (the manager of the bank) (up).*

The derivation of the first pair of sentences is schematized in Figure 5.16, in which we can see that **A detective hunted down the killer** and **A detective hunted the killer down** result from the same conceptual structure and involve the same lexical choices. By and large, the same set of syntactic rules apply in the derivation of these two sentences. The sole difference between them is that the Particle Shift rule applies in the derivation of one but not the other. Like many syntactic rules, this one is optional—it may apply but it does not have to. When it does, the sentence **A detective hunted the killer down** results. When it does not, **hunted** and **down** remain adjacent in the string, yielding **A detective hunted down the killer.**

Notice that neither sentence is derived from the other. Rather, both are manifestations of the same underlying structure, represented in Figure

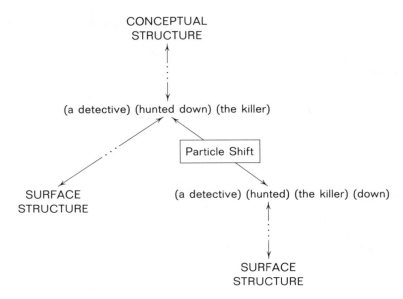

CONCEPTUAL
STRUCTURE

(a detective) (hunted down) (the killer)

Particle Shift

SURFACE
STRUCTURE

(a detective) (hunted) (the killer) (down)

SURFACE
STRUCTURE

FIGURE 5.16

5.16 as *(a detective) (hunted down) (the killer)*. This underlying structure is not the shared conceptual structure itself, but an intermediate structure derived from it by previous lexical choices and rule applications. The same will be true of all our examples of syntactic rules. Surface structures are the product of syntactic rules; these rules do not apply to them, but rather derive them from abstract underlying structures. At present, however, we cannot validly postulate for any sentence an underlying structure that is anywhere near as abstract as its conceptual structure must be.

SYNTACTIC RULES

In this section and the next, we will illustrate the nature of syntactic rules by taking a number of rules from English as concrete examples and showing how they combine in the derivation of a complex sentence. We should bear in mind, however, that there is still much to be learned about syntactic structure. Since linguists are unable at present to describe conceptual structures, they are severely limited in their ability to formulate definitive syntactic rules for connecting conceptual structures with surface structures. The following discussion is therefore tentative in many ways. Our description of various syntactic phenomena is only meant to be illustrative and will ultimately have to be refined.

Reduction Rules

Consider the sentence *My uncle has been dieting, and my aunt has been dieting, too*. This sentence is complex, manifesting a conceptual structure with two components. One component underlies *My uncle has been dieting*, while the other underlies *My aunt has been dieting*, which is conjoined with the first by *and* and *too*. There are many other ways in which this complex conceptual structure could be manifested instead, some of them involving radically different lexical choices and syntactic rules (for example, *Both my aunt and my uncle have been eating less than usual in order to lose weight*). However, we will be concerned only with three alternative sentences that result from the same basic lexical and syntactic options.

The similarity of the following four sentences is readily apparent:

My uncle has been dieting, and my aunt has been dieting, too.
My uncle has been dieting, and my aunt has been, too.
My uncle has been dieting, and my aunt has, too.
My uncle has been dieting, and my aunt, too.

Not only do they come from the same conceptual structure, but they are also very similar lexically and syntactically. Each sentence differs from the one that follows it only in that it contains one more verb word in the second conjunct. Thus, *My uncle has been dieting, and my aunt has been dieting, too* differs from *My uncle has been dieting, and my aunt has been, too* by the second occurrence of *dieting*. The second instance of *been* in the second sentence distinguishes it from *My uncle has been dieting, and my aunt has, too*. This differs from *My uncle has been dieting, and my aunt, too* by the second occurrence of *has*.

These four sentences come from a common underlying structure, in which the full verb sequence *has been dieting* is represented in the second conjunct. *My uncle has been dieting, and my aunt has been dieting, too*

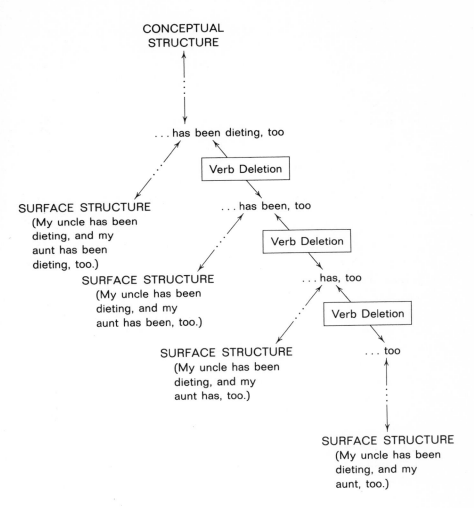

FIGURE 5.17

thus reflects this common underlying structure most directly, although the relationship may be quite distant. A syntactic rule of English that we will call Verb Deletion applies to the common underlying structure and provides for its alternate manifestations, as shown in Figure 5.17.

The Verb Deletion rule applies optionally to the second conjunct of a complex sentence structure that involves conjoining with *too*. What this

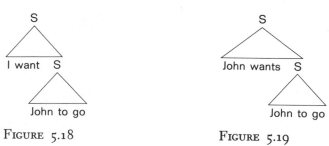

FIGURE 5.18   FIGURE 5.19

rule does (in somewhat simplified terms) is to delete the last in a sequence of verb words, provided that the same sequence of verb words also occurs in the first conjunct. The verb sequence *has been dieting* occurs in both conjuncts of the structure underlying *My uncle has been dieting, and my aunt has been dieting, too,* which allows Verb Deletion to apply. If this rule applies just once, *has been dieting* is reduced to *has been* in the second conjunct. If it applies a second time, *has been* is reduced to *has,* since *been* is now the last verb word in the sequence. A third application of Verb Deletion reduces *has* to zero. All four sentences therefore derive from the same underlying structure, the choice depending solely on how many times Verb Deletion applies.

Reduction rules such as Verb Deletion are very common. Every language has syntactic rules which, under certain conditions, allow constituents to be deleted from a sentence structure when identical constituents occur elsewhere within the same sentence. When *has been dieting* is deleted to produce *My uncle has been dieting, and my aunt, too,* there is no doubt about what is predicated of the aunt. A speaker of English immediately interprets this sentence to mean that the aunt has been dieting, despite the fact that no verb phrase occurs overtly with *my aunt.* Because a duplicate of the deleted sequence occurs in the first conjunct, the full significance of the surface string *and my aunt, too* can be ascertained by examining the rest of the sentence. The reduction of duplicated elements thus eliminates a great deal of potential repetition without a loss of semantic content.

Another example from English is a reduction rule that we will call Noun Phrase Deletion, which applies under certain conditions to embedded sentence structures. The sentence *I want John to go* is derived by embedding after *want* the structure underlying *John goes.* Because this structure occurs as an embedded clause and not in isolation as an independent sentence, it is modified by a syntactic rule that inserts **to** and deletes the present tense morpheme; the rule changes **John+go+PRESENT** to **John+to+go**. *I want John to go* is represented in Figure 5.18. *I* and *John* are both noun phrases, the former functioning as the subject of *want* and the latter as the subject of *go*.

It happens that these two noun phrases are different, but there is no reason why they have to be. In Figure 5.19, which is exactly parallel to Figure 5.18, the two noun phrases are identical. Notice, however, that we do not say *John wants John to go*—to convey this idea, we say *John wants to go*, in which *John* occurs only once. A syntactic principle of English specifies that the subject of an embedded clause is omitted after certain verbs like *want* when it is identical to the subject of the sentence in which the clause is embedded. This principle, the Noun Phrase Deletion rule, applies to the structure of Figure 5.19 and deletes the second occurrence of the noun phrase *John*, resulting in the surface string *John wants to go*.

The captain would like to leave the sinking ship and *The prisoner arranged to escape* are further examples. The former comes from the underlying structure *The captain would like the captain to leave the sinking ship* (parallel to *The captain would like the crew to leave the sinking ship*). Noun Phrase Deletion derives it from this underlying structure by deleting the second occurrence of *the captain*. *The prisoner arranged to escape* comes from the underlying structure *The prisoner arranged for the prisoner to escape* (parallel to *The prisoner arranged for me to escape*). After Noun Phrase Deletion eliminates the second occurrence of *the prisoner*, another rule deletes *for*.

Pro Forms

Reduction does not always mean full deletion, since a remnant is often left when a repeated constituent is erased. Such a remnant is called a **pro form**.

Consider the sentence *Howard trapped the bear and Peter skinned the bear*, which is represented in Figure 5.20. This sentence may be grammatical, but at best it seems clumsy and repetitious. The conceptual structure that underlies it finds a more acceptable manifestation in *Howard*

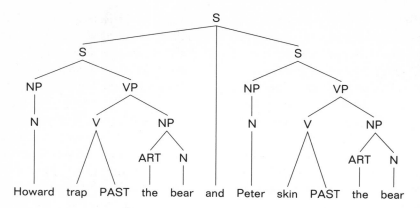

FIGURE 5.20

trapped the bear and Peter skinned it, shown in Figure 5.21. The structure of Figure 5.20 is reduced to that of Figure 5.21 by a syntactic rule that we will refer to as Pronominalization. When two identical noun phrases occur in the same sentence, the Pronominalization rule reduces one (usually the second) to a pronoun. In Figure 5.21, the pronoun *it* remains as a remnant of the fuller underlying noun phrase *the bear*, in a sense serving as a placeholder for it.

Personal pronouns such as *he, she, it,* and *they* are perhaps the most familiar kind of pro forms, but there are numerous others as well. For instance, the pro forms *there* and *then* substitute for adverbs of place and adverbs of time respectively, just as pronouns substitute for noun phrases. By way of illustration, an underlying structure of the form *Jack always plays in the sandbox on Thursday, but Mary never plays in the sandbox on Thursday* can undergo two reductions. The adverb of place *in the sandbox* reduces to *there,* and the adverb of time *on Thursday* reduces to *then,* the result being *Jack always plays in the sandbox on Thursday, but Mary never plays there then.*

This, that, and *which* will be our last examples of pro forms. They may substitute for embedded clauses, allowing the reduction of otherwise rather clumsy structures such as *The baby cried, and that the baby cried upset her mother.* Notice that the embedded clause *that the baby cried* duplicates the first conjunct of the sentence (leaving aside the semantically empty morpheme *that*). When this is the case, the entire embedded

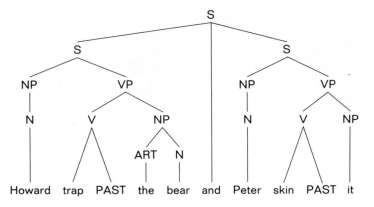

FIGURE 5.21

clause can be replaced by the pro form *this*, resulting in the sentence *The baby cried, and this upset her mother*. *That* can also be chosen as the pro form, producing *The baby cried, and that upset her mother*. An alternate reduction involves *which*; *which* replaces the embedded clause and at the same time entails the deletion of *and*: *The baby cried, which upset her mother*.

Sentence Trappings

Through the reduction of repeated constituents, large portions of underlying tree structures may fail to be manifested overtly in surface structure (although their conceptual import can be reconstructed on the basis of the rest of the sentence). On the other hand, some syntactic rules have the effect of introducing into surface structure elements that are semantically empty or that duplicate information represented elsewhere in the sentence. Such elements may be regarded as trappings on sentences, as syntactically introduced embellishments with no independent semantic content.

The morphemes *that, to,* and *ing*, which crop up in subordinate clauses, are good examples of sentence trappings. For instance, *that* is semantically empty in sentences like *I know that my cousin needs money*.

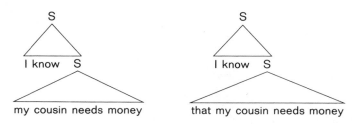

FIGURE 5.22

Notice that the corresponding sentences without *that*, in this case *I know my cousin needs money*, mean exactly the same thing. The structures underlying such pairs of synonymous sentences are connected by a rule that we will call That Insertion; That Insertion derives the second structure of Figure 5.22 from the first. *That* represents nothing in the conceptual structure underlying these two sentences but is inserted (in this case optionally) by a syntactic rule.

To and *ing* are inserted by syntactic rules in similar fashion, except that they replace the present or past tense morpheme of the subordinate clause in which they are inserted. Let us return to a previous example, *I want John to go*, which was diagramed in Figure 5.18. To form this sentence, the structure underlying *John goes* is embedded as a constituent after *want*. The To Insertion rule applies to this subordinate structure because it is embedded as a constituent of a more complex sentence and does not occur in isolation. Applied to the structure *John+go+PRESENT*, To Insertion produces *John+to+go*. The derivation of *John wants to go*, which has the underlying structure *John+want+PRESENT+John+go+PRESENT*, thus involves both To Insertion and Noun Phrase Deletion. To Insertion modifies this to *John+want+PRESENT+John+to+go*, from which Noun Phrase Deletion derives *John+want+PRESENT+to+go*, manifested as *John wants to go*.

Ing Insertion is more complex, since it affects the subject of the embedded clause as well as its tense morpheme. Take for example the sentence *I regretted his leaving*. *Ing* has been attached to the verb *leave* to replace the tense morpheme, but in addition we find that the possessive morpheme has been affixed to the subject of *leave*, the noun phrase *he*. Ing Insertion therefore applies to the embedded structure *he+leave+*

PAST and derives *he+POSSESSIVE+leave+ing*. *He+POSSESSIVE* is manifested phonologically as *his*, just as in expressions like *his book*. Notice that Noun Phrase Deletion can apply to clauses containing *ing*; instead of *I regretted my leaving*, for instance, we say *I regretted leaving*.

That Insertion, To Insertion, and Ing Insertion all serve to insert semantically empty morphemes in subordinate clauses as trappings. Which of these rules applies in a given case is constrained by the verb of the structure in which the clause is embedded. The verb *want*, for example, allows To Insertion to apply to a clause embedded after it, but neither of the other rules. *I want to go* is therefore grammatical, while *I want that I go* and *I want going* are both ungrammatical. The verb *advocate*, on the other hand, allows That Insertion and Ing Insertion to apply, but not To Insertion; *I advocated that she leave* and *I advocated her leaving* are both grammatical, but *I advocated her to leave* is not. The information about which of these rules can apply is part of the syntactic representations of such verbs.

Agreement rules also serve to introduce sentence trappings. There are relatively few agreement rules in English, one of them being Subject-Verb Agreement. This rule specifies that the first verb word in a simple sentence structure is marked to agree with its subject in number and in person. The first verb word of *I am tired* is *am*, which is the phonological result of the morpheme sequence *be+PRESENT* when it is marked first person singular to agree with *I*. *Be+PRESENT* is manifested instead as *is* when it agrees with a third person singular subject, as in *Rosemary is working tonight*. Although the Subject-Verb Agreement rule applies to all verbs, its overt consequences are greatest with *be*. *Be* has three forms in the present tense (*am, are, is*) and two in the past tense (*was, were*), but most verbs have only two present tense forms and one past tense form. *Sing+PRESENT*, for instance, is manifested as *sings* if it is marked third person singular, but as *sing* in all other cases. *Sing+PAST* is always spelled phonologically as *sang*, regardless of its specification for person and number.

Permutation Rules

In addition to inserting and deleting constituents and marking elements for agreement, syntactic rules rearrange tree structure by changing the linear order of constituents. We have already encountered a rule

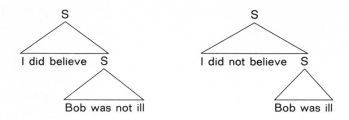

FIGURE 5.23

that changes the order of constituents—the Particle Shift rule, which applies to the structure underlying **A detective hunted down the killer** and permutes **down** with **the killer** to produce **A detective hunted the killer down**. Numerous examples of permutation rules can easily be found in English.

A permutation rule that we will call Not Promotion is an interesting example that accounts for a subtle type of ambiguity in negative sentences. Consider the sentence **I did not believe Bob was ill**. This sentence may mean that the speaker held a belief to the effect that Bob was not ill. On the other hand, it can mean that no belief concerning Bob's illness was involved at all; the speaker did not happen to believe Bob was ill, but he did not necessarily believe the opposite either. Under the first interpretation, **not** is semantically associated with **ill**—there was a belief that Bob was not ill. Under the second interpretation, **not** is semantically associated with **believe**—there was no belief that Bob was ill.

Since the sentence is ambiguous, **I did not believe Bob was ill** has two underlying structures. In one, **not** is associated with the subordinate clause containing **ill**. In the other, **not** is associated with the main clause containing **believe**. These two structures are schematized in Figure 5.23. Since either of these underlying structures can be manifested as **I did not believe Bob was ill**, there must be a syntactic rule that moves **not** from its position in the subordinate clause and places it in the main clause. This optional rule, to be called Not Promotion, derives the second structure of Figure 5.23 from the first. If Not Promotion applies, therefore, the first structure of Figure 5.23 is manifested as **I did not believe Bob was ill**. If it fails to apply and **not** remains in the subordinate clause, the result is **I did believe Bob was not ill** (alternately, **I believed Bob was not ill**), which is semantically equivalent.

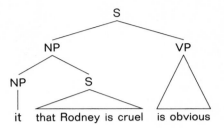

FIGURE 5.24

A syntactic principle commonly called Extraposition is another example of a permutation rule. The Extraposition rule accounts for the basic difference between synonymous pairs of sentences such as the following: *That Rodney is cruel is obvious/It is obvious that Rodney is cruel; That I am only interested in money is true/It is true that I am only interested in money; That he hasn't come yet bothers me/It bothers me that he hasn't come yet.* The sentences of each pair derive from the same underlying structure. For instance, *That Rodney is cruel is obvious* and *It is obvious that Rodney is cruel* both manifest the underlying structure of Figure 5.24. The subject noun phrase consists of the morpheme *it* and the embedded clause *that Rodney is cruel.* Notice that this noun phrase is parallel to others like *the fact that Rodney is cruel* and *the idea that Rodney is cruel,* which also contain an embedded *that* clause.

Since *That Rodney is cruel is obvious* and *It is obvious that Rodney is cruel* come from the same underlying structure, there must be syntactic rules that introduce the surface differences between them. One such rule is Extraposition, which moves the embedded clause to the end of the sentence and leaves behind, as a placeholder in subject position, the semantically empty form *it.* Extraposition, in other words, applies to the structure of Figure 5.24 and derives from it the structure of Figure 5.25. When the optional Extraposition rule applies, then, the result is surface strings like *It is obvious that Rodney is cruel, It is true that I am only interested in money,* and *It bothers me that he hasn't come yet.* When Extraposition does not apply, *it* is deleted by another rule, and the same underlying structures are manifested instead as *That Rodney is cruel is obvious, That I am only interested in money is true,* and *That he hasn't come yet bothers me.*

129

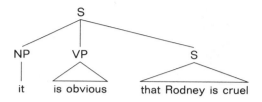

FIGURE 5.25

Relative Clauses

For further examples of syntactic rules, let us turn to the derivation of relative clauses. Consider the sentence *The brick with which I broke the window was heavy.* It is semantically equivalent to two simpler sentences, *The brick was heavy* and *I broke the window with the brick.* The structure underlying the complex sentence is formed by embedding one of the simpler sentence structures in the other, as shown in Figure 5.26. From this underlying structure, two rules that we will call Noun Phrase Advancement and Relativization derive the surface structure of *The brick with which I broke the window was heavy.* This surface structure is shown in Figure 5.27. If it were to occur in isolation as an independent sentence, the embedded structure would be manifested as *I broke the window with the brick.* Instead, because it is embedded as a constituent of a more complex sentence, its surface form is *with which I broke the window.* The embedded clauses of Figures 5.26 and 5.27 differ in two respects. First, the prepositional phrase comes at the end of the clause in Figure 5.26, but at the beginning of the clause in Figure 5.27. Second, the pro form *which* appears in Figure 5.27 in place of the noun phrase *the brick.* The Noun Phrase Advancement rule accounts for the first of these differences, and Relativization accounts for the second.

The embedded sentence structure contains a noun phrase, *the brick,* which is identical to the noun phrase that the structure modifies. The Noun Phrase Advancement rule moves the identical noun phrase to the beginning of the embedded clause; if a preposition precedes this noun phrase, it too can be transported, but it does not have to be. Applied to *I broke the window with the brick,* Noun Phrase Advancement derives the intermediate structure *with the brick I broke the window.* (If the

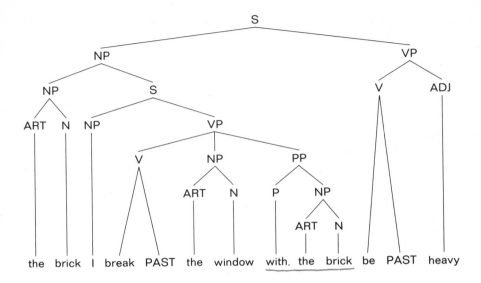

Figure 5.26

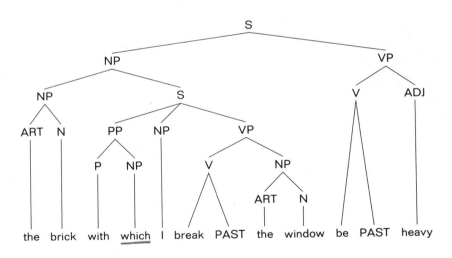

Figure 5.27 — Surface Structure

preposition *with* were left behind, producing instead *the brick I broke the window with,* the resulting surface structure would be *The brick which I broke the window with was heavy.*)

Enclosing the embedded clause in parentheses, we can now represent the structure of the entire sentence as *The brick (with the brick I broke the window) was heavy.* *The brick* occurs twice, and the Relativization rule reduces the second occurrence of this noun phrase to the pro form *which,* producing the structure of Figure 5.27. *Which* is the relative pronoun that substitutes for noun phrases designating nonhuman entities. *Who* is in general restricted to noun phrases designating humans, as in *the woman who came to see me.* The relative pronoun *that* can replace either but cannot follow a preposition; *the woman that I love* and *the books that I burned* are both well formed, therefore, but *the brick with that I broke the window* is ungrammatical.

For a slightly different example, consider the noun phrase *the flowers which are on the table.* The structure underlying *The flowers are on the table* is embedded as a relative clause after *flowers* to construct this complex expression. Because the repeated noun phrase is already at the beginning of the subordinate clause, Noun Phrase Advancement has no effect; it yields exactly the same structure, *the flowers (the flowers are on the table).* Relativization then reduces the second occurrence of *the flowers* to the relative pronoun *which.*

The flowers which are on the table can subsequently be reduced by the Relative Reduction rule. Relative Reduction optionally deletes a relative pronoun and a form of the verb *be* when a preposition or an adjective follows. Since *which are* is followed by the preposition *on* in *the flowers which are on the table,* this structure can be reduced to *the flowers on the table.* Similarly, Relative Reduction truncates the subject of *The woman who is ready to leave is my aunt,* forming *The woman ready to leave is my aunt.* The rule is applicable because *who is* precedes the adjective *ready.*

The woman ready to leave, with the complex modifier *ready to leave,* is a well-formed noun phrase. However, the same rules that we have been discussing will also derive ungrammatical noun phrases, such as *the woman happy.* Applied to the noun phrase *the woman who is happy,* Relative Reduction produces *the woman happy* by deleting *who is;* this rule can apply because *who is* precedes an adjective, *happy.*

Noun phrases like *the woman happy* are ungrammatical because they violate an obligatory syntactic principle of English, which we shall call the

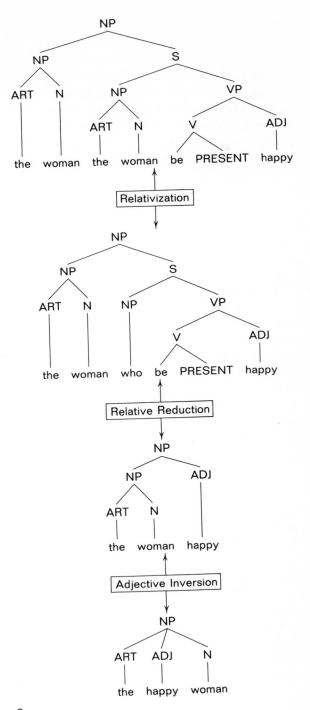

FIGURE 5.28

Adjective Inversion rule. This permutation rule specifies that a simple adjectival modifier (such as *happy*, but not *ready to leave*) must precede the noun it modifies instead of following it. Applied to the structure *the woman happy*, Adjective Inversion permutes *woman* and *happy* to produce the grammatical sequence *the happy woman*. The derivation of this noun phrase is diagramed in Figure 5.28. It exemplifies the derivation of a relatively simple surface structure from a more complex underlying structure through the application of a series of syntactic rules.

A SYNTACTIC SKETCH OF A SENTENCE

In examining the various syntactic rules of English, we have not explored the structure of any single sentence in depth. We have only gone far enough into the examples to see how these rules function. In order to illustrate the tremendous syntactic complexity of sentences, even sentences that seem rather simple on the surface, we will now examine in considerable detail the structure of a single sentence.

Let us take the sentence *I cannot believe that this cowardly man wants to drive the car in which it is not probable that he would survive a collision*. It is a sentence of only moderate length and complexity; you can easily make up more difficult ones. Nevertheless, even a partial and tentative analysis of its syntactic structure will reveal a long, intricate derivation.

The Underlying Structure

Figure 5.29 represents in skeletal form the surface structure of *I cannot believe that this cowardly man wants to drive the car in which it is not probable that he would survive a collision*. The complex structure *that this cowardly man wants to drive the car in which it is not probable that he would survive a collision* is embedded as a constituent after the main verb *believe*. *To drive the car in which it is not probable that he would survive a collision* is in turn a constituent of the embedded clause and is itself complex, containing the sentence constituent *in which it is not probable that he would survive a collision*. *That he would survive a collision* represents still another level of sentence embedding.

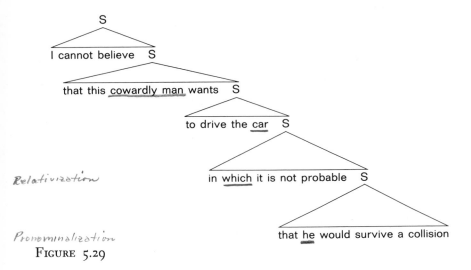

Relativization

Pronominalization

FIGURE 5.29

From the preceding section, it should be apparent that a number of elements in this surface structure are reduced versions of fuller underlying structures. *He*, for example, comes from the same underlying structure as *this cowardly man*; the Pronominalization rule reduces the second occurrence of this noun phrase to the pro form *he*. *This cowardly man* itself reflects a complex underlying structure, the same one that underlies *this man who is cowardly*, which is formed by embedding *this man is cowardly* as a relative clause modifying *this man*. The derivation of *this cowardly man* is exactly parallel to that of *the happy woman*, illustrated in Figure 5.28. *In which it is not probable that he would survive a collision*, a relative clause modifying *the car*, manifests the same underlying structure as *It is not probable that he would survive a collision in the car*; *the car* is reduced to *which* by the Relativization rule. Finally, *this cowardly man* is understood to be the subject of *drive*, although no trace of it remains overtly in the structure *to drive the car*.

There are other ways in which the surface structure of this sentence differs from more abstract representations of it. *To* and the two occurrences of *that* are devoid of semantic content, being introduced by syntactic rules, and the verbs are marked to agree with their respective subjects by the Subject-Verb Agreement rule. These trappings are purely grammatical entities and have no place in the conceptual structure. Fur-

135

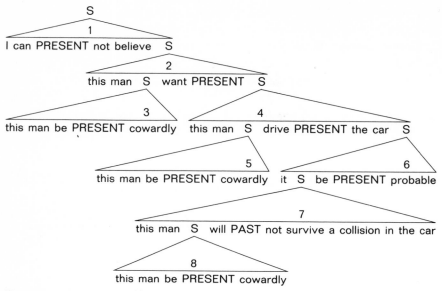

FIGURE 5.30

thermore, *It is not probable that he would survive a collision in the car,* which underlies *in which it is not probable that he would survive a collision,* can itself be related to a more abstract underlying structure.

Notice first that this string is ambiguous. On the one hand, it can mean that he would most probably not survive a collision in the car; under this interpretation, *not* is semantically associated with *survive.* On the other hand, it can mean that his survival in the event of a collision does not happen to be probable (but his death is not necessarily probable either—maybe the odds are even); under this interpretation, *not* is semantically associated with *probable.* We will consider only the former interpretation, so the underlying structure we postulate will find *not* associated with *survive* instead of with *probable.* Notice also that *It is not probable that he would survive a collision in the car* and *That he would survive a collision in the car is not probable* manifest the same underlying structure.

Putting together these varied observations, we can postulate for the entire sentence an underlying structure that is very abstract indeed. This structure is depicted in Figure 5.30, in which the simple sentence structures are numbered for reference. A long series of rule applications translates this abstract structure into the surface string *I cannot believe that this cowardly man wants to drive the car in which it is not probable that he would survive a collision.*

It must be emphasized that the structure of Figure 5.30 is by no means the conceptual structure of this sentence. The conceptual structure is far more abstract still, and at present we could not even make a reasonable guess as to what it looks like. The structure of Figure 5.30 is itself the product of lexical choices and an undetermined number of syntactic rules.

Derivation of the Surface Structure

That Insertion, To Insertion, and Subject-Verb Agreement all apply to this underlying structure and introduce sentence trappings. The verb *believe* and the adjective *probable* are both members of the class of forms which allow the insertion of *that* to head an embedded clause. Therefore, since structure 2 is embedded as a constituent of the clause containing *believe*, the That Insertion rule applies to produce the structure *that this man S want PRESENT S*. By the same token, structure 7 is modified to read *that this man S will PAST not survive a collision in the car* because it is embedded in the clause containing *probable*. The verb *want* requires the insertion of *to*, which substitutes for the present tense morpheme of the embedded clause. Structure 4 is thus transformed to *this man S to drive the car* by the application of To Insertion. Subject-Verb Agreement applies within each structure and marks the verb to agree with the subject in number and person. In clause 2, for example, *want+ PRESENT* will be spelled out phonologically as *wants* (not *want*) because it is marked third person singular to agree with *this man*.

The structure of Figure 5.30 contains three occurrences of the noun phrase *this man (this man be PRESENT cowardly)*, although the three occurrences are all manifested differently in surface structure. The third occurrence of this noun phrase, spanning clauses 7 and 8, is manifested as the pronoun *he* because of the Pronominalization rule. The second occurrence, in clauses 4 and 5, is deleted by the Noun Phrase Deletion rule and has no overt manifestation at all; the same rule, it will be recalled, reduces *John wants John to go* to its surface form, *John wants to go*. These two occurrences of *this man (this man be PRESENT cowardly)* can be reduced because they duplicate a noun phrase occurring in clauses 2 and 3.

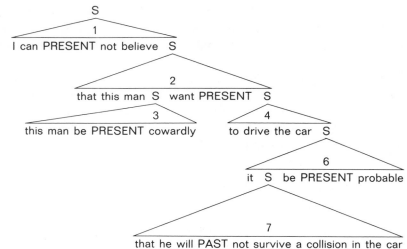

FIGURE 5.31

The result of these rule applications is the structure of Figure 5.31. This structure is derived from that of Figure 5.30 by the application of That Insertion, To Insertion, Subject-Verb Agreement, Pronominalization, and Noun Phrase Deletion.

A number of additional rules come into play in connecting this derived structure with its surface manifestation. The substructure comprising clauses 6 and 7 can be manifested in either of two ways. On the one hand, clause 7 can be moved to the end of clause 6 by the Extraposition rule, producing the structure that would come out in isolation as *It is probable that he would not survive a collision in the car*. On the other hand, clause 7 can remain where it is. *It* must be deleted in this case, the result being *That he would not survive a collision in the car is probable*. In the derivation of this sentence, Extraposition does apply, moving clause 7 to the end of the structure in which it is embedded. Not Promotion also applies in the derivation of this sentence, moving *not* from its position in clause 7 up into clause 6, where it appears in the surface structure.

From the structure of Figure 5.31, Extraposition and Not Promotion derive the structure of Figure 5.32. Structures 6 and 7 constitute a complex sentence constituent that is embedded after the noun phrase *the car* as a relative clause. The repeated noun phrase, *the car*, is moved to the begin-

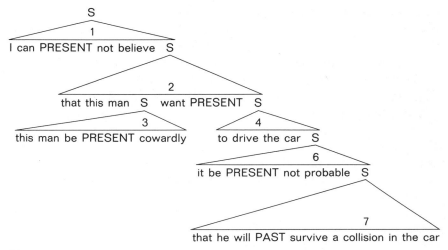

FIGURE 5.32

ning of the relative clause by the Noun Phrase Advancement rule, and the preposition *in* is carried with it. From ***the car (it be PRESENT not probable that he will PAST survive a collision in the car)***, Noun Phrase Advancement derives the structure ***the car (in the car it be PRESENT not probable that he will PAST survive a collision)***. The Relativization rule applies to the latter and reduces the second occurrence of ***the car*** to the relative pronoun ***which***. When the verbs are assigned their proper forms by phonological rules, therefore, the entire complex noun phrase is manifested as ***the car in which it is not probable that he would survive a collision***.

Noun Phrase Advancement and Relativization also apply to ***this man (this man be PRESENT cowardly)***. The former has no observable effect, since the repeated noun phrase ***this man*** is already at the beginning of the embedded clause. Relativization does have an effect, reducing ***this man*** to the pro form ***who***, yielding ***this man (who be PRESENT cowardly)***. If no other syntactic rules were to apply, this complex noun phrase would have the surface manifestation ***this man who is cowardly***. If the Relative Reduction rule applies, on the other hand, the relative pronoun ***who*** and the verb form ***be+PRESENT*** are deleted, leaving only the adjective ***cowardly*** to represent clause 3 of the underlying structure. ***This man*** *cowardly* must then be modified to *this cowardly man* by the Adjective Inversion rule. The result is the structure of Figure 5.29, the surface structure of *I cannot believe that this cowardly man wants to drive the car in which it is not probable that he would survive a collision.*

The derivation of this sentence thus involves That Insertion, To Insertion, Subject-Verb Agreement, Pronominalization, Noun Phrase Deletion, Extraposition, Not Promotion, Noun Phrase Advancement, Relativization, Relative Reduction, Adjective Inversion, and a great many other rules. This partial syntactic sketch of a single English sentence gives some indication of the tremendous abstractness and complexity of syntactic systems. Their abstractness and complexity is such that no human language—indeed, no sentence of any human language—has ever been fully described, and this will remain true for many decades to come. Every sentence, no matter how simple it may appear on the surface, manifests a conceptual structure through the mediation of a highly intricate set of syntactic principles. These principles are in no way subject to conscious inspection, although they constitute an important facet of our psychological organization. As native speakers of a language, we know a great deal that we are not ordinarily aware of.

CHAPTER
SIX _____

Phonological
Systems

ARTICULATORY PHONETICS

The sounds of speech can be studied from various points of view. One can investigate the physical properties of speech sounds as they are transmitted through the air, measuring the amount of energy present in the acoustic signal, its distribution over the frequency spectrum, how these measurements change in the course of an utterance, and so on. Another approach is to study sounds with respect to how we perceive them, asking questions like these: How much of a physical difference must there be between two sounds before a person can tell them apart? Which acoustic cues does the hearer rely on most heavily in speech perception? Which physical properties of sounds does he ignore altogether? A third way to study speech sounds is to examine the way they are produced, or **articulated,** by the speech organs. This approach is the oldest of all, going back at least to ancient India, and is also the most common. It is the one we will follow here.

The Speech Tract

The vocal organs of human beings all have more basic functions (such as eating and sucking), on which their articulatory functions are superimposed. Our vocal organs are thus not radically different from those of other primates. The fact that we vocalize in a highly systematic and coordinated manner, while they do not, must therefore be attributed to neurological factors rather than to gross anatomical differences.

When air is forced out of the lungs, it passes through the windpipe and exits through the mouth, the nose, or both. The outflow of air can be harnessed and channeled in various ways to form speech sounds. The path through which the air flows is sketched in Figure 6.1. This path is a sort of obstacle course in which the obstacles can be inserted and removed. When we exhale normally, the air is allowed to exit freely. Speech sounds are produced when various obstacles are moved into position.

The first potential obstacle that the outflowing air encounters is the vocal cords, two elastic membranes situated near the top of the windpipe in the little box that is popularly called the "Adam's apple." These membranes can assume various positions. When relaxed, they are separated and allow air to pass through unobstructed. When they become taut, they come together to close off the windpipe and prevent air from flowing through. In still a third position, they are drawn together, but not so tightly as to prevent air from being forced out through them, setting them in rapid vibration. This vibration of the vocal cords, called **voicing**, is the source of vowel sounds, which are produced when no other obstructions are placed in the path of the outflowing air. We will first examine the articulation of vowels and then consider the consonants.

Vowel Articulation

The sound produced by the vibration of the vocal cords is unavoidably modified by the configuration of the remainder of the vocal tract. For one thing, the tissues of the vocal tract absorb some of the original sound. More important, changes in the shape of the vocal tract affect its resonance properties. If the lips and tongue are in one position, the cavity through which the vibrating air passes will emphasize, or render more prominent, the sound components at certain frequencies. If the lips

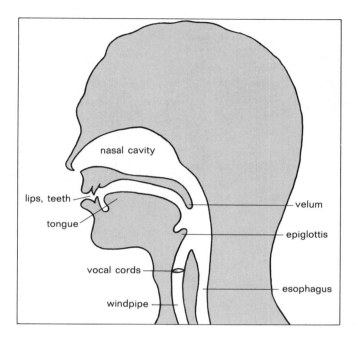

FIGURE 6.1

and tongue are in some other position, energy will be concentrated at other frequencies. (In similar fashion, an organ pipe emphasizes a tone at a frequency determined by its length and other characteristics.) The resulting differences in the distribution of energy over the frequency spectrum are what we perceive as differences in vowel quality. The vowels [i] and [a], for example, sound different because they are pronounced with the tongue in different positions, causing energy to be concentrated at different frequencies.

After the vocal cords, the most important organs in the articulation of vowel sounds are the tongue, the lips, and the velum (the fleshy rear part of the roof of the mouth). The tongue assumes many different postures and is of central importance in determining vowel quality. The lips may be rounded in various degrees or unrounded. The velum can be closed, as shown in Figure 6.1, blocking the opening to the nasal cavity so that air can pass out only through the mouth; or it can be lowered, allowing air into the upper chamber. For the moment, let us ignore the action of the

143

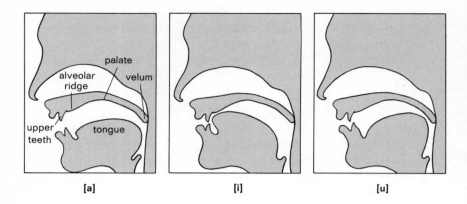

FIGURE 6.2

lips and the velum, taking the latter to be closed. This will permit us to concentrate on the effect of modifying the position of the tongue.

It is customary to talk about the position of the tongue in terms of two dimensions, high–low and front–back. The tongue may be held low in the mouth, or it may be extended upward at some point toward the roof of the mouth, or **palate**. Accordingly, a vowel sound is said to be **low** or **high**. The sound [a], as in *father*, is a low vowel. [i] and [u], as in *feet* and *boot*, are high vowels. The position of the tongue during the articulation of these three vowels is roughly indicated in Figure 6.2. Unlike [a], the sounds [i] and [u] are articulated with the tongue raised to constrict the vocal tract slightly at some point, though the constriction is not enough to cause any noticeable turbulence in the air passing through. [i] and [u] thus have a trait in common that distinguishes them from [a].

[i] and [u] are of course not the same. They differ with regard to the point of constriction. For [i], the constriction is formed by advancing the front of the tongue toward the **alveolar ridge**, the ridge just behind the upper teeth. For [u], however, the back of the tongue is raised and approaches the rear of the palate. [i] is said to be a **front** vowel, because the constriction is toward the front of the mouth, and [u] is a **back** vowel. Notice that [a] is like [u] with respect to the front-back dimension. It is at the rear of the mouth that the tongue is closest to the surface above it,

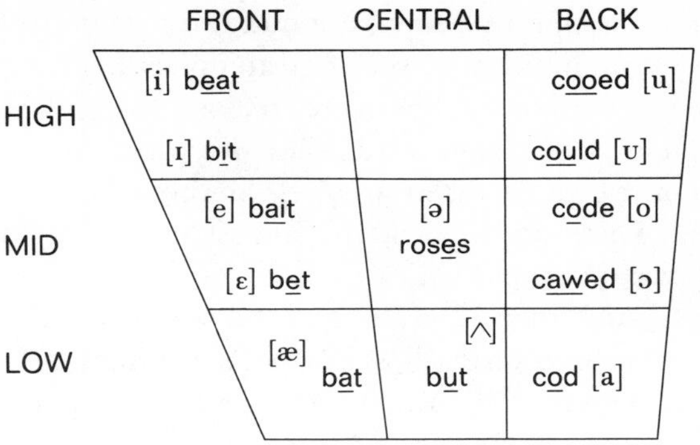

	FRONT	CENTRAL	BACK
HIGH	[i] b<u>ea</u>t [ɪ] b<u>i</u>t		c<u>oo</u>ed [u] c<u>ou</u>ld [ʊ]
MID	[e] b<u>ai</u>t [ɛ] b<u>e</u>t	[ə] ros<u>e</u>s	c<u>o</u>de [o] c<u>aw</u>ed [ɔ]
LOW	[æ] b<u>a</u>t	[ʌ] b<u>u</u>t	c<u>o</u>d [a]

FIGURE 6.3

although at no point are the two very near. [u] and [a] are both back vowels, therefore, and share a trait on which they differ from [i].

[a], [i], and [u] represent the extremes of vowel articulation. No vowel sound is pronounced with the tongue farther toward the front than it is for [i]; farther back than for [u] and [a]; higher than for [i] and [u]; or lower than for [a]. Between these extremes, of course, there are many possibilities. A vowel can be intermediate in height between high vowels like [u] and low vowels like [a]. Or a vowel can be intermediate in the front-back dimension, coming between front vowels like [i] and back vowels like [u]. The position of the tongue during the articulation of various vowel sounds is represented in Figure 6.3. The location of a vowel with regard to the front-back and high-low dimensions is indicated by the phonetic symbol for that vowel. An English word containing each vowel sound is provided to illustrate the values of the phonetic symbols that are employed. Both dimensions have been divided into three regions, front–central–back and high–mid–low. These divisions are often made, but the scales are really continuous, so the zones are mainly for ease of reference.

The interpretation of Figure 6.3 should be fairly obvious. Starting from the vowel [i], one can produce in series the vowels [ɪ], [e], [ɛ], and [æ] by gradually lowering the tongue (and also the jaw). In the same way, [u] can be successively modified to [ʊ], [o], [ɔ], and [a]. Moreover, the height of the tongue is roughly comparable for [i] and [u], as well as for the pairs [ɪ ʊ], [e o], [ɛ ɔ], and [æ a]. To identify a vowel, we give its location along

145

the two dimensions. [e], for instance, is a mid front vowel, [a] is a low back vowel, and [ə] is a mid central vowel. If greater precision is needed, we can divide the dimensions into smaller bands, making the grid finer.

The position of the tongue establishes the basic quality of a vowel. The precise phonetic character of a vowel, however, also depends on the lips and velum. These add two more dimensions to any fully adequate chart on which vowels are plotted.

Pronounce [i] and then [u]. Notice how radically different they are with respect to the shape of the lips. For [i], the corners of the mouth are drawn back as in a smile. For [u], on the other hand, the lips are rounded and protruded. [u], therefore, is said to be a **rounded** vowel, and [i] is **unrounded**. Of the vowels in Figure 6.3, [u ʊ o ɔ] are rounded, while all the others are unrounded. More often than not, a vowel is rounded if it is a back vowel and unrounded otherwise, but this is not always true. The dimension of rounding is independent from the horizontal and vertical dimensions; no matter what the position of the tongue, a vowel can be either rounded or unrounded. For example, it is easy to make a vowel like [i] except that it is rounded, or a vowel like [u] except that it is not. These sounds are not used in English, but they are in many languages.

Any of the sounds so far discussed can be modified by lowering the velum so that air is allowed to pass through the nasal cavity. Vowels articulated in this way are called **nasal** vowels; those articulated with the velum closed are said to be **oral** vowels. Nasal vowels are very common, although they do not happen to be used in English. They are in French, to take one well-known example. Low vowels are more frequently nasal than high vowels, but again this is only a tendency. The nasal-oral dimension is independent from the other three.

A speech sound can therefore be viewed as a bundle of articulatory properties. [i], for instance, can be described as a high front unrounded oral vowel. Five terms are included in its description. The term **vowel** establishes that the articulation of the sound involves the vibration of the vocal cords and that there are no other major obstructions in the vocal tract. The other four terms situate this sound in the classification of vowels just outlined; each term locates the sound along one dimension. To take another example, the French word *un* 'one' is manifested phonetically as a mid front rounded nasal vowel. Phonetic symbols, like [i], can be regarded as convenient notations for bundles of articulatory properties.

146

Consonant Articulation

There are many ways to make consonant sounds, and the mechanisms involved are sometimes quite intricate. Since this book is not a treatise on phonetics, we will have to be rather selective.

Perhaps the most fundamental of the consonants are the **stops**. These are sounds produced by closing off completely the flow of air, letting pressure build up behind the closure, and then releasing it in a sudden burst. [p], for example, is articulated by closing the lips, thereby effecting a stoppage in the flow of air, and then opening the lips to let the trapped air escape. This sound occurs before the vowel [a] in the word *pa*.

The stoppage of air may be made with the lips, the vocal cords, or the tongue. A stop articulated with the two lips is called **bilabial**. One made by the vocal cords is a **glottal** stop. With the tongue, of course, there are many points in the mouth where the closure can be effected. For the most part, the point at which the closure is made determines what part of the tongue is used; the tip of the tongue, for instance, can easily make a stoppage against the upper teeth, but hardly against the velum. Stops articulated with the tongue are said to be **dental, alveolar, palatal,** or **velar** if the stoppage is made, respectively, against the upper teeth, the alveolar ridge, the palate, or the velum (see Figure 6.2). The English [p], then, is a bilabial stop. [t], the first sound of *to*, is an alveolar stop. *Key* begins with the velar stop [k].

A stop produced by means of a closure at a particular point can assume many different specific phonetic forms. Just as with the vowels, there are a number of secondary dimensions along which a stop consonant may vary. We will consider only some, and these fairly briefly. These modifications are most relevant for stops, but they pertain to other kinds of sounds as well.

The vocal cords may cease to vibrate during the articulation of a consonant. If they do, the consonant is said to be **voiceless**. If they continue to vibrate, it is said to be **voiced**. English [p t k], for instance, are voiceless stops. All three have voiced counterparts: [b], as in *bib*, is a voiced bilabial stop; [d], as in *dud*, is a voiced alveolar stop; [g], as in *gag*, is a voiced velar stop.

English voiceless stops are normally produced with the emission of a puff of air as the closure is released. Pronounce *pa*, holding your fingers directly in front of your mouth as you do so; it should be easy to feel the

147

air emitted as [p] is articulated. Stops can be produced without the accompanying puff of air, and in fact, such sounds are very common. The stops of French and Spanish, for example, usually lack it. Stops accompanied by this puff of air are called **aspirated** stops; those that lack it are **unaspirated**. The [p] of English *pa* can now be described more precisely as a voiceless aspirated bilabial stop. The French [d] sound, as in *dans* 'in,' is a voiced unaspirated dental stop.

We should mention a few other modulations of stop articulations that, while relatively infrequent in the familiar European languages, are used in many languages of the world. A stop pronounced with an accompanying rounding of the lips is said to be **labialized**. (This is the same trait that characterizes rounded vowels.) Labialized alveolar and velar stops occur in English, but only in a few special environments. [t d k g] are labialized, for instance, when they precede the sound [w] (the initial sound of *wig*), in anticipation of the position of the lips that the pronunciation of [w] requires. Examples are *twig, Edward, liquid*, and *iguana*. Sounds can also be modified by changing the size of the upper throat, or **pharynx**. By moving the root of the tongue back, the pharyngeal cavity can be greatly constricted. Sounds that are accompanied by this constriction are said to be **pharyngealized**. Arabic is a language that has pharyngealized consonants. **Glottalized** consonants are produced by the simultaneous action of the box containing the vocal cords and some other articulator. This box is raised with the vocal cords closed, causing an increase in air pressure along the upper vocal tract. The trapped air then rushes out when the consonant articulation is released. Many American Indian languages have glottalized consonants.

In the production of stops, the lips, tongue, or vocal cords effect a stoppage in the flow of air along the vocal tract, and this stoppage is subsequently released. Another mode of consonant articulation is to obstruct, but not block entirely, the flow of air. This is done by moving an articulator very close to the position it assumes in making a closure but leaving a small opening through which the outflowing air can pass. The constriction of the vocal tract induces turbulence in the flow of air through the narrowed passage, a turbulence that we perceive as a kind of hissing. Sounds produced in this way are called **fricatives**.

Like stops, fricatives can be characterized by the point at which the narrowest constriction is made. A fricative produced with both lips would

148

be a bilabial fricative, a sound that is not used in English. The English sound [f] is a **labiodental** fricative, since its articulation has the upper teeth placed on the lower lip. [θ], the initial sound of *thing*, is a dental fricative; the tongue makes contact with the upper teeth, but, as is the case with [f], the flow of air is not completely blocked. [s], illustrated twice in *sis*, is alveolar. Articulated farther back on the tongue, and slightly behind the alveolar ridge, is the palatal fricative [š], the last sound of *fish*. English does not have a velar fricative; German and Russian do. [h], the first sound of *hand*, is a glottal fricative, although not much friction is produced as the air passes through the vocal cords. All of the above fricatives are voiceless. English also has a series of voiced fricatives, each of which matches a voiceless fricative in point of articulation. The voiced fricatives [v ð z ž] are the first consonants of *vile, this, zero,* and *azure* respectively.

A third mode of consonant articulation combines the features of stops and fricatives. A stoppage is made and then released, as for stops, but the release is made with the turbulence that is characteristic of fricatives. English has two of these sounds, called **affricates**. [č], the first and last sound of *church*, is voiceless. Its voiced counterpart, which occurs twice in *judge*, is symbolized [ǰ]. One is a voiceless palatal affricate, and the other is a voiced palatal affricate. The affricates used in English are, of course, only a small sample of those to be found in human languages.

Some consonants are articulated by making a closure in the mouth while lowering the velum to allow air to pass through the nasal cavity. These are called **nasal** consonants. Nasal consonants are distinguished from one another by the point where the oral closure is made. For English [m], as in *me*, the two lips are brought together, and [m] is thus a bilabial nasal. [n], as in *no*, is an alveolar nasal. The word *sing*, despite the orthography, ends phonetically in a single consonant, a velar nasal; this is symbolized as [ŋ]. Nasal consonants are usually voiced, but they do not have to be.

This brings us to the **liquids**, the *r*- and *l*-like sounds. We can only touch on the variety of liquids to be found in the languages of the world.

The various *l*-like sounds are called **laterals**. Pronounce an [l], as in *lap*. Notice that your tongue makes an alveolar closure in the center of your mouth. At the same time, however, air is permitted to escape on the sides, so that it is never completely blocked; hence the term lateral. The English lateral is voiced. Since no turbulence is caused by the closure in the center, and since the flow of air is continuous, it resembles vowels in acoustic quality. The same is true of voiced nasals and especially of the English [r] sound.

The English [r], as in *row*, involves no oral closure at all. It is therefore very much like a vowel. The articulatory trait that gives it its special character is the shape of the tongue. Either the front or the rear of the tongue is raised slightly toward the roof of the mouth in such a way that the upper surface of the tongue is shaped something like a cup. More commonly, *r*-like sounds are produced by flapping the front part of the tongue against the alveolar ridge, as in a very rapid pronunciation of [d]. One of the Spanish *r* sounds is produced in this manner. A common variant of this is the trilled *r*. A trill is a rapid series of flaps induced by the air stream as it is forced out. The Spanish word *pero* 'but' contains a flap *r*, while *perro* 'dog' has a trilled *r* in the same position. Trills are sometimes not produced with the tongue, but with the uvula, that slender finger of tissue that hangs down from the velum in the back of the mouth. This kind of *r* is used in many dialects of German and French.

We have now characterized all of the basic sounds of English except [w] and [y]. These are called **glides** or, because they are closely related to vowels, **semivowels**. The exclamation *wow* begins and ends with [w], and *yoyo* contains two occurrences of [y]. A glide is a rapid movement of the articulatory organs to or from the position they assume for the articulation of a certain vowel. The glide [w] is related to the vowel [u] in this way, and the glide [y] to [i]. The pronunciation of *wow*, for instance, starts from the articulatory position used to pronounce [u], with the lips rounded and the tongue high and back. Instead of actually articulating [u], however, the vocal organs glide rapidly into position for [a]. As [a] is being pronounced, the lips and tongue glide back where they came from, so that the word ends as they are approaching the [u] position. The articulation of [y] is parallel.

Usually, though not always, glides are related to high vowels, with [w] and [y] being the most common. To take one other example, French has in addition to these a glide from the high front rounded position, as in *lui* 'him.' In English, the vowels [e] and [o] are normally pronounced with an accompanying glide. [e] is regularly followed by [y], and [o] by [w]. *Bait* and *boat*, for instance, are [beyt] and [bowt] phonetically. Other vowel-plus-glide combinations to be found in English are [ay] (*eye*), [ɔy] (*boy*), and [aw] (*cow*, though in many dialects the combination is [æw] instead).

Suprasegmental Features

Thus far we have examined only sound segments. In closing, we should say a word about **length, stress,** and **tone,** phonological entities that can hardly be considered segments. They are commonly called **suprasegmental** phenomena because of the practice of writing them phonetically by means of marks made above the symbols indicating segments.

Length is commonly regarded as a suprasegmental feature. Two sounds, particularly in the case of vowels, may be the same in every respect except duration. The vowel of English *bed*, for example, is slightly longer than the vowel of *bet*. In general, English vowels are longer before voiced consonants than before voiceless ones. In many languages, the length of vowels or consonants plays a more important role, serving to distinguish morphemes.

Vowels can also differ in relative prominence, as we have already observed with respect to English compounds. In the compound *redskin,* *red* is articulated with greater emphasis, and the opposite is true in the phrase *red skin*. The usual term for this prominence is **stress.** Thus *red* is said to be stressed in *redskin*, but *skin* is stressed in *red skin*. Linguists do not fully understand just what constitutes stress. The best we can say is that stressed vowels are apparently different from unstressed ones in that they are of greater length, higher pitch, and greater articulatory force.

We can raise (or lower) the pitch of our voices simply by increasing (or decreasing) the tension of the vocal cords. In many languages, differences of pitch are systematically used to distinguish morphemes. Chinese is the standard example of such languages, which are called **tone** languages. A difference in tone may be a difference in pitch alone. For instance, the identification of a morpheme may depend on whether the vowel has high or low pitch. If a language has a number of tones, and not just two or three, the pitch **contour** becomes relevant. Speakers may distinguish, for example, among a high tone, a low tone, a falling tone, a rising tone, and a tone that falls and then rises. The maximum number of tones systematically used in any one language to distinguish morphemes seems to be about five.

151

DISTINCTIVE DIFFERENCES

Human beings can make an infinite number of speech sounds. This is true simply because some articulatory dimensions are continuous rather than discrete. Between the positions for [u] and [a], for instance, there are an infinite number of possible tongue heights, and hence an infinite number of corresponding vowel sounds. The point of closure for stop consonants, to take another example, can come at any point along the oral tract. Most of these minuscule phonetic differences, naturally, are below the threshold of perception. Moreover, many grosser, clearly perceptible differences are not exploited systematically by the speakers of a language for purposes of communication.

We have come to a crucial notion: the systematic exploitation of certain phonological differences by the speakers of a language for purposes of communication. A language can serve as an instrument of communication because it establishes pairings between meanings and pronunciations. The building blocks of these pairings are the individual morphemes, which (in addition to syntactic properties) have conceptual import and phonological representations. The phonological representation of a morpheme determines its pronunciation.

For this communication scheme to function effectively, it must by and large be true that different morphemes have different pronunciations. It must be possible, on the basis of its phonological shape, to identify a morpheme and recover its meaning; otherwise the hearer would have no way of knowing what a sentence said and the speaker would have no reason to produce it. To take an extreme case, we could hardly communicate with one another if all the morphemes of our language were pronounced identically. A few identically pronounced morphemes present no real difficulties (for example, *fire* = flame and *fire* = dismiss). Massive identities of phonological shape, on the other hand, could seriously disrupt communication.

Therefore it must be possible to tell morphemes apart on the basis of their pronunciations. In what ways, then, do the morphemes of a language differ from one another phonologically? One way is in the number of sound segments they contain. **Red** and **ready**, for instance, differ in that the former has three segments and the latter has four. Obviously, though, the identity of the segments is of vastly greater importance. **Tan** can be recognized, distinguished from other morphemes, when the first segment is identified as [t], the second as [æ], and the third as [n]. This information separates *tan* from, say, *can*, which has a different initial segment, as well as from other morphemes that resemble *tan* even less.

But in what sense is it meaningful to talk about identifying a sound segment? In purely objective terms, no two uttered sounds are ever exactly alike in all their phonetic detail. Whenever a sound is pronounced, that exact sound is pronounced for the first (and last) time. The differences between two uttered sounds may be minute, almost immeasurable, but they are always there. In what sense, then, do we identify sounds, since every one is unique?

The answer is that, as speakers of a particular language, we systematically ignore certain differences between sounds and pay attention to certain other differences. We learn which ones to pay heed to as part of mastering the phonological system of our language. As speakers of English, for example, we pay attention to whether or not a stop is voiced. This difference is used to distinguish between [p] and [b], between [t] and [d], and between [k] and [g], which for us are functionally different sounds. By paying heed to the voicing of stops, we tell *pun* from *bun*, *tin* from *din*, and *come* from *gum*. On the other hand, we ignore the feature of labialization with stops. The difference between a plain [t] and [t] articulated with the lips rounded is not a functional one in English. There are no two morphemes of English that differ solely in that one has a plain [t] in the same position where the other has a labialized [t]. Functional differences, differences to which the speakers of a language pay heed in determining the identity of morphemes, are called **distinctive**. Voicing is thus distinctive in English with respect to the stops, but labialization is not.

The phonological system of a language imposes structure on the phonetic continuum. Just as the largely continuous speech stream is treated psychologically as a series of discrete sound segments, so the continuous articulatory dimensions are broken up into discrete ranges by a linguistic system. A sound may be voiced throughout its articulation, voiceless throughout, voiced at the beginning then voiceless, voiceless until the last hundredth of a second—the possibilities are endless; but for speakers of a language in which voicing is distinctive, a segment is treated as either voiced or voiceless, with no middle ground. From the alveolar ridge to the velum, there are an unlimited number of places where the tongue can make contact with the roof of the mouth in articulating a stop. As speakers of English, however, we treat this continuum as if it were divided into two discrete regions. A voiceless stop articulated with the tongue is judged to be either a [t] or a [k]. There are no other possibilities; a stop pronounced with the tongue in an intermediate position is forced into one of the two molds.

The functionally different sounds of a language are opposed to one another in a network of distinctive differences. In English, for example, [s] is opposed to [z] by the distinctive difference between voiceless and voiced segments; to [f], [θ], and [š] by the distinctive opposition among alveolar, labial, dental, and palatal articulations; to [t] on the feature of nonclosure versus closure (that is, fricative versus stop); to [d] on the features of closure and voicing; and to the other sounds of English by these and other distinctive differences. A small number of distinctive differences are sufficient to distinguish all of the functionally different segment types of a language. The other, nondistinctive differences are ignored.

Languages vary with respect to which differences are treated as distinctive and used to tell morphemes apart. In English, we pay attention to whether or not a stop or fricative is voiced. It matters, since some morphemes are distinguished from one another solely on this basis (for example, *pig/big; fan/van; vat/fad*). In many languages, however, the voiced-voiceless distinction is not exploited at all; there are no morphemes that are differentiated on the basis of this feature alone. In some languages, the difference between aspirated and unaspirated stops is distinctive, but it is not in English. In others, both voicing and aspiration are distinctive. Similar observations hold for labialization, glottalization, and pharyngealization. The feature of voicing is not distinctive in English with respect to the liquids. There is only one distinctive [l] sound in English, and only one [r]; no two morphemes are distinguished just by virtue of the difference between a voiced and a voiceless liquid. Some languages, though, rely on the contrast between, say, a voiced and voiceless [l] to differentiate morphemes. We have to recognize several functional vowel heights for English, to distinguish, for example, among *bit, bet,* and *bat*. In various other languages, however, a simple dichotomy between high and low vowels suffices.

Part of learning a language consists of mastering the system of distinctive oppositions that the language uses to differentiate morphemes. Beyond this, a speaker must assimilate the phonological representations of all the individual morphemes of the language. These are not separate tasks; they are closely connected. The system of distinctive oppositions determines what phonological information has to be learned individually for each morpheme and what information can be supplied by general phonological rules that hold for all the morphemes of the language.

The phonological properties of a morpheme that have to be learned individually for that morpheme are precisely those properties that are distinctive. Phonological properties that can be supplied by general rules cannot serve as distinctive properties.

Consider the initial sound of the English word *tin*. Phonetically, it is an aspirated voiceless alveolar stop. The information that it is a voiceless alveolar stop is distinctive and has to be learned individually for this morpheme. The information that it is aspirated, however, can be predicted by a general phonological rule of English. The property of being aspirated or unaspirated is not distinctive.

There is no way to predict that the English word for this kind of metal begins with a voiceless alveolar stop as opposed to a voiced one. Both voiced and voiceless alveolar stops occur in initial position; it is just an arbitrary fact that the form happens to be *tin* and not *din*. The feature of voicelessness is therefore distinctive in this position, serving to specify which of the two potential forms is the correct one. In the same way, the information that this segment is alveolar and not bilabial or velar is distinctive information. It is an idiosyncratic property of this one morpheme and distinguishes it from the possible English forms *pin* and *kin*. Finally, it is necessary to learn individually for this morpheme that the first sound is a stop and not, say, a fricative. This phonological property differentiates the morphemes *tin* and *sin*.

However, the fact that the stop sound of *tin* is aspirated does not distinguish this form from any other possible form of English. This information has no contrastive value, since initial voiceless stops in English are always aspirated when the following vowel is stressed. Because this property is characteristic of all morphemes that begin with a voiceless stop, it cannot be used to tell them apart. It is redundant phonetic detail that is filled in by a general rule of English on the basis of other phonological information. When a speaker learns how the word *tin* is pronounced, he does not have to learn individually for this form that the initial stop is aspirated. He aspirates it automatically in accordance with a phonological principle that holds across the board for English.

A couple of additional examples may prove helpful. It is a general phonological principle of English that nonlow back vowels (that is, [u ʊ o ɔ]) are rounded while all other vowels are unrounded. The rounded or unrounded character of vowels therefore does not have to be learned individually, over and over again, for each of the thousands of morphemes of the language. In learning to pronounce *pen*, for example, a speaker must learn the distinctive information that its vowel is a front vowel (to distinguish it from *pawn*), and he must learn its height (to distinguish it from *pin, pan,* and so on), but he does not have to learn that it is unrounded. This nondistinctive phonetic detail is supplied by a phonological principle of English that applies to thousands of other morphemes as well. It is much less of a burden to master this one simple rule than to learn, individually for each morpheme, the thousands of phonetic facts that it accounts for.

As a final example, consider the second segment of the word *spin*. Phonetically, it is an unaspirated voiceless bilabial stop. Of these four traits, only the last two are distinctive. The information that it is a bilabial stop, and not velar or alveolar, distinguishes this morpheme from the morpheme *skin* and from *stin*, which is a possible English form that does not happen to occur. The distinctive property of being a stop distinguishes the second segment from [w l m n] and the vowels, which can also occur after initial [s]. But stops in English are always unaspirated after initial [s]; this is a general phonological rule and not an idiosyncratic property of *spin*. Therefore, the unaspirated character of [p] after initial [s] is not distinctive. There could be no two morphemes of English that were identical except that one had an unaspirated stop in this position whereas the other had an aspirated stop.

The feature of voicing is for the most part distinctive in English with respect to the stops, but it is not after initial [s]. In this phonological environment, stops are always voiceless. A speaker does not have to learn this information for every morpheme beginning with [s] plus a stop; he masters a single rule which specifies that all stops in this environment are voiceless. There could thus be no morphemes of English distinguished solely by the different initial sequences [sp] versus [sb]; [st] versus [sd]; or [sk] versus [sg]. The contrast between the pairs [p b], [t d], and [k g] is said to be **neutralized** in this environment. The difference between them is systematically exploited for purposes of communication in other phonological environments, but not after initial [s].

The phonological representation of a morpheme, therefore, is the information that a speaker has to learn individually for that morpheme in order for him to know how it is pronounced. A morpheme is represented phonologically as an ordered series of segments. Each segment is specified by all and only those properties that are distinctive for segments in that position.

PHONOLOGICAL RULES

The function of phonological rules, as we saw in Chapter Four, is to connect surface structures with their phonetic manifestations (see Figure 4.4, page 92). A surface structure, you will recall, is a tree structure that terminates in a linear string of morphemes. Each morpheme in the string has a phonological representation, a specification of the distinctive properties that determine its pronunciation. Phonological rules relate a sentence and its phonetic manifestation on the basis of these specifications.

The Specification of Nondistinctive Features

Phonological systems are anything but simple. The relation between surface structures and their phonetic manifestations is an indirect one, mediated by long and sometimes very intricate series of phonological rules. We will begin to illustrate this process by examining the derivation of the English morpheme *stack*.

Phonetically, *stack* consists of a sequence of four segments: [stæk]. [s] is a voiceless alveolar fricative; [t] is an unaspirated voiceless alveolar stop; [æ] is a low front unrounded nonnasal vowel; and [k] is an unaspirated voiceless velar stop. If we wanted to make our description complete, we would have to add many more nondistinctive phonetic details. We would have to note that none of the segments, for example, is labialized, pharyngealized, or glottalized. We would have to indicate the precise spot of the velar closure for the articulation of [k]. Somewhere we would have to specify that [s] and [t] are not articulated with the very tip of the tongue, but with a part of the tongue slightly behind it. The full series of rules responsible for the phonetic manifestation of *stack* therefore contains many rules in addition to those that we will explicitly consider.

Not all of the phonological properties listed above are distinctive. The unaspirated quality of [t], for instance, can be predicted by a general rule of English, as can the lack of rounding for [æ] and several other features. As indicated in Figure 6.4, the distinctive phonological properties of *stack*, the features that have to be learned individually for this morpheme, constitute its phonological representation, which underlies its full phonetic manifestation. In both the underlying and phonetic representations, a segment can be viewed as comprising a bundle of phonological properties. In Figure 6.4, each bundle is enclosed in square brackets. The nondistinctive phonetic properties of *stack* are in bold type. These are specified by the phonological rules that connect the underlying phonological representation with its phonetic manifestation.

By comparing the two representations of *stack* in Figure 6.4, we find that phonological rules are responsible for specifying the voiceless and alveolar features of [s]; the unaspirated and voiceless features of [t]; the unrounded and nonnasal features of [æ]; and the unaspirated feature of [k]. The addition of all this phonetic detail is the cumulative effect of a number of individual rules, each of which holds for all the morphemes of English.

Let us start with the vowel. The information that the third segment is a low front vowel is distinctive; these features distinguish [æ] from nonlow and nonfront vowels, as well as from the liquid [r], all of which can occur after initial [st] (for example, *stick, stool, strip*). The information that it is nonnasal, however, is not distinctive. There is a general phonological principle of English that specifies all vowels as being nonnasal. This is not an idiosyncratic property of any individual morpheme. None of the English vowels shown in Figure 6.3 is nasal, so the lack of nasality cannot be used to tell them (or morphemes) apart. We have already noted the existence of another rule of English to the effect that nonlow back vowels are rounded while all other vowels are not. Since [æ] is a front vowel, this rule fills in the nondistinctive detail that it is unrounded. Thus two rules combine to connect an underlying segment specified as a low front vowel with its phonetic manifestation as a low front unrounded nonnasal vowel.

We turn next to the initial segment. Normally, the voiceless and alveolar features are distinctive for the fricative [s]. At the beginning of a morpheme before a stop, however, they are not distinctive. [s] is the only fricative that can occur in this position; there are no English forms like *zdack* or *ftack*, where a voiced or nonalveolar fricative precedes a stop. The information that the first segment is a fricative, as opposed to a vowel,

UNDERLYING PHONOLOGICAL REPRESENTATION

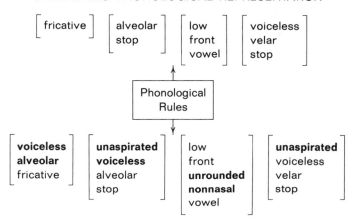

PHONETIC MANIFESTATION

FIGURE 6.4

is therefore sufficient to identify it. (In fact, the information that it is a consonant suffices.) The other features can be specified as redundant phonetic detail by the rule that a fricative is voiceless and alveolar in initial position before a stop. This is a general characteristic of English, not a property of individual morphemes.

We saw previously that the voiceless unaspirated character of stops after initial [s] is nondistinctive. These two features should probably be attributed to different rules. One rule specifies a stop as being unaspirated when it follows a fricative. The other pertains to consonant sequences— or **clusters**—composed of stops, fricatives, and affricates. It is a general principle of English that, when two or more of these sounds occur adjacent to one another in a string, either they are all voiced or they are all voiceless. For instance, **exit** can be pronounced in either of two ways, [ɛksɪt] or [ɛgzɪt]. The stop-fricative cluster can be completely voiceless, or completely voiced, but not mixed. The voicing feature of the stop determines that of the following fricative, ruling out combinations such as [kz] or [gs]. The plural morpheme, for another illustration, is usually an alveolar fricative, as in **books** and **beds**. However, it is pronounced as [s] in the first of these words and as [z] in the second. Evidently, the voiceless [s] of [bʊks] and the voiced [z] of [bɛdz] agree in voicing with the preceding stop. As a final example, take the past tense morpheme, which is an alveolar stop (for regular verbs). *Judged* and *reached* are phonetically [ǰʌǰd] and [ričt]. The past tense morpheme is manifested as the voiced [d] after *judge*, since this ends in a voiced affricate, and as [t] after the voiceless affricate of *reach*. This general rule, then, which has to be posited for the phonological system of English to handle many other cases, specifies the second segment of *stack* as voiceless to agree with the initial [s].

We described the final segment of *stack* as being phonetically unaspirated. This is indeed one possibility, but it does not happen to be the only possibility. The articulation of final stops is an area in which English speakers have some latitude. Final stops may be either aspirated or unaspirated, and there is even the third option of moving the tongue up to the roof of the mouth for the stop closure but omitting the stop burst. This is done by simply not releasing the closure. Thus the rules that serve to fill out the phonetic detail for final stops must provide for all three of these possibilities.

We have examined the derivation of the phonetic manifestation of *stack* by phonological rules from its underlying representation. Even ignoring minute phonetic specifications, we found at least six rules to be involved in connecting the two levels. Each of these rules specifies one or more nondistinctive features for some segment, putting phonetic flesh on the skeletal representations in terms of distinctive properties alone.

Other Kinds of Phonological Rules

It would be wrong to conclude from the above example that phonological rules do nothing more than to specify nondistinctive features. It would also be wrong to conclude that underlying phonological representations and their phonetic manifestations differ only in that the latter are fleshed out, more detailed versions of the former; the relation between the two levels can be extremely distant and abstract. Phonological rules insert segments, delete segments, and change the identity and even the order of segments. In addition, they introduce and modify suprasegmental features.

A hypothetical example will allow us to illustrate these remarks simply and coherently. Consider the phonetic data in the table below, which could

160

perfectly well be found in some real language. (An accent mark over a vowel indicates that the vowel is stressed.)

[béb]	'bird'	[bébib]	'birds'
[lót]	'tree'	[lódib]	'trees'
[mék]	'dog'	[mégib]	'dogs'
[rába]	'fire'	[rábib]	'fires'
[sónob]	'rock'	[sómbib]	'rocks'
[íf]	'run'	[ífa]	'ran'
[tíf]	'not run'	[tífa]	'did not run'
[éso]	'swim'	[ésa]	'swam'
[téso]	'not swim'	[tésa]	'did not swim'
[kínap]	'eat'	[kímba]	'ate'
[etkínap]	'not eat'	[etkímba]	'did not eat'
[síme]	'walk'	[síma]	'walked'
[estíme]	'not walk'	[estíma]	'did not walk'
[sárot]	'sleep'	[sárda]	'slept'
[estárot]	'not sleep'	[estárda]	'did not sleep'

Let us start by comparing the forms for 'bird' and 'birds,' [béb] and [bébib] respectively. [bébib] evidently consists of the morpheme [béb] 'bird' followed by the suffix [ib], which marks the plural. It seems, then, that the plural is marked in this language by the addition of [ib] as a suffix to the noun root.

The noun meaning 'tree' is [lót], and on the basis of the pair [béb] and [bébib], we would expect the form for 'trees' to be [lótib], which is what we obtain by adding [ib] to [lót] as a suffix. In fact, however, the form is not [lótib] but [lódib]. At first glance, therefore, the noun meaning 'tree' seems to be irregular with respect to plural formation; this root has two alternate forms, [lót] and [lód], depending on whether or not it is followed by the plural suffix. When we look at the words for 'dog' and 'dogs,' though, we find a similar alternation, suggesting that [lót] may not be irregular after all. The morpheme meaning 'dog' is [mék], but the plural form 'dogs' is [mégib] rather than [mékib]. [lót] and [mék] thus behave alike with respect to the formation of plurals; when the suffix [ib] is added, the underlying voiceless stop is manifested instead as a voiced stop.

In the phonetic data at hand, there is no instance of a voiceless stop that occurs between two vowels. It seems to be a general phonological

161

principle of this language that a stop is always voiced when it is flanked with vowels; let us call this principle the Stop Voicing rule. According to the Stop Voicing rule, then, [rába], [lódib], and [mégib] are possible phonetic sequences, but [rápa], [lótib], and [mékib], with voiceless stops occurring intervocalically, are not. In light of the general Stop Voicing rule, the forms [lódib] 'trees' and [mégib] 'dogs' are seen to be completely regular. Like [bébib] 'birds,' they are formed simply by adding [ib] as a suffix to the noun root. The underlying representations so obtained are [lótib] and [mékib], for 'trees' and 'dogs' respectively. The Stop Voicing rule applies to these underlying representations and makes the intervocalic stops voiced instead of voiceless, producing the phonetic manifestations [lódib] and [mégib]. [béb], [lót], and [mék] all form the plural in the same way, therefore, by the addition of [ib] as a suffix. It is a general phonological rule of the language that changes [t] to [d] and [k] to [g] between vowels. The surface irregularity turns out, on examination, to reflect a deeper regularity.

The root for 'fire' is [rába], but the plural form is simply [rábib] instead of the expected [rábaib]. Once again it seems that we are faced with a phonological irregularity, until we look into the matter further. The occurrence of [rábib] instead of [rábaib] is not at all surprising if we examine the rest of the data; in no case do we find more than one vowel after the stressed vowel of a word. This is apparently a phonological principle of the language. More specifically, let us postulate the existence of a Vowel Deletion rule, which applies within a word and deletes a vowel that follows a stressed syllable and precedes another syllable. Vowel Deletion thus applies to the regularly formed underlying representation [rábaib] and deletes [a] to yield the phonetic sequence [rábib]. [a] can be deleted because it follows a stressed syllable ([rá]) and precedes another syllable ([ib]).

We find further illustration of Vowel Deletion when we examine the noun [sónob] 'rock' and its plural [sómbib]. If the noun [sónob] is regular with respect to plural formation, then the phonetic sequence [sómbib] must manifest a more abstract phonological representation of the form [sónobib]. [sómbib] differs from this underlying representation in two ways. First, the unstressed [o] of [sónobib] is lacking. Second, the underlying segment [n] shows up phonetically as [m]. Both of these differences can be traced to the operation of general phonological rules. The Vowel Deletion rule specifies that an unstressed vowel is deleted when it follows a syllable containing a stressed vowel and precedes another syllable (in the same word). Since [o] follows a stressed syllable in [sónobib], and since another syllable follows [o], Vowel Deletion applies and reduces [sónobib] to [sónbib]. From the representation [sónbib] produced by Vowel Deletion, a rule that we will call Nasal Assimilation derives [sómbib]. This rule specifies that a nasal consonant is manifested as a bilabial when it precedes a bilabial stop, [b] in this instance. **Assimilation,** a very common phonological phenomenon, is the modification of a sound to make it more similar to neighboring sounds. In this case, the underlying segment [n] is assimilated to the following [b], so that both are manifested phonetically as bilabials. Nowhere in the data will one find the phonetic sequence [nb], where an alveolar precedes a bilabial stop; Nasal Assimilation thus appears to be a general principle of the language.

If the data contained only the above nouns and their plurals, one might reasonably doubt the existence of certain of the rules we have posited. It could perfectly well be the case, for instance, that [sónob], like the English morpheme *child,* has a special form used only with the plural morpheme and that we were wrong in attributing the variant [sómb] to the operation of general phonological rules. When we turn to the verb forms, however, we find further justification for the rules in question.

The verb meaning 'run,' when unspecified with respect to tense, has the form [íf]. By comparing this with the past tense form [ífa] 'ran,' we see that past tense is indicated by the addition of the suffix [a]. The negative forms [tíf] 'not run' and [tífa] 'did not run' support this analysis and at the same time show that negation is marked on the verb by the prefix [t].

Since 'swim' is pronounced [éso], we would expect the form for 'not swim' to be [téso], and this is indeed what the data shows. By the same token, we would expect the forms for 'swam' and 'did not swim' to be [ésoa] and [tésoa] respectively, for these result directly from the addition of the suffix [a] to indicate past tense. In fact, however, the forms are [ésa] and [tésa], not [ésoa] and [tésoa]. [ésa] and [tésa] thus seem irregular at first glance, but only until we recall the Vowel Deletion rule. In order to account for the occurrence of [rábib] 'fires' as the plural of [rába], and [sómbib] 'rocks' as the plural of [sónob], we posited the existence of this rule, which deletes a vowel that follows a stressed syllable and precedes another syllable in the same word. [éso] is seen to be perfectly regular with regard to past tense formation when viewed in light of the Vowel Deletion rule. The addition of the past tense suffix [a] to [éso] and [téso] yields the underlying representations [ésoa] and [tésoa]. Vowel Deletion applies automatically to these underlying representations and deletes [o] to produce the phonetic sequences [ésa] and [tésa]. The same phonological principle that accounts for the plural of the nouns [rába] and [sónob] therefore accounts as well for the past tense of the verb [éso].

[kínap] 'eat' and [kímba] 'ate' provide additional justification for Stop Voicing, Vowel Deletion, and Nasal Assimilation in similar fashion. Suffixing [a] to [kínap] produces the underlying representation [kínapa], whose phonetic manifestation, [kímba], results from it automatically by the application of these three rules. Stop Voicing specifies that a stop is voiced when it occurs between two vowels; the application of this rule to [kínapa] yields [kínaba]. Vowel Deletion requires the loss of a vowel that follows a stressed syllable and precedes another syllable, and from [kínaba] it produces [kínba]. Nasal Assimilation makes a nasal bilabial when it occurs directly before a bilabial stop, as [n] does in [kínba]. Nasal Assimilation thus connects [kínba] with the phonetic sequence [kímba].

The other affirmative forms, [síme] 'walk,' [síma] 'walked,' [sárot] 'sleep,' and [sárda] 'slept,' confirm our analysis. [síma] 'walked' results directly from the addition to [síme] 'walk' of the suffix [a], coupled with the principle of Vowel Deletion. The suffixation of [a] to [sárot] 'sleep' gives [sárota] as the underlying representation of [sárda] 'slept.' From this underlying representation, Stop Voicing produces [sároda], which Vowel Deletion reduces to [sárda].

On the basis of [tíf] 'not run' and [téso] 'not swim,' it is evident that negation is marked on the verb by the prefix [t]. Adding this prefix to [kínap] 'eat' yields for 'not eat' the underlying representation [tkínap], whose phonetic realization is [etkínap]. Other negative forms such as [estíme] 'not walk' and [estárot] 'not sleep' show that the appearance of [e] is a general phenomenon, not an idiosyncratic property of [kínap]. Consequently, we are justified in positing the existence of a Vowel Insertion rule, which inserts [e] before a cluster of two consonants that would otherwise begin a word. Vowel Insertion thus applies to the underlying representation [tkínap] and connects it with the phonetic sequence [etkínap]. [etkímba] 'did not eat,' the negative past tense form of [kínap] 'eat,' must have the underlying representation [tkínapa], from which it is derived by several rules, including Vowel Insertion. This derivation is outlined in Figure 6.5.

UNDERLYING REPRESENTATION

	[tkínapa]
Stop Voicing:	[tkínaba]
Vowel Deletion:	[tkínba]
Nasal Assimilation:	[tkímba]
Vowel Insertion:	[etkímba]

PHONETIC MANIFESTATION

FIGURE 6.5

Since 'walk' is [síme], the underlying representation of 'not walk' must be [tsíme] if this verb is regular. Vowel Insertion naturally applies to [tsíme], the result being [etsíme]. The form meaning 'not walk' that is given in the data, however, is [estíme] rather than [etsíme]. [estárot] 'not sleep,' the negative of [sárot] 'sleep,' similarly displays the cluster [st] where we would expect instead [ts]. Apparently, then, this language contains a rule that reverses the order of the segments [ts] under certain conditions. We will call this the Metathesis rule; **metathesis** is the term used to indicate a change in the order of sound segments. Metathesis derives [estíme] 'not walk' and [estárot] 'not sleep' from [etsíme] and [etsárot] respectively.

We have now established five rules, including rules that insert and delete segments, modify segments, and change the order of segments. The data testifies to the existence of yet another rule, one that determines the placement of stress. The location of stress is not an idiosyncratic property of individual words or morphemes; it is completely regular. The stress always falls on the first vowel of the root, never on the second vowel of the root or on an affix. Thus we find forms like [béb], [sómbib], and [etkínap], but none like [sombíb], [etkináp], or [étkinap]. Stress is therefore not marked in the most abstract underlying phonological representations, since it is not distinctive. Rather, it is inserted by the general rule of Stress Placement. The derivation of [estíma] 'did not walk' and [estárda] 'did not sleep,' outlined in Figure 6.6, provides further illustration of the rules we have examined.

UNDERLYING PHONOLOGICAL REPRESENTATION

	[tsimea]	[tsarota]
Stress Placement:	[tsímea]	[tsárota]
Stop Voicing:	(inapplicable)	[tsároda]
Vowel Deletion:	[tsíma]	[tsárda]
Nasal Assimilation:	(inapplicable)	(inapplicable)
Vowel Insertion:	[etsíma]	[etsárda]
Metathesis:	[estíma]	[estárda]

PHONETIC MANIFESTATION

FIGURE 6.6

The Abstractness of Phonological Systems

The preceding examples should give some indication as to how abstract the relation between underlying phonological representations and their phonetic manifestations can be. The derivation of a phonetic sequence from its underlying representation is the cumulative result of the application of a long series of phonological rules. Very often, in fact, such derivations involve much longer series of rules than the rather simple cases we have examined. We see also that what appear to be idiosyncrasies and irregularities quite often turn out to result from perfectly regular phonological processes. To uncover these regularities, we must view the phonological system of a language as a system of rules that derive phonetic manifestations from very abstract underlying representations. Quite commonly there are regularities in the underlying representations that are obscured at the phonetic level by the application of phonological rules. We learned similar lessons in our examination of syntactic systems.

Phonological and syntactic systems are further alike in that their rules must sometimes apply in a particular order. In the derivation of [kímba] from the underlying representation [kínapa], for example, Vowel Deletion applies before Nasal Assimilation. It is only after Stress Placement, Stop Voicing, and especially Vowel Deletion have applied to produce [kínba] that the nasal [n] and the bilabial stop [b] are adjacent, causing the nasal to be assimilated. To take a simple syntactic example from English,

Subject-Verb Agreement must apply before Relativization. *The flowers which are on the table*, for instance, is formed by embedding after *the flowers* the structure that underlies *The flowers are on the table*. Relativization reduces *the flowers* to *which* in the embedded structure, but Subject-Verb Agreement must apply first, marking the verb *be* to agree with its subject *the flowers* in number and person. Otherwise, if the reduction of *the flowers* to *which* occurred first, the plural subject with which *are* agrees would no longer be present and agreement could not be marked properly.

Because phonological rules can change the identity of segments, as well as insert and delete them, the inventory of sounds used in a language may be different for the underlying representations and phonetic manifestations. That is, some segment types may occur in underlying phonological representations even though they are never manifested overtly at the phonetic level, and vice versa. In speaking of the sounds of a language, therefore, we may be referring either to overtly occurring phonetic entities or to the abstract entities of underlying representations, and it is of course necessary to be clear as to which we mean. When we listed the sounds of English as part of our examination of articulatory phonetics, we were referring to the sounds that occur on the phonetic level (with certain minor phonetic variations being ignored).

MORPHOLOGY

We observed in Chapter Four that a morpheme may have a number of different phonetic manifestations. The plural morpheme of English, for example, appears variously as [z], [s], and [əz], and it has other phonetic shapes as well (in *children, sheep, men*, and so on). The term **morphology** is applied to those aspects of phonological systems that account for variations in the phonetic manifestations of morphemes, though there is no neat dividing line between morphology and the rest of phonology.

The area of morphology is one in which languages tend to display a considerable amount of irregularity, especially if one does not pry beneath the surface. Why, for instance, should the plural of *child* be *children*, and not the expected *childs*? Why *women* and *sheep* instead of *womans* and *sheeps*? Why should the past tense of *eat* be the irregular *ate* and not the regular *eated*? There would seem to be no principled reason for our using *went* instead of *goed*.

For those forms that are truly irregular, special rules are required. Some rule of English, for example, must say that the sequence *eat+PAST* is manifested as *ate*. As the statement of an irregularity, this rule does not hold for all the morphemes of English; it is a special rule that applies just to one morpheme and has to be learned individually for that morpheme. Similarly, a speaker of English has to learn as an arbitrary fact about the morpheme *woman* that *woman+PLURAL* is manifested as *women*; the rule that is required will be of no use to the speaker in predicting the plural form of other morphemes. (The plural of *man* is formed differently—do not confuse spelling and pronunciation!)

Phonological rules that apply to just one morpheme or morpheme sequence are at one extreme of the continuum which has at the other extreme general phonological rules that hold for all morphemes of the language. Between the extremes are rules specifying morphological alternations that are neither wholly idiosyncratic nor wholly regular. These rules apply to classes of morphemes, but not to all morphemes of the language. A number of English verbs, for instance, are put into the past tense by changing the vowel from [ɪ] to [æ]. The rule that manifests *PAST* in this way does not apply to all verbs of the language, but neither is it restricted to a single verb. The same rule accounts for the past tense forms *sat, spat, rang, sang, swam, began, drank, shrank, stank*, and *sprang*. A number of verbs are put into the past tense by substituting [ɔt] for everything after the initial consonant cluster: *brought, bought, caught, fought, sought, thought*, and *taught*. The past tense formation of this handful of verbs constitutes a subregularity of English morphology and can be expressed by a single rule that applies to them all. If these verbs were completely irregular, each would form the past tense in a separate, idiosyncratic manner, and each individual verb would require a special rule, as do *eat* and *go*.

It is very often the case, however, that apparent morphological irregularities turn out to be completely regular phenomena when examined carefully in relation to the entire phonological system. Consider, for instance, the English plurals formed with [əz], [s], and [z]. [əz] marks the plural in words like *glasses, sizes, bunches, judges, bushes*, and *rouges*. [s] occurs in plural words such as *hips, bits, books, fifes*, and *births*. [z] indicates the plural in words like *ribs, beds, eggs, elms, bins, bars, pills, loves, ways,* and *bras.* The choice of [əz], [s], or [z] to mark the plural is anything but random in this set of words. Notice that [əz] is used only when the last sound of the noun root is [s], [z], [č], [ǰ], [š], or [ž]. When the noun ends in some other sound, the form of the plural is determined by voicing; [s] occurs only after voiceless segments, and [z] occurs only after voiced segments.

For all these words, we may take the underlying phonological representation of the plural morpheme to be [z]. *Glasses, bunches, hips,* and *books,* for example, have the underlying representations [glæsz], [bʌnčz], [hɪpz], and [bʊkz], exactly parallel to those of *ribs* and *bras,* namely [rɪbz] and [braz]. The variants [əz] and [s] are derived from the underlying [z] by general phonological rules of English, rules that account for various other phonological phenomena as well.

Glasses and *bunches* are manifested phonetically as [glæsəz] and [bʌnčəz]. These phonetic forms are derived from the underlying representations [glæsz] and [bʌnčz] by a rule that inserts the vowel [ə] between the last segment of the noun and the suffix [z]. This rule is a general one; it inserts [ə] between a root and a suffix whenever the suffix consists of a single **obstruent** and the root ends in an obstruent of basically the same type. (An obstruent is a stop, fricative, or affricate—sounds formed by obstructing the flow of air.) In the relevant sense, [s z č ǰ š ž] are obstruents of basically the same type as [z]. They are fricatives articulated in the alveolar or palatal region (affricates such as [č ǰ], remember, end as fricatives after an initial stop-like closure). The sequences [sz zz čz ǰz šz žz] are thus changed respectively to [səz zəz čəz ǰəz šəz žəz] by the [ə] Insertion rule in determining the phonetic manifestations of *glasses, sizes, bunches, judges, bushes,* and *rouges.*

The possessive morpheme and the third person singular verb ending are also suffixes whose basic form is [z], as shown by words like *Bill's, Ed's, goes,* and *stabs,* phonetically [bɪlz], [ɛdz], [gowz], and [stæbz]. The underlying representations of *Chris's* and *reaches* are thus [krɪsz] and [ričz], parallel to the above forms. The rule that inserts [ə], being a general rule not restricted just to the plural morpheme, applies automatically to these underlying representations to yield the correct phonetic manifestations, [krɪsəz] and [ričəz]. Further evidence for the existence of the [ə] Insertion rule is provided by alternate forms of the past tense morpheme. Its underlying form is [d], showing up overtly as [d] in words such as *bribed*

169

[braybd] and *freed* [frid]. The underlying representations of **rotted** and **raided** are therefore [ratd] and [reydd], which are modified to [ratəd] and [reydəd]. The [ə] Insertion rule applies to produce these sequences because the final segment of the root is an obstruent of basically the same type (an alveolar stop) as the suffix.

The [əz] variant of the plural morpheme is therefore derived from the underlying form [z] by a general phonological rule of English, one that accounts for numerous other phenomena as well. The same is true of the [s] variant, which occurs after voiceless consonants other than [s č š]. We saw earlier that all of the consonants in a consonant cluster are voiceless if the first one is voiceless. Thus, while [ɛksɪt] is a possible English word, [ɛkzɪt] is not. This principle also specifies that the second segment of **stack** is voiceless, since it follows the voiceless fricative [s]. It is apparent that this same rule will apply to the underlying representations of **hips** and **books**, namely [hɪpz] and [bʊkz], to produce the phonetic manifestations [hɪps] and [bʊks].

This rule also accounts for variants of the possessive morpheme, the third person singular verb ending, and the past tense morpheme. Since these have the respective basic forms [z], [z], and [d], the underlying representations of **Nat's, kicks**, and **kicked** must be [nætz], [kɪkz], and [kɪkd]. The final voiceless consonants of the roots cause the endings to be voiceless as well, accounting for the phonetic manifestations [næts], [kɪks], and [kɪkt].

The three plural endings [əz s z] all derive, therefore, from the same underlying representation. General phonological rules apply to this abstract representation to produce the superficial phonetic diversity. Notice that the [ə] Insertion rule must apply before the rule that specifies voicelessness; if the two rules were not ordered in this way, they would give the wrong results. **Glasses**, for instance, would be assigned the phonetic shape [glæsəs] instead of [glæsəz], since the underlying representation [glæsz] would be modified to [glæss] before the [ə] Insertion rule applied.

The hypothetical data we examined in the previous section provides further illustration of how apparent morphological irregularities sometimes turn out to be completely regular phenomena when viewed in relation to the entire phonological system. If we examined only the phonetic data, for example, we would observe very little regularity in the formation of the past tense of verbs:

[íf]	'run'	[ífa]	'ran'
[éso]	'swim'	[ésa]	'swam'
[kínap]	'eat'	[kímba]	'ate'
[síme]	'walk'	[síma]	'walked'
[sárot]	'sleep'	[sárda]	'slept'

[íf] forms the past tense by the addition of [a]; [éso] by the substitution of [a] for the final [o]; [kínap] by the addition of [a] and the modification of [nap] to [mb]; [síme] by the substitution of [a] for the final [e]; and [sárot] by the addition of [a] and the modification of [ot] to [d]. On deeper examination, however, we found that all of these verbs form the past tense in exactly the same way—by the suffixation of [a]. The interaction of the abstract underlying representations so obtained with general phonological rules produces the surface diversity that is observed in the phonetic data.

To understand the morphological patterns of a language, therefore, it is not sufficient to examine the phonetic data alone. The phonological mechanisms involved can be uncovered only if we look beneath the phonetic surface and regard the phonological system as an integrated series of rules that apply to very abstract underlying representations. When we do, we find that surface disparity very often results in a completely regular fashion from underlying uniformity.

Linguistic

Relationships

Language

Change

BORROWING

Lexical Borrowing

Living languages never hold still. Every language is the product of change and continues to change as long as it is spoken. For the most part, these changes escape our attention as they occur. They are minor enough or gradual enough to be imperceptible. Over a span of centuries, however, their cumulative effect is appreciable. Shakespeare's English is difficult for modern readers, and Chaucer's is almost incomprehensible without formal instruction.

One way languages change is through the influence of other languages. At one time the English word *patio*, for example, was not part of the English vocabulary. Now it is. The addition of this word to our lexicon thus constitutes a change in our linguistic system, albeit a minor one. Moreover, the word *patio* was not created out of thin air by English speakers. Prior to its use as an English word, it was a Spanish word with comparable meaning (and still is). The addition of *patio* to our vocabulary clearly results from the influence of Spanish. Speakers familiar with the Spanish term started using it in English. Its use spread, and now it is a well-established word of our language. If this word had not existed in Spanish, or if English speakers had never had contact with it, it would not have become part of English. *Patio*, in short, was **borrowed** into English from Spanish.

Borrowing is a very common linguistic phenomenon. In all probability, no language whose speakers have ever had contact with any other language is completely free of borrowed forms. Languages differ radically, however, with respect to the proportion of lexical items in their vocabularies that can be attributed to borrowing. Albanian, for instance, has so many borrowed words in its lexicon that only a few hundred native words remain. Although English has borrowed much less than Albanian, it is often cited as a language that has borrowed heavily, since over half of the English lexicon is of foreign origin. In contrast, American Indian languages of the Athabaskan family tend to borrow relatively little. The reasons why languages differ in this regard are no doubt more historical and cultural than linguistic. Borrowing is never a linguistic necessity, since it is always possible to extend and modify the use of existing lexical items to meet new communicative needs.

An interesting variant of lexical borrowing is a phenomenon known as **loan translation**. The English expression *That goes without saying*, for example, is a literal translation from the French *Ça va sans dire*. What English speakers borrowed, in this case, was not actual lexical items, but rather a pattern for combining them figuratively to express a certain notion. The word *skyscraper* provides another illustration. French, with the term *gratte-ciel*, and Spanish, with *rascacielos*, have borrowed from English the metaphor of 'scraping the sky' to convey the idea of a very tall building. The German *Wolkenkratzer* is different only in that the form for 'clouds' occurs instead of the one for 'sky.'

Syntactic and Phonological Borrowing

Lexical items are borrowed relatively freely. This fact is not really surprising; one lexical item more or less matters little to a language, since the lexicon is for the most part simply a list of independent elements.

Changes in the syntax or phonology of a language also result from borrowing, but somewhat less frequently. Perhaps this is because a syntactic or phonological system consists of an integrated series of rules, and the modification of one rule could have drastic consequences elsewhere in the system. The extent to which languages can affect one another with respect to syntax and phonology is not really known, but there are cases that demonstrate the existence of this kind of influence.

For a syntactic example, we may cite the languages of the Balkan peninsula, such as Albanian, Bulgarian, Greek, and Rumanian. They are alike syntactically in that infinitival clauses are highly restricted in their use. Indeed, some of the Balkan languages lack infinitives entirely. Instead of *The children want to leave,* for instance, one would say something like *The children want that they leave.* The languages are related, but many of them only very indirectly, and it is clear that this shared syntactic trait is due to mutual borrowing.

The American Indian languages of the Pacific Northwest provide an example of borrowing in the realm of phonology. Many languages of this area have glottalized consonants; the percentage is much higher than it is in the languages of the world generally, and yet the languages displaying glottalized consonants are not all related. The explanation seems to be that glottalization spread among the tribes in the area through borrowing. Another example of phonological borrowing is seen in the many Indo-European languages of India that have **retroflex** consonants, consonants articulated with the tip of the tongue against the palate. It is fairly certain that these sounds developed in the Indo-European languages under the influence of the Dravidian family of languages, which are also spoken in India and which employ retroflex consonants.

Causes of Borrowing

A common cause of lexical borrowing is the need to find words for new objects, concepts, and places. It is easier to borrow an existing term from another language than to make one up. Many place names on the North American continent, for instance, were taken from Indian languages: **Mississippi, Michigan, Chicago, Dakota, Oklahoma, Kentucky, Manhattan,** and **Waukegan,** to cite just a few. From the American Indians we also received—along with the items themselves—the words **totem,** *wampum, moccasin, toboggan,* and *tomahawk.* From the aboriginal languages of Australia we get the words *kangaroo* and *wombat.* The word *gnu,* referring to an African antelope, is borrowed from the Bantu languages of that continent.

The paths of lexical borrowing reflect to a certain extent the paths of cultural influence. For example, a large proportion of the Arabic words in English pertain to the realm of science: *zero, cipher, zenith, alchemy, algebra, nadir, alcohol, bismuth,* and *alkali.* These borrowings, which came to English through Spanish, attest to Arabic influence in science and mathematics during the early medieval period. The importance of Italian influence in music and the other arts is apparent from the long list of Italian loan words that belong to this domain, such as *opera, tempo, adagio, soprano, piano, sonata, scherzo, virtuoso, sonnet, fresco, miniature, dilettante, balcony, cornice, corridor, colonnade, mezzanine, parapet,* and *niche.*

After the Norman conquest of England, great numbers of loan words came into English from French. Included among these borrowed words are scores of terms in such areas as government, the military, law, and religion, reflecting the fact that the Norman French, as the conquerors, exerted predominant influence in these areas. Governmental terms that came to English from French include *crown, power, state, reign, country, peer, court, duke, duchess, prince, realm, sovereign, minister, chancellor, council, authority, parliament, baron,* and *nation.* Borrowed terms pertaining to military matters are *battle, army, war, peace, lance, banner, ensign, officer, lieutenant, vessel, navy, admiral, soldier, sergeant, troops, arms, armor, assault, siege, enemy, challenge, gallant, march, company, guard, force,* and *danger.* Our legal vocabulary has been enriched by such words as *jury, judge, plaintiff, accuse, crime, justice, privilege, damage, traitor, felony, summon, defendant, sue, attorney, session, fee, plead, suit,* and *property.* Terms of religious and moral significance include *mercy, cruel, vice, nature, blame, save, pray, preach, angel, religion, virgin, saint, tempt, grace, pity, trinity, service, savior, relic, abbey, cloister, clergy, parish, baptism, friar, altar, miracle, sermon, sacrifice, virtue, charity, chaste, covet,* and *lechery.*

The influx of French borrowings into English during the Norman period was not matched by any comparable flow of loan words from English into French. The prestige factor, which was touched on in Chapter Three, is no doubt largely responsible. Since the French constituted an upper class, English speakers who desired social advancement were naturally led to learn French. The use of French words in English conversations became a common practice because of the air of prestige that accompanied them. The French, on the other hand, felt no corresponding pressure to master English, which was, after all, only the tongue of the masses.

The prestige factor is a very common cause of lexical borrowing. The great prestige of French culture was also strongly felt among the upper classes of Czarist Russia. It was commonplace for the members of high society to speak French instead of Russian, and French expressions of course found their way into Russian conversations. Consequently, modern Russian contains a great many French borrowings. American power and importance in today's world has brought on a trend of borrowing opposite to the one in Norman England. The number of English loan words in modern French is rising so rapidly that it is becoming a cause for alarm in some quarters (although it is hard to see why such a natural phenomenon as lexical borrowing should be considered alarming). Symptomatic of this modern "Anglomania" are scores of expressions such as *snack bar, self-service, parking* 'parking lot,' *check list, deep freeze, pullover, living* 'living room,' *expressway, pinup, whisky, sandwich, weekend,* and *dancing* 'night club.' In a singing commercial for soft drinks that is frequently aired on a Tijuana radio station, the line *a cada gusto,* which means 'for every taste,' is followed immediately by the line *a cada taste.* It is evidently felt that the prestige of an English word will induce Mexicans who desire to be modern and sophisticated to purchase these products.

Latin and Greek had great prestige in the world of scholarship during the Middle Ages. Consequently, words from Latin and Greek have been finding their way into English (often through French) and into other European languages ever since the Renaissance. By no means have all of them been taken from classical texts. A great many have been formed by combining Latin or Greek morphemes after the model of words of these languages, or just combining them in any way at all to make the result look scholarly. Words obtained from classical sources in these ways are sometimes called **learnèd words** (French *mots savants*); many thousands of them can be found in any large English dictionary.

The greatest concentration of learned words is probably to be found in the vocabulary of the sciences and other scholarly disciplines. Even the names of many of these disciplines are borrowed from the classical lan-

179

guages: *sociology, psychology, anthropology, philosophy, philology, biology*. Learned words are most certainly not limited to this domain, however. Hundreds of words in everyday use can be traced back to Latin and Greek. To take just one class of examples, consider these common English words starting with the Latin morpheme *ex* 'out of, from': *exact, exaggerate, exalt, exasperate, excerpt, exclude, excrete, excursion, execute, exempt, exert, exhaust, exhibit, expand, expect, expel, explain, explicit, explode, explore, export, extend, exterminate, extinct, extort, exude.* So prevalent are learned words in English that a number of Latin and Greek morphemes have come to be used productively. They can be combined with roots of any origin, not just those taken from the classical languages. *Ex-husband* and *ex-wife,* for instance, reveal the Latin *ex* prefixed to Germanic forms. The *able/ible* suffix, of Latin origin, combines with native roots in words such as *answerable, eatable, bearable, laughable,* and *salable.*

Effects of Borrowing

Normally, when a word is borrowed it is made to fit the phonological system of the borrowing language. The English word *rendezvous,* for example, was taken from French, but it obeys the phonological principles of English. It is pronounced with the English [r], not the French one; the first vowel is nonnasal, although it is nasalized in French; and so on. The reason is obvious—English speakers know English, but they do not, for the most part, know French.

Loan words are not always completely assimilated to the phonological system of the borrowing language, however. The same people who sprinkle their speech with French words for purposes of prestige may very well, for the same reason, attempt to preserve the French pronunciation. If enough people are familiar with the donor language, or if a great number of words are borrowed, the loan words may function as a phonological Trojan horse, sneaking new sounds into the inventory of sounds used in the borrowing language. As a matter of fact, the voiced fricatives [v z] worked their way into English from French in just this manner. They had occurred previously as variant phonetic manifestations of other sound types, but not as distinctive sounds. Loan words such as *very, veal, zeal,* and *zest* were responsible for their introduction.

Another result of heavy lexical borrowing can be the partitioning of the vocabulary with respect to the operation of phonological rules. Turkish, for example, has hundreds of loan words from Arabic, most of which do not follow the phonological rules of **vowel harmony** that apply to native Turkish words. (Vowel harmony means, roughly, that the vowels of a word are either all back vowels or all front vowels.) Thus, the Arabic loan words behave in one way with respect to the phonological rules of Turkish, and the native Turkish words behave in another. The child who masters Turkish must learn, for every word he picks up, which class it falls into, because this information determines the word's behavior with respect to phonological rules and is therefore partly responsible for determining its pronunciation. A similar partitioning of the vocabulary exists in numerous other languages.

The borrowing of lexical items, then, can have an important impact on the phonological system of a language. One can hypothesize, in fact, that this is the basic mechanism by which languages influence one another phonologically.

INTERNAL CHANGE

Lexical Changes

Not all changes in linguistic systems are brought about by the influence of other languages. Borrowing, in all its forms, can be called **external change**, since it results from external linguistic influence. Without pretending that any neat dichotomy exists, we can label changes that do not come about through borrowing as instances of **internal change**.

Internal change can be discerned at all levels of linguistic structure. It affects individual lexical items as well as general rules, and it occurs in the semantic, syntactic, and phonological systems of a language alike.

The simplest form of internal change is probably the addition and loss of lexical items. There used to be an English verb *cere*, meaning 'wax,' but it is now obsolete. In order to express the notion 'idol,' few contemporary speakers would think of the word *maumet*, but there was a time when this word was current. *Congree* 'agree' is no longer used, and the same is true of the word *neat* 'cattle' (a native word, not to be confused with the modern English word *neat,* which is borrowed from French). What these examples show, of course, is that words can drop out of common use into oblivion. Were it not for written records, we would have no knowledge at all of words like *maumet* and *cere.*

The loss of lexical items seldom comes to our attention. They do not suddenly go into hiding, causing us to wonder what ever became of them; the process of obsolescence is a gradual one. For one reason or another, certain words fall into disfavor and disuse, dropping from sight little by little until, over a period of decades or centuries, they disappear completely. We can put our finger on many lexical items that seem to be on their way toward oblivion. *Lo* is no longer a common word, for instance. Some speakers may not even recognize it without its caboose, *and behold. Fro* is reduced in its occurrence to the fixed phrase *to and fro. Verily* has a distinct Biblical flavor. Not even proper names and oaths are immune to the ebb and flow of linguistic fashion. Contemporary American parents do not often name a child *Egbert, Bertha,* or *Percival.* We never use *Zounds!* or *Egad!* without humorous intent. Some of these expressions may make a comeback in popularity, of course, but the odds would seem to be against it.

In a highly technical and complex society such as ours, there is a constant need for new lexical items. Where borrowing does not suggest itself as a way of obtaining a new term, alternative methods are available. A new term can be made up from scratch, coined just to meet the new need. Another possibility is to combine existing lexical items to form more complex ones that are in some way descriptive or appropriate. Still a third way to obtain a new term is to extend the use of an old one, making it applicable to new situations.

Of these three methods, the first is by far the least frequent. For the most part, people tend to readapt existing lexical material rather than to create entirely new material. Trade names for new products might be considered one area in which new coinages are frequent, but even here most terms have some relation to existing lexical items. Most trade names are taken either from proper names (*Ford, Edsel*) or from other already existing morphemes (*Rambler, Thunderbird, Mustang*). Of those that are not, the vast majority are clearly modeled after existing morphemes in a fairly transparent manner. *Vel, Lux, Jello, Brillo,* and *Fab,* for example, bear strong resemblances to *velvet, luxury, gelatin, brilliant,* and *fabulous;*

the similarities are anything but accidental. Slang would seem to be an important source of linguistic inventions, such as *hip/hep, mooch, fink, moola,* and *barf.* Even slang expressions, however, most often consist of old lexical items in new semantic garb.

The creation of complex lexical items is such a frequent means of obtaining new terms that it is perhaps sufficient to give a few examples. When linguists started talking about *tree structure, spelling pronunciation, hypercorrection, loan translation, surface structure,* and *idiolects,* they combined previously existing lexical items into more complex ones for use as technical terms. The word *hippie* does not represent an entirely new creation; it consists of the diminutive suffix *y/ie* (as in *sonny, birdie*) added to the older morpheme *hip.* Similarly, new words such as *beatnik, peacenik,* and *Vietnik* were formed by adding to an existing word the morpheme *nik,* which entered the language as part of the Russian loan word *sputnik.* The word *hamburger* (originally from the place name *Hamburg*), was evidently analyzed as *ham+burger* by English speakers. The resulting lexical item *burger* has been the source of an endless stream of creations, among them *cheeseburger, pizzaburger, chiliburger, tomato-burger, mushroomburger, tunaburger, beefburger, doubleburger, steak-burger,* and *Burger Chef.* The list of new creations from old lexical material could be lengthened *ad nauseam.*

The extension of existing lexical items to new situations involves both the metaphorical side of language and semantic change. Metaphorical extensions occur in such diverse domains as scientific terminology (electro-magnetic *wave,* radiation *belt,* solar *storm*); marketing (*Salvo* laundry detergent, Plymouth *Fury, Spring* cigarettes); and slang (LSD *trip,* to *snow* a professor, to *squeal* to the cops). Not all extensions involve meta-phor, of course. It is a common practice, for instance, to use a proper name to designate a new product, as in *Kent, Newport, Salem, Chesterfield, Marlboro, Winston,* and so on. In other cases, a label is adopted simply because it has a favorable or unfavorable connotation, or just for the sake of finding a label. *True* and *Lucky Strike* were no doubt chosen as names for cigarettes because of their favorable connotations. *Fuzz* was adopted to designate police for the opposite reason. The trade name *Pure Oil* is transparently propagandistic, but *Shell* seems to represent an arbitrary choice.

Metaphorical extension is one way in which semantic change comes about, though certainly not the only way. *Squeal to the cops* was no doubt a very vivid expression when it was new, but metaphors fade with continued use. The figurative force of *squeal to the cops* is now lost on us, since the expression is so familiar. *Squeal*, in short, has acquired the sense 'inform,' which it did not have originally. This extension in its use constitutes a change in the semantic system of English.

Over a period of centuries, a great many of the lexical items of a language change in meaning. The French verb *traire*, for example, used to have the general meaning 'pull' or 'draw.' In modern French, it is restricted to the specialized sense 'milk.' *Cuisse* 'thigh' originally meant 'hip' (Latin *coxa*). In English, *nice* used to mean 'foolish.' *Silly* had the sense 'happy, blessed, innocent.' *Cheek* is the modern continuation of the Old English word for 'jaw.' The word *meat* once meant 'food,' but it has narrowed in scope and now designates only one kind of food. *Bird* has broadened in scope, since it used to mean 'birdling, young bird.' *Bead* used to mean 'prayer'; it came to assume its present sense because of the practice of keeping track of one's prayers on what we now call the *beads* of a rosary. It should be apparent that there is no neat formula to describe the relationship between the old and the new meaning of a lexical item that has undergone semantic change. The relationship is sometimes very indirect, and it is often mediated by nonlinguistic factors. If there had been no such thing as rosaries, for instance, *bead* would not now mean what it does.

A lexical item can be characterized as a bundle of semantic, syntactic, and phonological properties. We have just observed that it is not at all unusual for a lexical item to change with respect to its semantic representation. It may be somewhat less common for the syntactic or phonological representation of a lexical item to undergo change, but this also occurs.

The English morpheme *friend* has undergone a change in its syntactic representation, resulting in expressions like *I'm friends with Harvey*. This expression is related to *Harvey and I are friends* by syntactic rules. Whatever their precise formulation may be, these rules are the same ones responsible for relating pairs of expressions such as *Paul and Mary came/ Mary came with Paul; The car and the truck collided/The truck collided with the car; The water and the oil mixed/The oil mixed with the water*. Normally these rules cannot apply when the verb phrase consists of *be* plus a noun phrase. Thus, *Harvey and I are a team* cannot be related to *I'm a team with Harvey*, which is ungrammatical; *Harvey and I are enemies* cannot be manifested instead as *I'm enemies with Harvey*. *Friend* is therefore exceptional. Its syntactic representation has changed, allowing the rules in question to apply to it. It now has slightly different syntactic properties from those of *enemy*, since *I'm friends with Harvey* is possible, but not *I'm enemies with Harvey*.

This change in the morpheme *friend* was a purely syntactic one, since *friend* means the same in *Harvey and I are friends* and *I'm friends with Harvey*. Quite frequently, though, syntactic change and semantic change accompany one another. When a morpheme is extended to a new syntactic class, it acquires a new meaning. The preposition/adverb *up*, for instance, can now be used as a verb (*The manager upped the prices*). Its new syntactic use is accompanied by a new meaning, 'raise.' *Down* has also become a verb, with the meanings 'drink' and 'knock from the air' (*He downed the medicine, Snoopy downed the Red Baron's plane*). Hundreds of examples of dual change of this sort can be found in English. If we wish to count this as syntactic change, then lexical items can be said to change very frequently in their syntactic properties.

Individual lexical items are also susceptible to change in their phonological representations. Under the influence of its spelling, as we saw earlier, *often* is now pronounced with a [t] by many people. These idiolects reflect a change in the phonological representation of *often*, because the [t] was not pronounced at an earlier period of English. More often, the phonological changes that morphemes undergo are of a morphological nature. The plural of *brother* used to be *brethren*, but now it is *brothers*; *brethren* survives only as a religious archaism. For some speakers, the plural of *ox* is not *oxen* but *oxes*. For these speakers, the morpheme *ox* is no longer an exception to the general rules that account for the phonetic manifestation of the plural morpheme. Its phonological properties have changed, since it interacts differently with the phonological rules of English. The conjugation of the French verb *aimer* 'love' will be our final example. As a regular development from Latin, it had the present tense forms *j'aime* 'I love,' *tu aimes* 'you love,' *il aime* 'he loves,' *nous amons* 'we love,' *vous amez* 'you (plural) love,' *ils aiment* 'they love.' Notice that the root vowel is *ai* [ɛ] in four forms, but simply *a* [a] in the other two. In modern French, *ai* has been extended to all the forms: *nous aimons* 'we love,' *vous aimez* 'you (plural) love.'

Rule Changes

Changes in the properties of individual lexical items are for the most part sporadic and idiosyncratic. Being limited to single lexical units, their effect on the linguistic system is minimal. Of much greater importance are changes in the rules of a language. Since rules apply to whole classes of lexical items and to infinite sets of sentence structures, the surface effect of modifying a rule may be extensive. Changes occur in the rules of both the syntactic and phonological systems of languages. They may take the form of the addition or loss of rules or the modification of existing rules.

In modern French, possessive expressions like *mon livre* 'my book' and *le mien* 'mine' are syntactically related. To take an example, the two sentences *Ce livre est mon livre* 'This book is my book' (which is awkward, but grammatical) and *Ce livre est le mien* 'This book is mine' manifest the same underlying structure. In particular, the two noun phrases *mon livre* and *le mien* manifest the same underlying structure. Various syntactic rules cooperate to produce an abstract structure of the form *le mien livre*, literally 'the mine book' (parallel to *le grand livre* 'the large book'). Either of two rules can then apply to this abstract structure. Since *livre* duplicates a noun that occurs previously in the sentence, it can be deleted, leaving *le mien*; when the Noun Deletion rule applies, the resulting sentence is *Ce livre est le mien* 'This book is mine.' On the other hand, *le mien livre* can be reduced to *mien livre* by the deletion of the definite article. When this happens, phonological rules manifest the possessive word as *mon* 'my' instead of *mien*. Thus the Article Deletion rule accounts for the sentence *Ce livre est mon livre* 'This book is my book.'

It is the Article Deletion rule that interests us. In modern French, this rule can apply only if the noun has not been deleted, and if the noun is still present, then the deletion of the article is obligatory. If the noun has been deleted, yielding *le mien* 'mine,' the article cannot be deleted, since *mien* by itself is ungrammatical. If, however, the noun has not been deleted from *le mien livre*, the article has to be deleted, since *mon livre* 'my book' is grammatical to the exclusion of *le mien livre*.

The Article Deletion rule was part of Old French, but it applied in slightly different circumstances. In Old French, around the twelfth century, the article could be deleted regardless of whether or not the noun was present, and the rule was optional rather than obligatory. Thus expressions such as *L'abaie est moie* 'The abbey is mine' and *li nostre deu* '(the) our God' were well formed, though their counterparts would not be in modern French. The Article Deletion rule has therefore been modified during the historical development of French, in that the conditions for its application have changed.

Let us turn to English for another example of historical change in syntactic rules. In modern English, the negative form *not* can come directly after certain verb words but not others. The modals (words like *can, may, will,* and *must*) can directly precede *not*, and so can *have, be,* and *do.* Sentences like *He cannot come, He has not come, He is not coming,* and *He does not come* are grammatical, in other words, while sentences like *He comes not* or *He likes not chicken* are ungrammatical. It used to be the case, however, that *not* could follow any verb, not just this handful. Some examples are *It aperteneth nat to a wys man* 'It is not suitable for a wise man' and *Yff the maters went not to my maister entent* 'If the matters did not go according to what my master had planned,' in which *not* follows the verb forms *aperteneth* and *went.* Thus, the syntactic rules responsible for the position of *not* in English sentences have changed.

For a final example, consider English possessive expressions such as *John's friend.* There is good reason to believe that such noun phrases result from underlying structures of the form *the friend of John's* (parallel to *a friend of John's*). Syntactic rules serve to permute the possessor noun phrase *John's* with *friend* (and also to delete *of* and *the*), thus producing *John's friend* from the postulated underlying structure. In modern English, the entire possessor noun phrase can be permuted, even if it is quite complex. (One can even get away with monstrosities like *The woman who I went to the party with's husband.*) Formerly, however, the permutation rule was considerably more restricted, since clauses or phrases modifying the possessor noun phrase could not be moved. Instead of *the King of England's throne,* one said *the King's throne of England;* the modifying phrase *of England* was left behind after the noun. The rule effecting this permutation has consequently been liberalized as part of the historical development of English.

The study of phonological systems uncovers a multitude of instances in which change has occurred through the addition or loss of phonological rules. Consider, for example, the phonological rules that accounted for the morphological patterns of Old English. English was at one time a highly inflected language; it was characterized by variations in the endings of words to distinguish case, gender, number, person, tense, and so on, much as Latin, German, and Russian are. The word *scip* 'ship,' for instance, had various endings that depended on its grammatical function in the sentence (case) and on whether it was singular or plural (number). *Scip* was used as the nominative and accusative singular form; *scipes* was the genitive singular form; *scipe* was dative singular. The corresponding three forms in the plural were *scipu, scipa,* and *scipum.*

Even without a close examination of the phonological structure of Old English, it is apparent that there must have been a fair number of phonological rules whose prime function was to specify the forms of all these inflectional endings. In modern English, however, there is relatively little in the way of inflection. Nouns have only a plural and a genitive or possessive ending, both of which are [z] in most cases, as we have seen. The inflection of verbs and pronouns has been vastly simplified, and the inflection of adjectives has been eliminated completely, except for comparative and superlative forms (**stronger, strongest**). Many phonological rules of English have therefore been dropped from the language. Some syntactic rules marking case and agreement must have been lost as well.

Comparing Latin and French, we find an instance of a phonological rule that has been retained but modified over the centuries. The rule in question is the one that assigns stress. In Latin, stress falls on the second syllable from the end of a word if this syllable is "heavy"; otherwise the third syllable from the end is stressed. A heavy syllable is one that either has a long vowel or is followed by two or more consonants (if the second is not a liquid). *Antepônō* 'I prefer' is therefore stressed on the second syllable from the end; this is a heavy syllable because the vowel is long (a bar over a vowel indicates length). Similarly, *advérsus* 'opposite' is stressed on the second syllable from the end because the vowel *e* is followed by two consonants. *Diffícilis* 'difficult,' on the other hand, is stressed on the third syllable from the end, since the second from the end is not heavy. To complete the statement of the rule, we must add that a word of less than three syllables is stressed on the first syllable (for example, *béne* 'well,' *rĕs* 'thing').

The evolution of Latin into modern French has involved, along with many other changes, modification of the stress rule. The rule in modern French is simply that the last vowel of a word is stressed. For example, *ami* 'friend,' *cheval* 'horse,' *finira* 'he will finish,' and *examiner* 'examine' are represented phonetically with stress as [amí], [šəvál], [finirá], and [εgzaminé]. The only qualification is that a final [ə] is ignored in the determination of stress placement. *Femme* 'woman' may be pronounced as either [fámə] or [fám], for instance, but [a] bears the stress in either case.

A comparison of Latin and modern French also provides an example of phonological change through the addition of a new rule. French has a rule that changes stressed [a] to [ε] in a large class of morphemes, illustrated by the following words:

mer	[mέr]	'sea'	*marine*	[marínə]	'marine'
sel	[sέl]	'salt'	*saline*	[salínə]	'saline'
clair	[klέr]	'clear'	*clarté*	[klarté]	'clarity'

Mer, sel, and *clair* have the underlying representations [mar], [sal], and [klar]. The vowel [a] shows up overtly in these morphemes when the ending *ine* or *té* is added to them, since the ending bears the stress. When these morphemes stand alone as full words, on the other hand, [a] is the final vowel and is consequently stressed, yielding [már], [sál], and [klár]. The rule changing stressed [a] to [ε] is applicable to these forms, and from them it derives the phonetic sequences [mέr], [sέl], and [klέr]. This rule was not part of Latin phonology, as shown by the words *máre* 'sea,' *sǎl* 'salt,' and *clǎrus* 'clear,' the respective sources of French *mer, sel,* and *clair*.

CHANGE AND LANGUAGE ACQUISITION

Changes in the structure of a language do not come about instantaneously. Within a single idiolect, the linguistic system of a single speaker, we may find that certain minor changes are effected in an instant, and not over a period of time; a speaker may open a dictionary and learn a new word, for example. This is not the case, though, when we regard a language as a system shared by many speakers, and it is probably not even typical of idiolectal changes.

Take the word *hippie*, for instance, which has spread very rapidly through much of the English-speaking world. Someone must have used this word first, or maybe a small number of people created it independently. In either case, many weeks or months must have gone by between the time it was coined and the time it became an item of general use. It is safe to say that there are still many English speakers who are not familiar with it. Most new lexical items spread and come into general use much more slowly, if they ever do at all. Moreover, an individual speaker may master a new lexical item only gradually. Perhaps, as a visitor in San Francisco, a speaker sees the word *hippie* in a newspaper headline; only much later, when its use is more widespread and he has encountered it on numerous occasions and in various contexts, does he come to realize just what it means.

Changes in the rules of a language spread even more slowly than do lexical changes. Consider the rule of some English dialects that [ɛ] is manifested phonetically as [ɪ] before [n]. For the speakers who have this rule, *pen* and *pin* are both pronounced [pɪn], and *penny* rhymes with *mini*. This rule is fairly widespread. The speech of certain radio and television announcers is characterized by the manifestation of [ɛ] as [ɪ] before [n], so virtually all speakers of American English have been exposed to this linguistic trait. But while most speakers who have repeatedly encountered the word *hippie* have picked it up, so that it belongs to their linguistic system, the same is not true of the phonological rule in question. Although virtually all Americans have encountered speech in which *pin* and *pen* are pronounced alike, most of them have not picked up the phonological rule that is responsible.

Idiolects that have this rule thus coexist with idiolects that lack it. This linguistic difference does not hinder communication (indeed, it is usually not even noticed), and communication has not as yet wiped out the difference. Maybe it never will. Suppose, though, that we came back to American English several centuries from now and found that all speakers possessed the rule for manifesting [ɛ] as [ɪ] before [n]. With this greater time perspective, we would say that English had undergone a phonological change; this rule had been added to the phonological system. It had taken decades or centuries to spread to all speakers, however, and was anything but instantaneous. Whenever we speak of changes that a language has undergone in its historical development, we understand that the widespread adoption of the innovations may have taken a very long time.

Adults are thought to have limited linguistic flexibility. An adult who learns a foreign language can achieve near-native competence in it only with great difficulty, and he will almost always speak it with an accent (in part because of interference from the phonological system he already possesses). Despite the linguistic rigidity of adults, innovations are indeed made in their speech. Even the oldest of codgers can pick up the word *hippie*, for example. Moreover, adults can modify their speech with respect to rules, consciously or unconsciously patterning it after the model of another dialect. An adult Texan who takes up residence in the Midwest is quite likely to make adjustments in his pronunciation, minimizing the differences between it and that of the speakers around him. An adult who desires social advancement may, with some success, study to "improve" his grammar.

Although we can only speculate at present, it is quite possible that the rule innovations of an adult speaker tend to be but a thin veneer over the system of rules he mastered as a child. In moments of excitement, fine points of grammar and pronunciation that an adult has carefully cultivated may go out the window. Regardless of whether this assessment is accurate, however, it is important for our ultimate understanding of language change that we understand the child's acquisition of his native language.

A linguistic trait that constitutes an innovation for adult speakers will not be so regarded by children who learn the modified linguistic system as their native language. An adult who learns a recently coined lexical item will be able to recognize it as an innovation. For children of succeeding generations, on the other hand, this item will have no aura of newness at all, since it will belong to their idiolects right from the start. If its status with mature speakers is insecure, the insecurity will disappear as the form is learned on a par with older lexical items by new waves of native speakers.

The difference between the language learning of children and that of adults, such as it is, is no doubt more important with respect to innovations in linguistic rules, since even adults can pick up new lexical items quite easily. It has been hypothesized that new syntactic or phonological rules can achieve only secondary status in the linguistic systems of adults, that they remain peripheral to the system of rules acquired when the adults were first learning to talk. Consider, however, the child who is exposed to speech characterized by rule innovations. Since he has no previous linguistic experience in which the innovations were lacking, he will naturally treat the new speech traits on a par with all the other traits of the language he is trying to learn. Consequently, the child will learn the new rules as an integral part of the linguistic system he acquires, not as superficial appendages to it.

The linguistic system that the child constructs for himself when he learns to talk may actually be simpler than the corresponding system of adults, particularly when the adult system includes rule innovations. Suppose, for the sake of discussion, that an adult's phonological system is modified by the addition of several rules, and that these rules have only secondary, peripheral status for him. When a child learns the modified dialect, the new rules are accommodated as an integral part of his linguistic system, not as isolated additions to it. In the context of the entire phonological system, the innovations may be significantly simpler than when they are learned independently. Children thus take a fresh look at a language when they go about learning it, and their efforts may entail a **restructuring** of the system.

Let us take a hypothetical example by way of illustration. Suppose there is a language that contains a rule to the effect that [t] is aspirated at the end of a word. A morpheme with the underlying representation [kit] would thus be manifested phonetically as [kitʰ], where the raised *h* after a segment indicates that the segment is aspirated. Suppose further that an innovation occurs in this language; for some unknown reason, perhaps just because of its stylistic value, speakers start pronouncing words using [s] instead of [tʰ]. By virtue of this innovation, then, the morpheme whose underlying representation is [kit] will be pronounced [kis]. If we assume that adult speakers learn new rules as essentially independent entities, the innovation for them consists in the addition of a phonological rule, a rule which manifests [tʰ] as [s]. The translation of [kit] into the phonetic sequence [kis] is thereby accomplished in two steps. First, the previously existing rule modifies [kit] to [kitʰ], since [t] comes at the end of the word. Second, the new rule manifests [kitʰ] as [kis].

When children become native speakers of this hypothetical language, they take a fresh look at things. Let us assume that there is structural evidence for positing [kit] as the underlying form of the phonetic sequence [kis] (for example, perhaps this morpheme is a verb, and in the past tense it is manifested as [kita], with the underlying [t] showing up overtly). The learners of this language will thus be confronted with underlying representations like [kit] that are paired with phonetic sequences like [kis], and as part of mastering the phonological system of the language they must construct some rule which effects all such pairings. The rule they come up with will probably be this one: Manifest [t] as a fricative in word-final position. Unlike the adult speakers, they will have no structural reason to posit a stage [tʰ] intermediate between [t] and [s], and one rule will suffice instead of two. The only reason why [tʰ] mediates [t] and [s] in the adult system is that the adult speakers, previous to the innovation, had mastered a system in which [t] was manifested as [tʰ]; children first learning the language will of course lack this motivation. The restructured phonological system they arrive at will be simpler than the adult one, for it contains only one rule connecting [t] and [s], while the adult system contains two.

In this plausible but hypothetical example, the adult dialect with the innovation is equivalent to the dialect learned by new speakers. Both pronounce our sample verb [kis], though they differ as to the rules that produce [kis] from the underlying representation [kit]. The speakers will be conscious of no difference at all, since linguistic rules cannot be directly observed, introspectively or by other speakers. A structural change in the language has nevertheless occurred; the phonological system has been restructured, and this restructuring can be attributed directly to the process of native language acquisition.

This is not the only mechanism by means of which change can stem from the child's acquisition of his native language. Another obvious mechanism is that of **imperfect learning**. In the transmission of a linguistic system from one generation to the next, some modifications are bound to creep in; the system the child constructs will inevitably diverge in at least minor ways from that of his linguistic models. In this case, we would expect the newly acquired system and the adult system not to be fully equivalent. The differences between them will have overtly manifested consequences.

Take the learning of vocabulary, for instance. Since thousands of lexical items must be mastered, there are bound to be some that the child learns not at all or only imperfectly. There may be some lexical items that are used only rarely, so that they fail, purely by chance, to occur in the child's linguistic experience. If he never encounters them, he will of course never learn them. He may become familiar with other lexical items without fully realizing what they mean, perhaps because they are used too infrequently or because they happen not to occur in a context that will allow him to deduce their meaning. It is not unusual to discover that a word does not mean for other people what it means for us.

Irregular morphological phenomena are no doubt frequent victims of imperfect learning. With very common morphemes, morphological irregularities can be sustained indefinitely. The English verb *go* is quite irregular; the past tense form is not *goed* but *went*, and the past participle is *gone*, whereas with regular verbs the past participle is the same as the past tense form. Since *go* is such a frequently occurring verb, however, these irregular forms are easily learned and retained. On the other hand, take a less common irregular verb like *strive*. *Strive* is not a verb we have occasion to use every day, and particular forms of it, like the past participle, may be used only rarely in the linguistic experience of a given speaker. It is not surprising, therefore, that the irregular past tense and past participle forms, *strove* and *striven*, are commonly replaced by the regular form *strived*. A child who learns English may never happen to hear *strove* and *striven*, or he may hear them so infrequently that they do not register with him. In the absence of information to the contrary, he will treat *strive* as if it were a regular verb.

Imperfect learning must be a significant factor in the modification of general rules as well. The child must construct his linguistic system on the basis of the speech traits he observes in the linguistic performance of others. The data that he has at his disposal is thus haphazard, distorted, and fragmentary. It contains errors that his models commit while talking, and it is likely to contain important gaps, since the sentences the child has occasion to witness constitute only a minute portion of the unbounded set of sentences that a language comprises. If only because of the imperfect character of the data the child has to go on, therefore, the rules he formulates may well differ in minor respects from those of his models. The consequences of this divergence may be so subtle that it is never noticed or corrected.

One should by no means conclude from this discussion that language change is fully understood. Many of the remarks in this section are quite tentative, particularly those pertaining to language acquisition. Much remains to be discovered about linguistic and psychological organization before all our questions about language change can be answered.

DIALECTS REVISITED

The Underlying Uniformity of Dialects

In our discussion of linguistic diversity, we noted that no two people possess precisely the same linguistic system. Idiolectal differences can be found between any two speakers, regardless of whether these differences are consciously perceived. They are not to be taken at face value, however. When viewed in relation to the system of rules and abstract underlying representations in which linguistic structure resides, surface differences quite often appear to be much less numerous and important than they do at first glance.

For illustration, let us return to the dialect divisions indicated in Figure 3.2, page 47. Dialect B_1, you may recall, was distinguished from the other varieties of language B because its speakers shared numerous speech traits that distinguished them from other speakers of B. Speakers of B_1 were said to pronounce [u] in words in which other speakers pronounced [ʊ]; they were said to pronounce [i] in forms pronounced with [ɪ] in other dialects; and a number of other traits combined with these to set B_1 apart from B_2 and B_3.

If one were to concentrate on the surface differences alone, they might seem impressive. It would be possible to list thousands of words pronounced differently by speakers of B_1 and by other speakers of B. The former, for instance, might say [tup], [kitane], [isu], [gilipumay], and [sumo], whereas the latter would say instead [tʊp], [kɪtane], [ɪsʊ], [gɪlɪpumay], and [sʊmo]. On the phonetic level, then, B_1 differs from B_2 and B_3 in thousands of individual details.

These differences all but disappear when we regard phonetic details as merely the surface manifestation of a system of phonological rules that apply to abstract underlying representations. Notice, first of all, that these phonetic differences are quite regular. Whenever a word in B_1 is pronounced with [i], the corresponding word in B_2 and B_3 is pronounced with [ɪ] in the same position. Whenever a word of B_1 is pronounced with [u], the corresponding word in B_2 and B_3 is pronounced with [ʊ] in the same position. In comparing B_1 and the other dialects, therefore, we find a systematic **correspondence** between [i] and [ɪ] and between [u] and [ʊ]. The phonetic differences are not random, sporadic, and peculiar to individual lexical items. Rather, they are regular, follow a constant pattern, and hold for all morphemes of B.

B_1, we may suppose, has five distinctive vowels, whose phonetic manifestations are [i u e o a]. The difference between high, mid, and low vowels is distinctive; it separates [i u] from [e o] from [a]. For the high and mid vowels, the difference between front and back is distinctive; it distinguishes [i] and [u], as well as [e] and [o]. In the underlying phonological representations of morphemes, then, the segment [i] will be listed as a high front vowel, to distinguish it from the mid and low vowels [e o a] and from the high back vowel [u]. Similarly, [u] will be listed simply as a high back vowel. The precise phonetic shape of these distinctive underlying vowel segments will be determined by rules that specify nondistinctive phonetic detail and are of relatively minor interest.

But B_2 and B_3 are characterized by exactly the same scheme. They too have five distinctive vowels, which include a low vowel, phonetically [a]; two mid vowels, phonetically [e o]; and two high vowels. The only difference resides in the phonetic manifestation of the two high vowels, which is [ɪ ʊ] instead of [i u]. The underlying representations will be identical, since [i ɪ] are both high front vowels and [u ʊ] are both high back vowels. The vowel segment of [tup]/[tʊp], for instance, would be listed simply as high and back in all dialects of B; so far as distinctive phonological information is concerned, the representations of morphemes are uniform for all dialects of B. Moreover, almost all of the relevant phonological rules will be identical for B_1 and for the other dialects. The rule that all vowels are nonnasal, for instance, is shared. So is the rule that front and low back vowels are unrounded while nonlow back vowels are rounded. The differences boil down to this: High vowels are articulated with the tongue slightly higher in dialect B_1 than in B_2 and B_3. That is, the rule specifying tongue height makes a slightly (but not radically) different phonetic specification for the speakers of B_1. Only one rule is involved, since [i u] differ from [ɪ ʊ] respectively in the same way. This one minute difference in a single phonological rule accounts for the thousands of differences in phonetic detail.

Naturally, not all dialect differences turn out to be as minor as this one. Two dialects of the same language may differ in very significant respects, even in terms of their rules. The important point to remember is that differences in speech traits should not be accepted at face value. When we look below the surface, we usually find that the dialects of a language are similar in many more respects than they are different. The differences, furthermore, are more often than not of a superficial nature.

Divergence into Distinct Dialects

The dialect picture of a language is never a static one. Over a period of years, various isoglosses indicating the boundaries of linguistic traits will shift. If two speakers or communities of speakers have frequent linguistic contact with each other, the dialect differences between them may tend to diminish through borrowing. An innovation that occurs in one dialect is likely to spread to the other if there is communication between the two.

But language change also contains the seeds of increased dialect diversity. Suppose, for example, that a relatively homogeneous group of speakers is divided by some accident of history into two smaller groups between which there is little or no subsequent communication. This separation might come about through the migration of a portion of the community, through the imposition of political barriers, because of a feud—the cause is irrelevant. What will be the linguistic fate of the two groups, once communication between them has ceased?

The linguistic system of both groups will of course change with time, and over a period of centuries the cumulative effect of the many individual changes that occur will be substantial. If the linguistic evolution of the two groups remains independent, the result will be divergence into two distinct dialects. Changes in the dialect of one will have no effect on the development of the dialect of the other. An innovation that spreads throughout one group will not be able to bridge the gap in the network of communication and spread to the second. Isoglosses will pile up along this gap to form a bundle, and the isogloss bundle will grow thicker and thicker as time passes and more and more features come to separate the two dialects.

The phenomenon of language change will therefore bring about increased linguistic diversity in a community of speakers unless there is enough communication and mutual linguistic influence within the group to offset this tendency. As long as the bulk of changes that occur within a group eventually spread to all its members, it will remain relatively homogeneous from the linguistic point of view. The dialect in question may change radically over a period of centuries, but the changes will be uniform within the group itself. When the changes are not coordinated for all speakers of the group, however, they will lead to increased diversity. The linguistic system of each subgroup will develop independently away from the common point of origin.

This mechanism is of extreme importance for the historical study of languages, so let us represent it diagrammatically. In Figure 7.1, L represents the shared linguistic system of a group of speakers, and the arrow symbolizes the passage of time. If the group coheres and the speakers con-

FIGURE 7.1   FIGURE 7.2

tinue to influence one another linguistically, the result will be a modified but still relatively uniform linguistic system, L'.

Suppose, on the other hand, that half of the speakers migrate to a distant island and that the two subgroups no longer communicate with each other. As time passes, the linguistic systems of the two subgroups diverge more and more. This situation is depicted in Figure 7.2. As the bundle of isoglosses between the two systems grows thicker, the split of L into two dialects, L_1 and L_2, becomes more and more apparent. Over a period of many centuries, L_1 and L_2 may become so different from one another that we would be inclined to call them two different languages, rather than dialects of the same language. In this case, L_1 and L_2 are said to be **related** languages.

For two languages to be related, therefore, means that they are divergent continuations of the same, historically earlier language. The Romance languages are a good example. French, Spanish, Italian, Portuguese, Rumanian, Catalan, and several others are related languages in this sense. They are all divergent continuations of spoken Latin, which developed independently in the various regions where spoken Latin was carried by the Roman conquerors. They remain similar enough so that their relationship is apparent, but at the same time they are different enough from one another to be considered separate languages. They could just as well be called dialects of the same language, however. It should be evident that the distinction between related languages and dialects of a single language is only a matter of degree.

CHAPTER EIGHT

Genetic

Relationships

FAMILY TREES

Direct and Indirect Relationships

Two languages are said to be related if they are divergent continuations of the same earlier language. L_1 and L_2 were seen to be related languages in Figure 7.2, since both are later stages of L. A language that occupies the position of L in such a situation is called a **proto** language; L is the prototype of L_1 and L_2. Spoken Latin can therefore be referred to as Proto Romance, since it is the language from which the contemporary Romance languages have descended. The various Slavic languages are divergent continuations of Proto Slavic.

Linguists have always found irresistible the temptation to speak of linguistic relationships with kinship terminology. A proto language can also be called a **parent** language, and its divergent continuations referred to as **daughter** languages. L would thus be the parent of L_1 and L_2. L_1 and L_2, since they are daughters of the same parent, are **sister** languages.

A parent language and its daughters constitute a language **family**. Latin and French, Spanish, Italian, Portuguese, and their sisters make up a language family, and so do Proto Slavic and the modern Slavic languages. Relationships of this type are called **genetic** relationships.

A daughter language, with the passage of time, itself becomes a parent language. Its historical evolution may involve divergence into a number of distinct dialects, and if the divergence becomes marked enough, these dialects can be considered separate but related languages. The "family tree" representing genetic relationships can therefore be quite complex. Consider Figure 8.1, for example. B, C, D, and E are shown as daughters of A, the proto language. As the historical development of this language family continues, each of the daughters of A splits into a number of daughters of which it is the parent. F and G, for instance, are divergent continuations of B; so B is a daughter of A but the parent of F and G. G in turn serves as the proto language from which Q and R descend. Proto Slavic, to take a real example, is one of the daughters of Proto Indo-European. The contemporary Slavic languages, such as Russian, Czech, and Polish, are in turn daughters of Proto Slavic. The continued historical development of this family may see Russian or Polish in the role of a parent language.

From Figure 8.1, we see that the connection between related languages can be either direct or indirect. Q and R are directly related, since they are continuations of G, which is the most immediate predecessor of both. S, T, and U are directly related in similar fashion. The relationship between Q and S, on the other hand, is quite indirect. They both descend from A, but this common ancestor is very far removed. Since they have both diverged so far from A, Q and S may be very different indeed. The sister languages Q and R will resemble each other much more closely than either will resemble S. English and German, for example, are very similar to one another, since they both descend from Proto Germanic. Likewise, Russian and Polish are quite similar, being directly related through Proto Slavic. English and Russian are also related, but only indirectly; Proto Germanic and Proto Slavic are both daughters of Proto Indo-European, and the latter mediates the genetic relationship of English and Russian. Because English and Russian are related only indirectly, they are much less similar to one another than they are to their respective sister tongues.

It is natural to ask whether all human languages are related, however

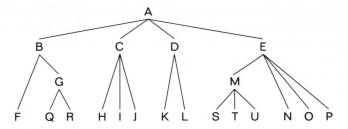

FIGURE 8.1

indirectly. Are all human languages, in other words, linked in a single, vast family tree? This is something that we do not know at present, and we may never know. It has never been demonstrated that all languages are members of a single, giant family. On the other hand, the opposite has never been proved either, and in principle could not be proved. It is possible to prove that two languages are related, by demonstrating that they display extensive similarities in structure that can reasonably be accounted for only by assuming them to be divergent continuations of the same proto language. How, on the other hand, would it be possible to show that two languages are not related? If they are radically different, it is clear that they are not directly related, but differences in structure can never rule out the possibility that they may be related indirectly. The common ancestor that connects them may lie so far in the past that all the original structural similarities have been wiped out during their long, divergent courses of development. It is perfectly conceivable, then, that all human languages are in fact related but that proof of this universal genetic relationship will never be forthcoming. It is equally conceivable that human languages are not all related; in this event, proof is ruled out in principle.

The Techniques of Historical Investigation

Establishing conclusively that a number of languages are related and identifying the genetic relationships that connect them is no simple matter. Languages do not carry signs saying "I belong to the X family of languages." Nor do family trees grow in linguists' back yards where they can be observed at leisure. We can today speak of the Indo-European family of languages and sketch the broad outlines of the genetic relationships among them only because of the genius of preceding generations of scholars. Discovering what languages are related, and how they are related, is a scholarly and analytical task of the first order.

For the most part, only descriptions of contemporary languages are available to work from in establishing genetic relationships. Sometimes, however, the investigator has at his disposal written records of earlier stages of a language, and these can be extremely valuable. We have written records of English covering more than a thousand years of its development; without them we would be very much in the dark concerning many aspects of its evolution. In some cases, written records preserve knowledge of a language that is no longer spoken and could not otherwise be taken into account. Our knowledge of Gothic, for example, has been a valuable resource in the historical investigation of the Germanic languages. Gothic has been extinct since the sixteenth century, but it is known from written documents. Of even greater significance for the study of genetic relationships is the preservation via writing of the proto language of a family. Because we have extensive written records of Latin, including some reflecting spoken Latin, our knowledge of Proto Romance is reasonably complete. We are aware of many features of the proto language that could not be discovered just by examining the contemporary Romance languages.

Linguistic scholars are rarely fortunate enough to have direct knowledge of a proto language. Very often, in fact, historical investigation must proceed without any written records at all. Let us put ourselves in the shoes of a linguist who finds himself in this situation. Suppose he stumbles on the language family of Figure 8.1. Available to him as evidence are the contemporary languages F, Q, R, H, I, J, K, L, S, T, U, N, O, and P. He can observe that they are similar in various respects (other than those respects in which all languages are similar). Thus he is led to the hypothesis that these languages are genetically related. How, and to what extent, can he discover the nature of these genetic relationships without written records to guide him?

Clearly, there will be some things he will not be able to discover at all. He may posit the prior existence of M, for instance, the parent of S, T, and U (if he notices that these three are especially similar). He may even be able to ascertain some of the properties of M by comparing its three daughters. But he will never be able to reconstruct a picture of M that is as complete as his information about the daughter languages. Many important structural details are bound to have been lost in the historical shuffle. Suppose, to take a plausible example, that M was highly inflected, but that the three daughter languages have independently lost the original inflections. From S, T, and U alone, then, it will be impossible to determine completely the details of the inflectional processes of M.

To some extent, one can reconstruct certain features of earlier stages of the individual contemporary languages. This technique is known as **internal reconstruction**, in which earlier stages of a language are partially reconstructed on the basis of structural properties of its later stages. Suppose, for example, that [č] occurs only before [i] in language S, and that [t] never occurs before [i]. S thus has morphemes like [čik] and [tak], but none like [čak] or [tik]. [č], it seems, is the variety of [t] that occurs before [i]. If we now find in S the morphemes [mač] and [kač], we are naturally led to the conclusion that these forms once ended phonetically in [i]. The final [i] conditioned the modification of [t] to [č] in these morphemes. On the basis of internal, nonhistorical evidence, we can reasonably posit the existence of final [i] in such morphemes at an earlier stage of the language. (In fact, they probably still contain final [i] in their underlying phonological representations; this [i] causes [t] to become [č] and is later deleted by a phonological rule.)

The limitations of internal reconstruction are rather severe, however. An earlier structural feature of a language can be reconstructed only if evidence for positing it happens to have been retained, and this is by no means always the case. For an obvious example, consider the loss of a lexical item. If S used to have a word [tal] but no longer does, it is quite possible that no features of contemporary S will lead one to suspect this word's previous existence.

A much more powerful technique is available for investigating the historical origins and development of a group of languages that seem to be related. Instead of examining individual languages, as in internal reconstruction, one can compare two or more languages, with the object of figuring out what their common ancestor must have been like. If Q and R appear to be much more similar to one another than to other languages of the putative family, it is reasonable to hypothesize that Q and R constitute a subfamily, that they are divergent continuations of the same earlier language. By pooling and contrasting the evidence from two or more daughters, one can obtain a much clearer picture of the proto language than by examining just one.

The technique of comparing sister languages to arrive at a reconstruction of the proto language is known as the **comparative method** and was developed in the nineteenth century. In its classic form, the comparative method concerns primarily the sounds of a parent language and how these sounds are reflected in the daughters. It is a technique both for showing that several languages are related and for reconstructing the sounds of the parent.

Of course, we are not limited to the sounds alone when we compare two or more related languages. Extensive similarities in the morphology of two languages can be counted as evidence in favor of the claim that they are related; the same is true of syntactic similarities. Moreover, by comparing the morphological and syntactic properties of the daughters, conclusions can naturally be drawn regarding those of the proto language.

The linguist is therefore not at a total loss to trace the historical relationship and development of a group of languages when there are no written records to guide him. The close examination of an individual language will provide him with some clues concerning earlier stages of it. By comparing and contrasting two or more languages that seem to be related, he can ascertain various characteristics of the proto language; the proto language can be partially reconstructed by a process of triangulation.

Nevertheless, there are limitations. A proto language can never be reconstructed completely, no matter how many of its daughters are known. Since less can be ascertained about the structure of a proto language than about the structure of a living language, reconstructed parent languages are not in general known in enough detail to be used for further reconstructions. The farther back we delve into the historical antecedents of a family of languages, the less data there is to work with.

Take the family of Figure 8.1 once again. Suppose it is correctly surmised that Q and R constitute a subfamily, and that F is more closely related to Q and R than to the other languages. From Q and R, it will be possible to partially reconstruct the proto language G, but G will be known much less completely than its daughters. Consequently, the usefulness of G in reconstructing the parent of it and F will be minimal. The reconstruction of B will be more tentative and incomplete than that of G. The reconstructions of B, C, D, and E may not contain enough information to allow any reconstruction of A at all, since none of A's daughters is known directly. Because of the increasing paucity of data as one digs farther and farther into the past, there is a point at which all known techniques of historical reconstruction cease to yield reliable results.

The situation is not basically different when written records are available. Written records allow us to pry a little deeper into the linguistic past, since they show earlier stages of languages in more detail, but they carry us back only a short distance. We have Gothic texts from as early as the sixth century, for example, but we have only scratched the historical surface even when we have gone back that far.

It should now be clear why no one has ever demonstrated that all human languages are related. The claim that they are related can be made, but it is an empty one. For the claim to be meaningful, one would have to show which established language families belong together in more comprehensive families, which of these belong together as members of still more inclusive families, and so on, until all human languages were accommodated. At each stage, it would be necessary to partially reconstruct a proto language and to demonstrate that its putative daughters were similar in ways that could best be explained by the hypothesis that they were divergent continuations of it. Even if all languages are in fact genetically related (which is a big assumption), it is simply not possible to reconstruct the family tree that links them all, thus establishing their relatedness. The time span is so great, and so many echelons of proto languages are involved, that the data supplied by contemporary languages will not take us back far enough.

The Problem of Borrowing

Complicating the whole picture of genetic relationship is the phenomenon of borrowing. When one language borrows a trait from another, the two are subsequently more similar to each other than they were before. If only one or a handful of traits are borrowed, the adjustment will of course be minute. It sometimes happens, however, that two languages influence one another on a grand scale. If the mutual influence should be extensive enough, the languages involved may appear on cursory examination to be related when they really are not. In order to avoid false hypotheses of genetic relationship, one must be careful to distinguish similarities that are attributable to a common heritage from those due to borrowing.

The problem that borrowing poses is usually much more subtle than this, however, and concerns the process of working out the genetic relationships of a group of languages that are in fact related. The problem, essentially, is that linguistic traits introduced through borrowing cannot be used for reconstructing a proto language; the amount of data that can validly be used for reconstruction is reduced significantly if one or more of the daughter languages has borrowed heavily. Suppose, for example, that two sister languages have been subjected to strong lexical influence from languages of other families, so that over half of the native lexical items have been replaced in each. Since the native lexical items are by definition those that descend from lexical items of the proto language, their loss inevitably diminishes the portion of the proto language that can be reconstructed.

The same is true when a language borrows from a related language. Such borrowing is very common, since speakers of divergent dialects usually continue to have some contact with one another during the historical evolution that leads to separate languages; it is an idealization to suppose that the speakers of a proto language suddenly split up into smaller speech communities between which there is absolutely no subsequent communication. (It is also an idealization to attribute complete linguistic homogeneity to speakers of the proto language.) If language Q has borrowed heavily from language R during their divergent evolution from the proto language G, the borrowed features of Q will add little information that cannot be provided by an examination of R. Moreover, the features of Q that have been dropped under the influence of R will not be available for establishing the relatedness of Q and R or for reconstructing the proto language. A good case in point is Albanian. Because it has borrowed so extensively from other languages, including Greek and the Slavic and Romance languages, only a few hundred native words remain. In addition, the inflectional endings have undergone considerable modification. As a result, the recognition of Albanian's place in the Indo-European family was relatively late.

THE COMPARATIVE METHOD

We will examine the comparative method first in its classic form and then in light of more recent insights, taking into account the necessity of viewing the sounds of a language in relation to a system of phonological rules and abstract underlying representations. The clearest and easiest way to introduce the comparative method is by means of a concrete example of its application. We will use a hypothetical example in order to keep the data down to a manageable amount, but the phenomena that will be illustrated are typical of those found in the more complex cases of reality.

The Data

Suppose that four new languages are discovered on a large island in the Pacific. For purposes of identification, we will call them L_1, L_2, L_3, and L_4. In addition to extensive syntactic and morphological congruence, these languages display striking similarities in their lexicons. A representative list of lexical items is given below with their meanings. (The symbol [x] stands for a voiceless velar fricative.)

L_1	L_2	L_3	L_4	Meaning
[puxa]	[buga]	[puka]	[puk]	'tree'
[lisu]	[lisu]	[risu]	[lis]	'bug'
[mani]	[mani]	[meni]	[man]	'sky'
[lana]	[lana]	[rena]	[rena]	'stone'
[kaxa]	[gaga]	[kaka]	[kak]	'hut'
[tupi]	[dubi]	[tupi]	[tup]	'thunder'
[palmufo]	[nili]	[niri]	[nil]	'spear'
[samu]	[samu]	[semu]	[sam]	'river'
[matu]	[madu]	[matu]	[mat]	'arrow'
[nipa]	[niba]	[nipa]	[nip]	'ocean'

From the very first glance, it is apparent that the four languages have lexical similarities that go far beyond the few that could be expected to occur by chance. In word after word, we find resemblances in both sound and meaning. The words for 'tree' in the four languages, [puxa], [buga], [puka], and [puk], differ from one another only in minor respects, and this is typical of each set of words with the same meaning. Furthermore, the pervasiveness of the similarities is such that borrowing would not seem to be a likely explanation for them. We would not expect each of three languages to borrow in such a uniform and exceptionless manner from a fourth. Borrowing is a common phenomenon, but not a very regular one. Since chance and borrowing are both ruled out as reasonable explanations for the resemblance of the four languages, we are left with the hypothesis that they are genetically related, that they are similar because they are divergent continuations of the same, historically earlier language.

Before examining more carefully the regularities in the data, however, we must deal with two forms that are not at all what we would expect. The word for 'spear' in L_1 stands out from the rest; [palmufo] has virtually nothing in common with [nili], [niri], or [nil], the words for 'spear' in L_2, L_3, and L_4. Furthermore, [palmufo] seems to violate otherwise valid phonological principles of L_1. All the other words of L_1 contain precisely two syllables, each of the form consonant plus vowel; consonants do not occur adjacent to one another within a word. [palmufo] is odd on both counts, for it has three syllables, not two, and contains the consonant sequence [lm]. The most likely explanation for these peculiarities is that [palmufo] was borrowed into L_1 from some other, unrelated language. Coming from another language, it has certain phonological properties not shared by native words of L_1; it has probably been modified by the borrowing speakers in the direction of L_1, but not completely. Our hypothesis that [palmufo] represents a borrowing would of course be confirmed if we should find another language spoken on the island in which [palmufo], or something very similar, is the word for 'spear.'

The other suspicious form is [rena], the word for 'stone' in L_4. It is the only word in L_4 that ends in a vowel, and in addition it is the only one containing the vowel [e] or the consonant [r]. If it is a borrowed word, however, it must have been borrowed from a related language, since the words for 'stone' in L_1, L_2, and L_3 are so similar: [lana], [lana], [rena]. In fact, the most likely explanation is that L_4 borrowed the word for 'stone' from L_3. This accounts both for the identity of the words in the two languages and for the oddness of [rena] with respect to the phonological properties of L_4. [rena] is not at all unusual as a word of L_3. [r] and [e] occur in other words of L_3, and it is normal for words of L_3 to end in vowels.

Since [palmufo] and [rena] entered L_1 and L_4 by borrowing, they cannot properly be used in reconstructing the proto language. The reduced body of data from which we can work is given below.

L_1	L_2	L_3	L_4	Meaning
[puxa]	[buga]	[puka]	[puk]	'tree'
[lisu]	[lisu]	[risu]	[lis]	'bug'
[mani]	[mani]	[meni]	[man]	'sky'
[lana]	[lana]	[rena]		'stone'
[kaxa]	[gaga]	[kaka]	[kak]	'hut'
[tupi]	[dubi]	[tupi]	[tup]	'thunder'
	[nili]	[niri]	[nil]	'spear'
[samu]	[samu]	[semu]	[sam]	'river'
[matu]	[madu]	[matu]	[mat]	'arrow'
[nipa]	[niba]	[nipa]	[nip]	'ocean'

Sound Correspondences

The crucial observation to be made concerning this data is not that the words for each concept are similar in the four languages, but rather that their similarities and differences follow fixed patterns. The sounds of the four daughter languages **correspond** in a completely regular fashion.

Take the sound [m], for instance. The word for 'sky' in L_1 starts with [m], but so do the corresponding words in the other three languages: [mani], [mani], [meni], [man]. The word for 'river' has [m] as the third segment, not in just one or two of the languages, but in all of them. All four words for 'arrow' have [m] in initial position. Without exception, an [m] in L_1 always corresponds to an [m] in L_2, L_3, and L_4. The corresponding sounds in the four languages are thus [m] - [m] - [m] - [m].

Another regular sound correspondence is [n] - [n] - [n] - [n], and a third is [s] - [s] - [s] - [s]. For every word in L_1 that contains [n], the corresponding words in the other three languages also contain [n], and in the same position. Thus we find [mani], [mani], [meni], and [man] for 'sky,' as well as [nipa], [niba], [nipa], [nip] for 'ocean.' With regard to the words for 'stone' and 'spear,' we only have data from three languages to work with, but the available forms follow the same pattern: [lana], [lana], [rena]; [nili], [niri], [nil]. In the same way, [s] in one language corresponds to [s] in the other three. All four words for 'bug' have [s] as the third segment, and all four words for 'river' have [s] as the initial segment: [lisu], [lisu], [risu], [lis]; [samu], [samu], [semu], [sam]. These correspondences are therefore completely regular.

Still a fourth exceptionless correspondence is [l] - [l] - [r] - [l]. In every position where L_1 has [l], so do L_2 and L_4; in the corresponding position, L_3 always has [r]. Alongside [lisu] in L_1, we thus find [lisu], [risu], and [lis] in L_2, L_3, and L_4 respectively. The data for 'stone' and 'spear' is incomplete, but the available words conform to the pattern perfectly. Notice that a sound correspondence can be completely regular even though the members of the correspondence differ from language to language. L_3 is different from the other languages because it has [r] instead of [l], but this difference is an entirely systematic one. It is possible to give a formula ([l] - [l] - [r] - [l]) that will hold uniformly for all lexical items of the sister languages, and it is this regularity, rather than phonetic identity, that is of greatest interest for reconstructing the proto language.

Two other fully regular correspondences of this type are [p] - [b] - [p] - [p] and [t] - [d] - [t] - [t]. From the words for 'tree,' 'thunder,' and 'ocean,' we see that whenever a word of L_1 has [p], the corresponding word in L_2 has [b] in the same position; the parallel forms in L_3 and L_4 agree with L_1 in having [p]. 'Tree,' for example, is rendered as [puxa], [buga], [puka], and [puk], and 'thunder' as [tupi], [dubi], [tupi], and [tup]. The latter series also illustrates the [t] - [d] - [t] - [t] correspondence, as do the words for 'arrow,' [matu], [madu], [matu], and [mat].

We have now established six completely regular correspondences: [m] - [m] - [m] - [m]; [n] - [n] - [n] - [n]; [s] - [s] - [s] - [s]; [l] - [l] - [r] - [l]; [p] - [b] - [p] - [p]; and [t] - [d] - [t] - [t]. When we try to find others, however, there seem to be exceptions. Take the sound [k] in L_3, for example. On the basis of the word for 'tree,' it appears that [k] in L_3 corresponds to [x], [g], and [k] in L_1, L_2, and L_4 respectively: [puxa], [buga], [puka], [puk]. This would lead us to set up the correspondence [x] - [g] - [k] - [k]. On the basis of this formula and the L_3 word for 'hut,' [kaka], we would expect the parallel words in the other three languages to be [xaxa], [gaga], and [kak] (with respect to the consonants). Our expectations are not fully borne out, though, since the L_1 word is not [xaxa], but rather [kaxa]. The initial consonant violates the pattern.

What this means is that some (but not all) correspondences have to be stated relative to a specific phonological environment. In the case at hand, the [x] - [g] - [k] - [k] correspondence is valid, but only if we exclude initial consonants. The noninitial velar consonants of [kaxa], [gaga], [kaka], and [kak] conform perfectly to the pattern observed in the words for 'tree.' Another formula is needed for initial velar consonants, namely [k] - [g] - [k] - [k]. We would expect other lexical sets to confirm this environmentally conditioned correspondence; for instance, the four corresponding words [kili], [gili], [kiri], and [kil] would constitute evidence that the L_1 word for 'hut' is not exceptional.

The correspondences involving the vowels [u] and [i] are relative to specific phonological environments in the same way. From the words for 'tree' and 'ocean,' the correspondences would appear to be [u] - [u] - [u] - [u] and [i] - [i] - [i] - [i]: [puxa], [buga], [puka], [puk]; [nipa], [niba], [nipa], [nip]. In both sets of words, the vowel in question occurs in nonfinal position. A glance at the words of L_4, though, shows that special provisions have to be made for word-final vowels, since L_4 has none. The words for 'river,' [samu], [samu], [semu], and [sam], show that the [u] series is [u] - [u] - [u] - [ ] at the end of a word (the empty brackets indicate the absence of a segment). The word-final [i] series, similarly, is [i] - [i] - [i] - [ ], as we can see from the words for 'sky': [mani], [mani], [meni], [man].

The [a] series in word-final position is comparable; from [nipa], [niba], [nipa], [nip] we see that it must be [a] - [a] - [a] - [ ]. This is confirmed by the words for 'tree' and 'hut.' In other cases, however, [a] in L_1, L_2, and L_4 corresponds sometimes to [a] in L_3 and sometimes to [e]. Thus we have [matu], [madu], [matu], and [mat] for 'arrow,' but [mani], [mani], [meni], and [man] for 'sky.' Is this then an irregularity in the system of correspondences, or is there a general principle that determines when L_3 has [a] and when it has [e]? If we examine the words of L_3, we find that [e] occurs only before a nasal consonant, and that [a] never occurs before a nasal: [puka], [meni], [rena], [kaka], [semu], [matu], [nipa]. The variation between [a] and [e] as the counterpart of [a] in the other languages is not an irregularity, therefore, but rather a subregularity. The correspondence is [a] - [a] - [e] - [a] before a nasal and [a] - [a] - [a] - [a] elsewhere.

The correspondences we have found are summarized in the table below.

(1)	[m] - [m] - [m] - [m]	
(2)	[n] - [n] - [n] - [n]	
(3)	[s] - [s] - [s] - [s]	
(4)	[l] - [l] - [r] - [l]	
(5)	[p] - [b] - [p] - [p]	
(6)	[t] - [d] - [t] - [t]	
(7a)	[k] - [g] - [k] - [k]	(in word-initial position)
(7b)	[x] - [g] - [k] - [k]	(elsewhere)
(8a)	[u] - [u] - [u] - [ ]	(in word-final position)
(8b)	[u] - [u] - [u] - [u]	(elsewhere)
(9a)	[i] - [i] - [i] - [ ]	(in word-final position)
(9b)	[i] - [i] - [i] - [i]	(elsewhere)
(10a)	[a] - [a] - [a] - [ ]	(in word-final position)
(10b)	[a] - [a] - [e] - [a]	(before a nasal)
(10c)	[a] - [a] - [a] - [a]	(elsewhere)

The words of the four sister languages are locked together with respect to their phonetic shapes by these formulas. This tabulation of regularities allows us to predict the pronunciation of a word in one language if we know how it is pronounced in its sisters. The native L_1 word for 'spear,' for instance, was replaced by the borrowed word [palmufo], but from [nili], [niri], and [nil] (the corresponding words in the sister languages), and from the established correspondences, it is easy to figure out that the native L_1 word would have been [nili] had it survived. Similarly, we know from [lana], [lana], and [rena] that the native L_4 word for 'stone' would have been [lan] if the borrowed word [rena] had not replaced it.

The Regularity of Sound Change

By the process of elimination, we concluded earlier that the similarities in the four languages were due to genetic relationship. More explicitly, we will now hypothesize that they are divergent continuations of the same proto language, which we will call PL, as shown in Figure 8.2. The observed regularities can be explained in part by this hypothesis; it is not surprising, for example, that the words for 'tree' in the daughter languages are similar, since they all descend from the same form, the word for 'tree' in PL.

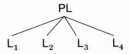

FIGURE 8.2

Nevertheless, the hypothesis of genetic relationship does not in itself explain the existence of systematic sound correspondences. It would be perfectly conceivable for each set of four words to be similar but for the nature of the similarities to be different for each set. This would be the case if the historical development of each word of the proto language were idiosyncratic. Initial [m], for instance, might develop one way in the word for 'sky,' and another way in the word for 'arrow.' If changes in the sounds of the proto language were idiosyncratic, or peculiar to individual lexical items, it would not be possible to find systematic sound correspondences linking the words of the daughters and holding across the board for all sets of words with the same origin.

In order to explain the existence of systematic sound correspondences, therefore, a double-barreled hypothesis is necessary. We must add to the hypothesis of genetic relationship the assumption that sound changes are basically regular. If initial [m] of PL is reflected as [m] in the L_1 word for 'sky,' it will be so reflected in all words of L_1. If an [a] of PL is reflected as [e] in L_3 when the next segment is a nasal, [a] will always be reflected as [e] in this environment. There may be sporadic exceptions, as there are to any rule, but sound change is envisaged as a fundamentally regular process. The common origin of each set of words, together with the assumption that sound change is regular, explains both the phonetic similarity of the words of each set and the fact that they are linked systematically by correspondence formulas that are valid for all words having a common origin.

A set of words that are genetically related in this way is said to constitute a **cognate set**, and the members of such a set are called **cognates**. The daughter words for 'tree,' to take one example, constitute a cognate set; [puxa], [buga], [puka], and [puk] are cognates. For each cognate set, there is by definition some proto form of which the members of the set are divergent continuations. The next step is to attempt the reconstruction of these proto forms and to state the sound changes that must have taken place in the development of each of the daughter languages.

Reconstruction

The existence of cognate sets linked by systematic sound correspondences is very strong evidence that the four languages are genetically related. The next step of the comparative method—partially reconstructing the proto language and stating the sound changes that have taken place— provides additional confirmation of the hypothesis. It demonstrates in detail the plausibility of explaining the observed regularities in terms of genetic relationship, since it shows that a real language could in fact have existed and diverged into the daughters by means of reasonable sound changes.

For each sound correspondence, we can set up a segment type of the proto language. If the correspondence is relative to a specific phonological environment, the reconstructed segment type will also be relative to that environment.

Take the correspondence [m] - [m] - [m] - [m], for instance. Whenever [m] occurs in some word of a daughter language, its cognates also contain [m], and in the same position. It is reasonable to suppose that this agreement comes about because the underlying word in the proto language also contained [m] in that position. The supposition, in other words, is that [mani], [mani], [meni], and [man] all start with [m] because the word for 'sky' in PL started with [m]; that the third segment of [samu], [samu], [semu], and [sam] is in each case [m] because the third segment of the PL word for 'river' was [m]; and so on. To underlie the segment [m] in the daughter languages, then, we reconstruct for PL the segment *[m]. (An asterisk always precedes reconstructed entities that have not been observed directly.) The resulting situation is depicted in Figure 8.3. In this case, no sound changes affecting the reconstructed segment have occurred.

Similarly, we can reconstruct the segments *[n] and *[s] for PL. The former underlies the [n] - [n] - [n] - [n] correspondence observed in the daughter languages, and the latter underlies the series [s] - [s] - [s] - [s]. Once again it appears that no sound changes have affected the proto segments in question, since their **reflexes**—their manifestations in the daughter languages—are uniform.

This uniformity is lacking in the [l] - [l] - [r] - [l] correspondence. The reflex of the proto segment in L$_3$ does not match the reflexes in the other daughters. What segment should we then reconstruct to underlie this

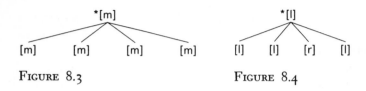

FIGURE 8.3   FIGURE 8.4

correspondence? The most important requirement is that the reconstructed segment be capable of developing historically to both [l] and [r], since we are claiming that such a development took place. On this basis alone, either [l] or [r] could be postulated as the proto segment, since the two sounds are very similar and the interchange of [l] and [r] is a frequent linguistic phenomenon. [l] often changes to [r], that is, and the opposite development also occurs.

We will reconstruct *[l] to underlie the series [l] - [l] - [r] - [l], as shown in Figure 8.4. In making this decision, we implicitly claim that the historical development of PL into L_3 involved, along with many other changes, the change of [l] to [r]. This claim is somewhat more reasonable than the opposite one. If we were to reconstruct *[r] instead, we would be claiming that [r] changed to [l] independently in L_1, L_2, and L_4, being retained only in L_3. While this is not impossible, it is somewhat less likely than the single change of [l] to [r]. We see from this example that it is not always possible to conclude with certainty what the precise phonetic shape of a proto segment must have been. Clearly, a single segment type must have been present to underlie its observed reflexes in the daughter languages, but beyond a certain point we can only speculate as to its exact character.

The next two correspondences present a similar problem, and we will suggest a similar solution—the majority rules, unless there is evidence to the contrary. For [p] - [b] - [p] - [p] we will reconstruct *[p], and for [t] - [d] - [t] - [t] we will reconstruct *[t]. With each reconstruction, we are claiming that a sound change occurred in L_2; the claim is that [p] changed to [b] in L_2, and that [t] changed to [d]. It is simpler to assume that changes occurred in L_2 than to assume that [b] and [d] are historically basic. With the latter assumption, we would have to accept that parallel innovations took place in L_1, L_3, and L_4, which is somewhat less likely.

The correspondence [k] - [g] - [k] - [k] was limited to word-initial position. By the same reasoning used above, we can reconstruct *[k] for PL in this position, claiming at the same time that [k] changed to [g] in L_2.

215

If we were correct in reconstructing *[p] and *[t], the third reconstructed stop almost has to be *[k] and not *[g]. The reason is that the inventory of sounds used in a language tends to display a certain symmetry, especially with regard to stops, fricatives, and nasals. It is very common for a language to have three voiceless stops, say [p t k], but it is not at all common for a language to have two voiceless stops and a voiced one, say [p t g]. With our reconstructed stops *[p t k], we take this tendency toward symmetry into account.

If PL had the stop *[k] in initial position, the same stop probably occurred in noninitial position as well. Therefore, the same segment no doubt also underlies the correspondence [x] - [g] - [k] - [k]. Both correspondences are illustrated in the cognate set for 'hut': [kaxa], [gaga], [kaka], and [kak]. The proto word for 'hut' evidently contained two occurrences of *[k]. Both occurrences are retained in the L_3 and L_4 words; no sound changes affected [k] in these languages. The sound change that occurred in L_2 was not restricted to any special environment; [k] became [g] in all environments. Thus both instances of *[k] in the proto word are reflected as [g] in the L_2 word. In L_1, on the other hand, a sound change must have taken place that was relative to a specific environment: [k] became [x] when it occurred between two vowels. The word-initial [k] was retained, but the intervocalic [k] underwent this sound change to be reflected in L_1 as [x]. The situation is represented in Figure 8.5. The postulated sound change is a quite reasonable one, for it often happens that a stop becomes a fricative, especially when it occurs intervocalically. The opposite development, where a fricative becomes a stop, is less usual.

This brings us to the vowel correspondences. We found the correspondence [u] - [u] - [u] - [ ] to be valid in word-final position, while [u] - [u] - [u] - [u] held in other environments. The obvious solution is to postulate *[u] for all positions in PL, together with this sound change for L_4: [u] was lost in final position. The same solution is appropriate for the two correspondences with [i], namely [i] - [i] - [i] - [ ] in final position and [i] - [i] - [i] - [i] elsewhere. The proto segment was no doubt *[i], and L_4 underwent this change: [i] was lost in final position.

With respect to [a], we found three correspondences. In word-final position, the correspondence was [a] - [a] - [a] - [ ]; before nasals, it was [a] - [a] - [e] - [a]; and elsewhere, it was [a] - [a] - [a] - [a]. For each correspondence, we will set up the proto segment *[a]. The following two sound changes then account for the data: In L_3, [a] became [e] before a nasal; in L_4, [a]

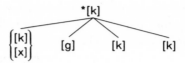

FIGURE 8.5

was lost in final position. It is readily seen that this solution is simpler and more reasonable than any obvious alternative.

In effect, we have now reconstructed the ten proto words underlying the data from which we started. Every segment in the data was accounted for by some correspondence, and for each correspondence we have reconstructed a proto segment. Reconstructing the proto words is only a matter of summarizing what we have already done. The reconstructed proto words are given in the table below with their cognate sets, and the postulated sound changes, which derive the cognate sets from the proto words, are recapitulated.

PL	L₁	L₂	L₃	L₄	Meaning
*[puka]	[puxa]	[buga]	[puka]	[puk]	'tree'
*[lisu]	[lisu]	[lisu]	[risu]	[lis]	'bug'
*[mani]	[mani]	[mani]	[meni]	[man]	'sky'
*[lana]	[lana]	[lana]	[rena]		'stone'
*[kaka]	[kaxa]	[gaga]	[kaka]	[kak]	'hut'
*[tupi]	[tupi]	[dubi]	[tupi]	[tup]	'thunder'
*[nili]		[nili]	[niri]	[nil]	'spear'
*[samu]	[samu]	[samu]	[semu]	[sam]	'river'
*[matu]	[matu]	[madu]	[matu]	[mat]	'arrow'
*[nipa]	[nipa]	[niba]	[nipa]	[nip]	'ocean'

In L₁, [k] became [x] between vowels.

In L₂, [p] became [b]; [t] became [d]; and [k] became [g].

In L₃, [l] became [r]; and [a] became [e] before a nasal.

In L₄, [u] was lost in final position; [i] was lost in final position; and [a] was lost in final position.

Let us go through a couple of examples for illustration. We will reconstruct the PL words for 'tree' and 'stone' and then trace the reconstructed forms in their historical development.

The cognate set for 'tree' is [puxa], [buga], [puka], and [puk]. The initial segment of these forms represents the correspondence [p] - [b] - [p] - [p], for which we reconstructed *[p]. For the [u] - [u] - [u] - [u] correspondence, we reconstructed *[u]; the second segment of the proto word must therefore have been *[u]. The last two segments represent the correspondences [x] - [g] - [k] - [k] and [a] - [a] - [a] - [ ], for which we reconstructed *[k] and *[a] respectively. Putting the proto segments together, we find that the proto word for 'tree' must have been *[puka].

In its development from PL, L_1 underwent a sound change: [k] changed to [x] between vowels. One specific effect of this change was the manifestation of *[puka] as [puxa] in L_1. The change, we notice, was a regular one, affecting all morphemes containing intervocalic [k]. Thus *[kaka] developed to [kaxa] in L_1 in the same manner. Two of the sound changes of L_2 are applicable to *[puka]: [p] became [b] and [k] became [g]. The result of these two regular changes was the L_2 word [buga]. Neither of the sound changes characteristic of L_3 could affect *[puka], so the L_3 word for 'tree' is identical to the PL word. Finally, *[puka] became [puk] in L_4 by the loss of [a] in final position.

Only three cognates are available for 'stone,' [lana], [lana], and [rena], but this leads to no difficulty in setting up the proto form. The first segment exemplifies the correspondence [l] - [l] - [r] - [l]; the second, [a] - [a] - [e] - [a]; the third, [n] - [n] - [n] - [n]; and the fourth, [a] - [a] - [a] - [ ]. Respectively, we reconstructed for these the proto segments *[l], *[a], *[n], and *[a]. The PL word for 'stone' must therefore have been *[lana].

[lana] is retained as the form in both L_1 and L_2, because the sound changes that took place in these languages affected only stops. Both sound changes of L_3 were applicable to *[lana]: [l] became [r], and [a] became [e] before a nasal. Consequently, the L_3 word for 'stone' is [rena]. The L_4 term was replaced through borrowing, but the principles we have uncovered make it clear that it would have been [lan] had it survived, since final [a] was regularly lost in L_4.

In its classic form, then, the comparative method can be viewed as comprising several steps. First, apparent cognates are isolated. Second, the systematic sound correspondences linking the cognate sets are uncovered.

Third, words of the proto language are reconstructed on the basis of the cognate sets. Fourth, the sound changes that have occurred in the development of each daughter language from the parent are stated. These changes must account for the evolution of each set of cognates from their common proto form. Moreover, the proto language, insofar as it can be reconstructed, must look like a real language, and the postulated sound changes must be reasonable ones, changes of the kind that are known to occur. If all these steps are taken, and if all the conditions are met, two things have been accomplished: It has been demonstrated that the putative sister languages are in fact genetically related, and the parent language has been partially reconstructed.

Needless to say, historical reconstruction is not always as easy as our hypothetical example might indicate. Many more segment types are involved with real languages; seldom are there so few gaps in the data; it is normally not so easy to recognize borrowed forms; the sound changes responsible for deriving the daughters from the proto language are usually much more numerous; syntactic and morphological evidence has to be taken into account as well; there is no *a priori* way to determine whether or how the related languages cluster into subfamilies—this list of problems could be extended. Nevertheless, the principles illustrated here are fully applicable to the data provided by real languages. The comparative method is a valid instrument for establishing the genetic relationship of a group of languages and for reconstructing proto forms.

THE INTERPRETATION OF SOUND CHANGE

In our hypothetical example, we were able to establish genetic relationship, and to reconstruct proto forms, without ever scratching below the phonetic surface. We worked from the phonetic shapes of the daughter words alone, never taking into account their underlying representations or the phonological rules responsible for their manifestation. Proceeding in this manner, we uncovered a rather surprising fact: Sound change is regular. If [a] became [e] before a nasal in L_3, it did so in all words containing [a] before a nasal, not in just one or a handful. The modification of [a] to [e] was not peculiar to individual morphemes but held across the board for all morphemes of the language. The common proto forms, together with the regularity of sound change, account for the observed sound correspondences that relate cognates in the daughter languages and relate the members of each cognate set in the same way. Since their development from the common proto forms is regular, cognates are related to one another in phonological shape according to regular patterns.

But why should sound change be regular? The regular character of sound change was a revolutionary discovery for the nineteenth-century philologists who developed the comparative method, but they never gave a satisfactory explanation of why it should be so. For this we must reinterpret things in terms of the more recent view of phonological systems outlined in Chapter Six. When the phonetic data we were working with is treated as the manifestation by phonological rules of abstract underlying representations, the regularity of sound change is quite understandable.

Let us reexamine the data that illustrates the change of [a] to [e] before a nasal in L_3. The ten L_3 forms available to us are [puka], [risu], [meni], [rena], [kaka], [tupi], [niri], [semu], [matu], and [nipa]. Phonetically, L_3 has both [a] and [e]. We notice, however, that the difference between them is not distinctive. There are no two morphemes that are distinguished solely by the fact that one has [a] in the same position where the other has [e]. Moreover, this could not be the case (if we take our small lexical sample to be indicative of the whole language). Since [e] occurs only before nasals, and since [a] never occurs before nasals, the difference between [e] and [a] in some position could never be the sole trait differentiating morphemes.

In L_3, therefore, [e] is nothing but a variant manifestation of [a]. It is the form that [a] assumes overtly when the following segment is a nasal. In the underlying representations, [a] and [e] are not differentiated, since the difference between them is not distinctive. The first vowel of both [semu] and [matu], for instance, would be listed simply as being low (to distinguish [a]/[e] from the high vowels [i u]). In most circumstances, a low vowel is ultimately specified as [a], as in [matu]. The [e] of [semu], however, results from the application of this rule of L_3: A low vowel is manifested as a mid front vowel before a nasal. If we use [a] to indicate a low vowel, we can say that the underlying representation is [samu], and that the above rule is responsible for its surface manifestation as [semu]. Similarly, [meni] and [rena] result from the more abstract representations [mani] and [rana].

In L₃, then, there is an underlying segment type [a] (that is, a low vowel) and a phonological rule to the effect that [a] is manifested as [e] before a nasal. Turning now to the proto language PL, we find that there is no [e] at all, only the reconstructed low vowel *[a], whose precise pronunciation cannot be surmised. By comparing L₃ with its earlier stage PL, we find that the difference between them, insofar as the vowels are concerned, is nothing more than the existence in L₃ of the rule manifesting [a] as [e]. The two stages are identical with respect to the underlying representation of the vowel segments in question; at both stages it is sufficient to specify the vowel as being low. In PL, an underlying low vowel was presumably always manifested phonetically as a low vowel (at least there is no evidence to the contrary); in L₃, a low vowel can be manifested as either a mid or low vowel depending on its phonological environment.

We said earlier that L₃ underwent a sound change in its development from PL, namely [a] changed to [e] before a nasal. The nature of this sound change should now be quite evident; the rule that [a] is manifested as [e] before a nasal was added to the phonological system of L₃. The change was not a change in the sounds *per se*, but rather in the system of rules responsible for them. It should also be apparent why this sound change was regular, why it held for all morphemes of the language instead of being peculiar to individual morphemes. The change consisted in the addition of a general rule, and a general phonological rule is by definition a principle that holds across the board, not an idiosyncratic property of individual lexical items.

The regularity of the other sound changes we postulated can be explained in a similar manner. In L₁, [k] became [x] between vowels, giving us forms like [puxa] and [kaxa]. The difference between [k] and [x] is not distinctive, however, since [x] occurs only intervocalically and [k] never occurs in this position. In both PL and L₁, therefore, there is a single underlying velar consonant. The sound change consisted in the addition of this rule to the phonological system of L₁: [k] is manifested as a fricative between vowels. The change was regular because the phonological representations of individual morphemes were not affected; a rule was added instead.

Three sound changes were postulated for L_2: [p] became [b]; [t] became [d]; and [k] became [g]. In neither PL nor L_2 is the difference between voiced and voiceless stops distinctive. All stops were presumably voiceless in PL, and all stops are voiced in L_2. At both stages, then, the specification of voicing for stops is redundant phonetic detail, detail that is added by a phonological rule. The rule for PL is simply that stops are voiceless, while the rule for L_2 is simply that stops are voiced. The sound change consisted in the modification of this rule specifying voicing, so that stops were subsequently specified as being voiced rather than voiceless. Since a rule was modified, not individual phonological representations, the change was regular. Notice also that a single, general rule is involved. All stops are specified as voiceless in PL and as voiced in L_2; the rule in question applies to the class of all stops. There is no reason to adopt the more complex, less general, and less insightful analysis whereby three separate rules are postulated, one for each kind of stop. Three separate sound changes took place, so far as surface phonetic facts are concerned, but all three are consequences of the same minor rule modification.

The change of [l] to [r] in L_3 is parallel. In neither PL nor L_3 is the difference between [l] and [r] a distinctive one. At both stages, it is sufficient to specify the underlying segment as a liquid, with its precise phonetic shape being determined by phonological rules. The change of [l] to [r] was thus a minor rule modification similar to the one affecting stops in L_2.

Three changes occurred in L_4: [u] was lost in final position; [i] was lost in final position; and [a] was lost in final position. By now it should be obvious that these three changes are consequences of the same historical phenomenon, not isolated events. To know just what this historical phenomenon was, however, we have to know a little more about L_4.

One possibility is that the underlying phonological representations have not changed in the development of PL into L_4, but that a rule deleting final vowels has been added to the phonological system. If this is the case, the underlying representations [puka], [lisu], and [mani] are translated into the phonetic shapes [puk], [lis], and [man] by this deletion rule. For the underlying vowels to be retained in final position despite their phonetic absence, however, there must be nonhistorical structural evidence in the language to posit them. Suppose, for example, that [n] is added as a suffix to form the plural of nouns, and that the plurals of the above nouns are [pukan], [lisun], and [manin]. Since the underlying vowels show up overtly in the plural (where the [n] suffix keeps them from being in final position and hence blocks their deletion), there is structural evidence for their existence. When children learn L_4, they have a reason to learn phonological representations for these nouns which include the specification of final vowels.

Suppose, on the other hand, that there is no such evidence. Suppose that all words of L_4 have just one syllable, and that the child who learns this language has no structural reason whatever to set up abstract underlying representations containing final vowels. In this case, the difference between PL and L_4 does not reside in the phonological rules, but rather in the underlying representations, since morphemes do end in vowels in the underlying representations of PL. But if the representations of individual morphemes have been altered, and not rules, why was the change regular? Why do morphemes not vary idiosyncratically as to whether they retain the final vowel?

The answer is that this change originated as a rule change. At some point in the historical evolution of PL into L_4, speakers adopted a rule dropping vowels in final position. Perhaps this mode of pronunciation spread because of its stylistic value, or perhaps there was some other reason. In any event, speakers who had learned phonological representations with final vowels started omitting these vowels when they pronounced words. The phenomenon was essentially regular, for a rule was responsible.

Children who learned to talk under these conditions took a fresh look at things. Hearing no final vowels, and having no reason to postulate them, they learned phonological representations in which all of the final vowels were lacking. Consequently, they had no reason to learn the rule for deleting these vowels. The change in underlying representations thus came about through restructuring. After final vowels had disappeared phonetically, by virtue of a new rule added to the phonological systems of adult speakers, children who subsequently learned to talk arrived at a simpler system, one in which final vowels were lacking entirely.

In all but one case, sound changes in the daughter languages turned out to be rule changes; there was only one possible instance of change in the underlying phonological representations, and even this presupposed a previous rule change. Our hypothetical example may not be completely representative, but rule changes do seem to preponderate in reality. The limited but growing amount of investigation in this area suggests that rule changes occur frequently in phonological systems, while underlying representations are fairly stable by comparison.

LANGUAGE FAMILIES OF THE WORLD

A note of caution is appropriate to preface this outline of the major language families of the world. When we leave the well-worn path of Indo-European and turn to languages that have been studied less thoroughly, genetic classifications are often more tentative. There are thousands of languages in the world, and many of them have been described very sketchily or not at all. When languages are known only poorly, of course, attempts to group them into families can easily go astray. Although we will concentrate on classifications that seem fairly well established, avoiding the more speculative ones, it should be kept in mind that not all of these putative families have been shown conclusively to be families by a rigorous application of the comparative method.

Indo-European

There is least doubt of all about the Indo-European family. In fact, the genetic relationships of this family were established concurrently with the development of the comparative method. Proto Indo-European has been reconstructed, to the extent that such a distant language can be reconstructed, and the historical evolution of the Indo-European languages has been traced in considerable detail.

The Indo-European family comprises ten subfamilies, as shown in Figure 8.6. All attempts to combine these subfamilies into larger ones have failed. The exact relationship of Anatolian to the rest of Indo-European is still not agreed on; Anatolian is sometimes claimed to be a sister of Proto Indo-European rather than a daughter of it.

The Anatolian languages, long since extinct, were spoken in Asia Minor. They are known through inscriptions dating from around 1400 B.C. and spanning about a millennium. The Anatolian language known in most detail is Hittite, but records have also been preserved of Luwian, Palaic,

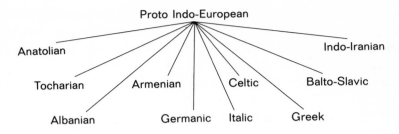

FIGURE 8.6

and Lydian. Because it was spoken at such an early period, Hittite is quite important for the reconstruction of Proto Indo-European, which dates from before 3000 B.C.

Tocharian is also extinct and known only from records. These fragmentary records, which cover the sixth to the eighth centuries A.D., were found in Chinese Turkestan. Two dialects are evidently represented, called Tocharian A and B.

Albanian apparently belongs by itself as a subfamily, and the same is true of Armenian. The former is spoken in Albania and extends into Italy and Greece. Armenian is spoken in the southern Caucasus as well as in parts of Turkey.

The first major subfamily we will treat is Germanic. Along with Gothic, which was last spoken in the Crimea in the sixteenth century, Scandinavian and West Germanic are usually considered to be subgroups of Germanic. Scandinavian includes Icelandic, Danish, Swedish, and Norwegian, the last three being quite similar.

English belongs to the West Germanic group. Its closest relative is Frisian, which is spoken along the coast of the Netherlands and on islands in the North Sea. The West Germanic languages of continental Europe are commonly divided into High German and Low German. High German, so called because it is spoken in the higher, more mountainous regions to the south, includes the dialects of Austria, southern Germany, and Switzerland. Low German includes Dutch, Flemish (spoken in Belgium), and the dialects of northern Germany. Yiddish, the language of Jews who settled in eastern Europe centuries ago, is High German. Afrikaans is a development of Dutch, spoken in South Africa.

The Italic subfamily comprises the languages that were spoken in

225

ancient Italy, together with their descendants. Besides Latin, which eventually displaced all the others, they included Oscan, Umbrian, and Venetic, which have long been extinct. Latin of course survives in the modern Romance languages. In addition to French, Spanish, Italian, Portuguese, and Rumanian, which everyone has heard of, they include Provençal, Catalan, Ladin, Sardinian, and Dalmatian. Provençal is a collective term for the dialects of southern France. During the early Middle Ages, it was a literary language and rivaled the Parisian dialect. Catalan is spoken in the eastern part of Spain, around Barcelona. Ladin, also known as Rhaeto-Romance and Romansch, coexists in Switzerland with French and Swiss German, extending as well into northern Italy. Sardinian is spoken on the island of Sardinia, oddly enough, while Dalmatian, extinct since the death of its last speaker in 1898, was centered in what is now Yugoslavia.

The Celtic peoples were once an important force in Europe, spreading across the continent into Asia Minor. The Celtic languages have given ground steadily, however, and survive today only in the British Isles and in France. Breton is the tongue of Brittany, in the northwest of France. In the British Isles we find Welsh, Irish, Scots Gaelic, and Manx. Another Celtic language, Cornish, has been extinct since the eighteenth century.

Greek has a known history of over three thousand years. Ancient Greek was composed of many local dialects, the most important of which was Attic Greek, the dialect of Athens. Attic Greek rose to prominence because of the cultural ascendancy of Athens and spread throughout the Greek empire. Virtually all the modern dialects descend from Attic Greek.

It is a matter of contention whether the Baltic and Slavic languages are similar because they constitute a subfamily or because of mutual influence. Instead of a Balto-Slavic subfamily, therefore, it may be proper to speak of two subfamilies, Baltic and Slavic. In any case, the Baltic group comprises Lithuanian and Latvian, as well as Old Prussian, extinct for several centuries. The Slavic languages are often divided into the South, East, and West Slavic groups. South Slavic includes Serbo-Croatian, Slovenian, and Bulgarian. In the East Slavic group are Russian, Ukrainian, and Byelorussian, which are very similar to one another. Czech and Slovak, which are dialects of one language, belong with Polish in the West Slavic group. The earliest written records of Slavic are from a ninth-century translation of the Bible. The language of this translation is known alternately as Old Church Slavonic, Old Church Slavic, and Old Bulgarian, and it has survived as a liturgical language.

The remaining subfamily is Indo-Iranian. Modern representatives of the Iranian group are Persian, spoken in Iran; Pashto, spoken in Afghanistan; Ossetic, spoken in the northern Caucasus; Kurdish, spoken in Iran, Iraq, and Turkey; as well as others. Two ancient Iranian languages are known through texts and inscriptions: Old Persian is known from as early as the sixth century B.C., while Avestan, the language of the Avesta (the Zoroastrian scriptures), dates from the same period but is preserved only in later manuscripts. The Indic group includes Sanskrit, which can be traced as far back as 1200 B.C., and many modern languages of northern India and Pakistan, among them Hindi, Urdu, Bengali, Panjabi, Gujerati, Marathi, Nepali, and Kashmiri.

The Rest of Eurasia

The Indo-European family includes almost all the languages of Europe; in addition, it covers parts of Asia and has been carried by colonizers to many other regions of the world. Two other families are represented in Europe. Basque, a language spoken in the Pyrenees, apparently constitutes a family in itself. It has no proven affiliations with any other known language. The remaining family of Europe is Finno-Ugric.

Of the large number of Finno-Ugric languages to be found in Europe and Asia, the most important are Finnish and Hungarian, the latter constituting a Finno-Ugric island surrounded by Indo-European languages. The other languages of this family extend eastward from Scandinavia into Siberia. They include Estonian, Lappish, Cheremiss, Mordvin, and the Samoyed languages.

The Altaic family is spread across much of central and northern Asia from the Mediterranean to the Pacific. Farthest to the west is the Turkic branch, which includes Turkish and a number of related languages, among them Azerbaijani, Uzbek, and Kirghiz. To the east lie the Mongol and Manchu branches. It is sometimes speculated that the Finno-Ugric and Altaic families should be joined in a larger family called Ural-Altaic. Korean and Japanese, which have been shown to be related to each other but not to any other major languages, are also contemplated as members of Ural-Altaic. If we wish to rely on something more than speculation, however, for the time being we must take Finno-Ugric, Altaic, and Japanese-Korean as constituting three separate families.

Two families are found in the Caucasus, the region between the Black Sea and the Caspian Sea. Among the better known members of the North Caucasian family are Kabardian, Avar, and Abkhasian. Georgian is the best known member of the South Caucasian family. To complete this survey of central and northern Asia, we might mention Ainu, a language of Japan, as well as a number of languages, among them Chukchi and Gilyak, that belong to other families and are found in the extreme northeast portion of the continent.

Most of the languages in the north of India are Indo-European. In southern India, the Dravidian family predominates. As far as the number of speakers is concerned, Telugu and Tamil are among the most important languages of India. Other important Dravidian languages are Kanarese, Malayalam, Brahui, Gondi, Kurukh, and Kui. Still a third language family of India is Munda. Munda is thought to be related to various languages found in Southeast Asia, the most notable being Mon, Khmer, and Vietnamese. This suggested family is called Austro-Asiatic.

The genetic relationships of the major languages of Southeast Asia are not completely clear, and there are conflicting proposals. The various dialects of Chinese constitute one family; Tibetan, Burmese, and many other lesser languages form another family, known as Tibeto-Burman; still another, called Tai or Kadai, has Laotian and Thai as its major members. The proposals conflict as to how these should be grouped into larger families, if at all. Under one proposal, they are all to be gathered into the inclusive Sino-Tibetan family. Another suggestion is that Tibeto-Burman should be left out, with Chinese and Tai being grouped together as the Sino-Thai family. Yet another view is that Chinese and Tai are not related at all.

The Pacific

The languages of the Pacific are generally grouped into four families. The numerous languages of the Australian aborigines are thought to form one family, and the same is true of the languages of Tasmania (an island just south of Australia), now extinct. The languages indigenous to New Guinea and adjacent islands are not known very well as yet; they are tentatively grouped under the label Papuan, but it is by no means certain that the Papuan languages constitute a single family.

The fourth Pacific family, Malayo-Polynesian, is by far the largest. It stretches from Madagascar in the west, through the East Indies, to Hawaii and Easter Island in the east, also taking in New Zealand to the south. The Malayo-Polynesian family is commonly divided into three groups: Indonesian, Melanesian, and Polynesian. The Indonesian subfamily includes Malagasy, spoken on Madagascar, and the languages of Malaysia, Indonesia, Formosa, and the Philippines. Among the more important of the latter are Malay, Indonesian, Javanese, Sundanese, Dayak, Maduran, Balinese, Macassar, Formosan, Tagalog, Ilocano, and Visayan. The Melanesian languages are spoken in the South Pacific; Fiji is the best known language of this group. Polynesian is the easternmost branch of Malayo-Polynesian. The most important of its languages are Samoan, Hawaiian, Tahitian, and Maori (spoken in New Zealand).

Africa

The linguistic situation of Africa is a complex one. Much remains tentative, although the Afro-Asiatic family, which occupies the northern part of the continent, has been extensively studied. The five main branches of Afro-Asiatic are Semitic, Egyptian, Berber, Cushitic, and Chad. The Semitic group includes such languages of antiquity as Hebrew, Akkadian, Aramaic, and Phoenician, as well as Arabic and the contemporary languages of Ethiopia. Ancient Egyptian, which is known from as far back as 4000 B.C., survived until the seventh century A.D., when it was replaced by Arabic through the Arab conquest of North Africa. Known as Coptic, Egyptian still survives as a liturgical language, however. The Berber languages, among them Tuareg, Zenaga, Kabyl, and Shilh, are spoken in various parts of North Africa. Somali and Galla are two of the more important Cushitic languages, which are spoken in eastern Africa, below Saudi Arabia. Of the Chad languages, spoken in and around Nigeria, Hausa is by far the most important.

Most of the southern half of Africa is occupied by the Niger-Congo family, of which the major subfamily is Bantu. The best known of the Bantu languages is probably Swahili, which is used in much of East Africa as a trade language. Others include Zulu, Nyanja, Xhosa, and Sotho. The other subfamilies of Niger-Congo are centered in the southern portion of the western horn of Africa. Some of the languages found there and to the east are Ibo, Yoruba, Ewe, Twi, Fanti, Malinke, Fulani, Wolof, and Sango.

Bushman and Hottentot constitute the Khoisan family; it extends from the southern tip of Africa northward, surrounded by Bantu. Sandwiched between the Afro-Asiatic family to the north and the Niger-Congo family to the south are the languages of three other families, Chari-Nile, Songhai, and Central Saharan.

The New World

We have now covered everything except the native languages of the New World. Compared with those of North America, the languages and language families of Central and South America are poorly known. The situation in South America is so unclear that we can do little more than mention some linguistic groups, without speculating as to how they combine in larger families. One of the best known is Quechua, located in Peru. Among the others are Chibchan, Huelche, Cariban, Pano, Jivaro, Tucano, Arawakan, and Tupi-Guaraní.

The situation in Central America is somewhat better. Restricting ourselves for the moment to southern Mexico and points south, the Mayan family is most easily distinguished. It occupies the Yucatan peninsula of Mexico, as well as parts of Guatemala, Honduras, and El Salvador. To the east and south of this region are languages of the Chibchan and other families. To the north and west are found various languages and language groups that are tentatively believed to be related; Otomanguian is the name used to designate this putative family, which is said to include Mixteco, Zapoteco, Trique, Amusgo, Zoque, Popoloca, Otomi, and others.

Relatively speaking, a great deal of work has been done on the indigenous languages of North America. The major families have been established quite firmly; disagreement stems mainly from attempts to combine these into more inclusive families. It is customary to discuss the geographical arrangement of the American Indian languages in terms of their location when Europeans first came into contact with them. Since then, of course, the picture we will sketch has changed considerably.

The Eskimo-Aleut family rims the continent on the north. It extends from the Aleutian islands, along the Alaskan coast, across northern Canada, to the coast of Greenland. Its two neighbors to the south are the Athabaskan and Algonkian families. The Athabaskan family occupies Alaska and northwestern Canada. It includes Chipewyan, Sarsi, Carrier, Hare, and quite a few others; Tlingit and Haida, found along the coast, are related to Athabaskan. Enclaves of Athabaskan are also found farther south, in California and Oregon. In addition, Navaho and the Apache languages, found in New Mexico and Texas, are Athabaskan. The Algonkian family is spread over central and eastern Canada, taking in parts of the United States as well, particularly the Great Lakes region and the upper Atlantic coast. Among the languages of this family are Blackfoot, Cree, Ojibwa, Illinois, Shawnee, Miami, Potawatomi, Kickapoo, Sauk, Fox, Menomini, Micmac, Abnaki, Delaware, Cheyenne, and Arapaho.

Located around Lake Erie and Lake Ontario is the Iroquoian family, which includes such languages as Mohawk, Wyandot, Oneida, Onondaga, Cayuga, Seneca, and Cherokee. The Natchez-Muskogean family is situated in the southeastern corner of the United States. The more familiar names among these languages are Natchez, Choctaw, Chickasaw, Creek, and Alabama. Continuing west along the Gulf of Mexico, we encounter a small family known as Tunican. Farther west, on the Gulf coast of Texas and northeastern Mexico, we find the Coahuiltecan family, which is entirely extinct.

Several families are represented in the Great Plains and farther west. A major one is the Siouan family, including Crow, Hidatsa, Mandan, Omaha, Iowa, Missouri, Osage, Winnebago, and a number of others. Other families found in this area are Caddoan (Wichita, Caddo, Arikara, Pawnee) and Kiowa-Tanoan (Kiowa, Jemez, Tewa, Taos, Tano, and some others). The Uto-Aztecan family occupies much of the western United States and northwestern Mexico. To the far south lies Aztec or Nahuatl, which survives in various modern dialects in the area of Mexico City. Others, extending north from Mexico, include Cora, Huichol, Yaqui, Papago, Cahuilla, Luiseño, Northern Paiute, Southern Paiute, Ute, Shoshoni, Hopi, and Comanche.

By far the greatest diversity of American Indian languages is found along the Pacific coast. Among the Hokan languages, found in Baja California, California, and Arizona, are Diegueño, Maricopa, Walapai, Havasupai, Yavapai, Washo, Achomawi, Shasta, and Karok. The California Penutian family (including Yokuts, Miwok, Maidu, Costanoan, Wintu, and Patwin) occupies much of the central and northern part of California.

Continuing north, we find Takelman (Takelma, Coos, Siuslaw, and others), Chinookan, and Plateau Penutian (including Klamath, Modoc, Nez Percé, Cayuse, and Yakima). The Mosan family occupies the northern part of Washington and extends into Canada. The two subfamilies of Mosan are Wakashan (Nootka, Kwakiutl) and Salishan (Spokane, Columbia Salish, Chehalis, Squamish, Bella Coola). Directly to the north of Mosan lies the small Tsimshian family, beyond which are found Athabaskan and Eskimo-Aleut, with which we started.

CHAPTER NINE

The Universality of
Language Design

ON THE NATURE OF LANGUAGE ACQUISITION

What the Child Accomplishes

Every human child, provided he is given a fighting chance by heredity and environment, acquires a native language during the first few years of his life. Language acquisition can take place despite very severe mental or physical handicaps, and it requires no special tutoring; sufficient exposure to the use of a language seems to be all that is needed. By about the age of six, the child has mastered the essentials of his native language. He is in possession of a linguistic system that specifies an unbounded class of sentences that he can draw upon in speaking and understanding. He has the ability to create and comprehend, effortlessly and spontaneously, sentences that are completely novel to his experience.

When you stop to think about it, this is quite a remarkable achievement. The magnitude of the accomplishment should be apparent to anyone past adolescence who has ever tried to gain near-native fluency in a foreign language; it is not something that can be taken lightly or for granted. Native language acquisition is one of the major events in the psychological development of the human child. As such, it is something that deserves explanation. If we can understand it, we will have learned something important about ourselves.

In some respects, the child learning to talk is in the same situation as a linguist investigating a language. The child must, in a manner of speaking, deduce the structure of the language spoken around him. Like the linguist, he is unable to observe this structure directly. He can only base his deductions on the linguistic performance that he monitors, which is determined in part by the abstract linguistic system but which reflects it at best indirectly and imperfectly.

The linguistic system that a child constructs for himself thus constitutes a hypothesis as to the structure of the language that the people around him use. By testing the consequences of this hypothesis against his further linguistic experience, the child continually refines it, until it is for all practical purposes equivalent to the system of his models. Since the systems are never compared directly, however, the possibility of restructuring or imperfect learning is always present.

Unlike the linguist, the child is not trying to render the structural principles of a language explicit and accessible to conscious inspection; he is simply learning to talk. He is trying, for the most part subconsciously, to make an abstract linguistic system part of his psychological organization. Only in a metaphorical sense does the child formulate a theory of linguistic structure and look for empirical evidence to verify or falsify it, but the metaphor is an instructive one. The child must somehow discover the structure of his native language; no one hands it to him ready to use.

When the child has learned to talk, when he has mastered his native tongue, he is in possession of an abstract system of rules that specify an unbounded class of well-formed sentences. He is not conscious that he possesses such a system of rules; nor can he determine their character by introspection. He possesses this system in the sense that its structural patterns have been imposed on his psychological processes, so that these patterns are a factor in determining the course of his verbal activity. Learning to talk, like learning to ride a bicycle, involves the mastery of a set of principles; it involves the addition of structure to the body of psychological skill or competence that shapes our mentally directed behavior. These rules are thus no more accessible to conscious inspection than the rules for keeping one's balance while riding a bike. We talk, and we keep our balance on bicycles, but in neither case do we know, at the level of consciousness, precisely what the guiding principles are. The activity of a computer, by way of analogy, is directed by a program, but the program is not the object of its activity; the computer carries out calculations related to other things, not to the program that guides it.

Empiricism and Rationalism

The problem of understanding language acquisition is that of finding out precisely how the child comes to possess the abstract linguistic system that is largely responsible for shaping his verbal activity. For the most part, the nature of this process is not known. We have no adequate theory to explain, stage by stage, the child's discovery of the structure of his language.

Consequently, we will focus our attention on a more restricted question, but one that is of primary importance for a full understanding of language acquisition: How much of linguistic structure is innately specified? To put it another way, how much of the linguistic system that he ultimately commands is the child born with, and how much must he discover on the basis of his linguistic experience?

At one extreme, it could be claimed that no linguistic structure is innately specified, that language is learned entirely through experience. This is the empiricist view, mentioned briefly in Chapter One. It holds that we have no special, inborn capacity to acquire language. The fact that we acquire language and the structure of the language we learn are both due to the training we receive as children. From the linguistic point of view, we start out as blank slates. The linguistic system that is ultimately written on these slates is somehow built up from scratch, its structure being determined by experience alone. Language is thus viewed as a culturally transmitted entity, like stamp collecting or the use of forks.

At the opposite extreme, we find the rationalist view that language is innately specified almost in its entirety. Children learn to talk because the capacity for language, as well as most of the structure of language, is built into them. The function of linguistic experience, according to the rationalist view, is not so much to shape language as to activate the linguistic competence with which we are born. The blueprints for any possible linguistic system are provided as part of the innate neural equipment with which every human child is born. The role of learning is thus minimal. The child has only to learn those details of structure that differentiate the language spoken around him from other possible human languages. He has only to put flesh on the skeletal linguistic system he already possesses. In this view, then, the bulk of language is genetically transmitted. Only the peripheral structural details that make languages superficially different from one another are acquired on the basis of environmental influence.

The empiricist and rationalist views are thus in disagreement as to how much of linguistic structure is learned, but they do not conflict completely. Even adherents of the empiricist position would concede that the structure of the human organism places certain restrictions on the kind of linguistic system that it can master. Any such system must be finite, for example, since the human organism is finite; no one could learn an infinite number of rules. Moreover, it must be assumed that children are born with some innate ability to learn, with some genetically transmitted capacity for combining simple psychological structures to form more complex ones. Otherwise, if the child had no inborn capacity to learn, he never would. This primitive ability to learn is usually conceived as being a relatively simple one, like the ability to form associations (for example, candy and sweetness are associated because they occur together so often in our experience; each one calls the other to mind).

The empiricist position, therefore, admits that innate properties of the organism are in some measure responsible for determining the organization of language. By the same token, the rationalist position does not deny that learning plays a significant role in language acquisition. What the child inherits genetically is not a specific language, but only the capacity for language. When he is born, the organizational and structural properties that all languages share are built into him, but these properties are not exhaustive of the structure of any particular language. Using the inborn, skeletal linguistic system as a base, the child must proceed to discover those structural details that translate this base into the fully specified system that is used around him. It is here that learning is involved. In learning which language, of all possible human languages, is spoken around him, the child formulates structural hypotheses (in a manner of speaking) and tests them against further linguistic experience, continually refining them until he possesses a linguistic system equivalent to that of his models. But this process of discovery takes place within limits that are narrowly prescribed by genetic endowment, and the role of learning is thus minimal.

The empiricist and rationalist positions differ in two important respects. The empiricist holds that very little of psychological structure is innately specified, while the rationalist claims that a great deal of it is. This difference is one of degree, but the other difference is absolute. In the empiricist view, the human child is born with no special capacity for language, only a general ability to learn. A linguistic system is built up through experience by means of the same basic intellectual ability (association, for example) that is responsible for shaping all other aspects of cognitive structure. In the rationalist view, on the other hand, there is, in addition to general intelligence, a special inborn capacity for language. Above and beyond our natural ability to form and manipulate concepts, we are endowed with an innately specified predisposition to acquire a linguistic system having certain properties as opposed to all other conceivable ones.

The Evidence for Innate Specification

The evidence for the rationalist claim is very strong. Consider first the uniformity of language acquisition throughout the human race. We have seen that every human child learns a language unless he is the victim of extreme mental deficiency or isolation from language use. There are all sorts of physical and intellectual skills that children can fail to master despite a considerable amount of instruction, but talking is not among them. This is precisely what one would expect on the basis of the assumption that language is innately specified almost fully, with linguistic experience serving mainly to activate the genetically specified system.

While the species uniformity of language acquisition fits in perfectly with the rationalist position, it conflicts with what we would expect on the basis of the empiricist viewpoint. If the acquisition of language depended mainly on the training the child receives, we would expect differences in training to correlate directly with differences in language acquisition (if general intelligence is held constant). In fact, however, this expectation turns out to be false. A child learns to talk regardless of whether or not his parents constantly pursue him, correct him, and put him through linguistic drills. Some parents do this, others do not, and some children don't even have parents—but they all learn to talk. Despite wide variations in the amount of speech they are exposed to, all children acquire a full-blown linguistic system. There are no cases on record of children who have only learned half a language, who have failed to master any syntactic rules, who lack underlying phonological representations, or who have not picked up any complex lexical items. The vicissitudes of early linguistic experience are not matched by any comparable variations in linguistic structure.

A second argument in favor of the rationalist position is provided by the fact that only human beings learn to talk. The most likely nonhuman candidates, of course, would be the higher apes—chimpanzees, for example. They are anatomically similar to humans and are also reasonably intelligent; they can learn to use tools and to solve simple problems. The difference in intelligence between apes and human beings is thus not absolute, but only a matter of degree. When we consider language, however, we find an absolute distinction. The progress that apes can make toward mastering a human language is not proportional to their intelligence—in fact, they can make no progress whatsoever. Experiment has shown that a chimpanzee, even when raised exactly like a child, acquires nothing that bears even the faintest resemblance to the linguistic systems that human children learn so easily. Language is therefore peculiar to our species. Moreover, it is not directly tied to intelligence. These observations are perfectly compatible with the view that language develops in the human child because of a special, inborn linguistic capacity. Apes cannot learn to talk because they do not possess this innate structure.

This simple and natural explanation is not available if one adheres to the empiricist position. If language is a function of general intelligence and not of any special linguistic capacity, then other animals should, given proper training, succeed in acquiring language to a degree proportional to their intelligence. Experiment has shown that this is not the case. There is absolutely no evidence to indicate that anything even remotely resembling the complex system of rules and abstract underlying representations of a human language can arise in other species.

The relative perfection of language acquisition is a third argument for innate specification. If language reflected general intelligence and not a special linguistic capacity, we would expect differences in intelligence to correlate directly with differences in language acquisition (if training is held constant). We would expect bright children to do better than stupid ones in mastering a linguistic system. We would also expect some children to fail miserably at acquiring language, just as many children fail to learn geography or the procedure for extracting square roots. We would expect some children to wind up with linguistic systems so deficient or so distorted as to be unrecognizable.

These expectations are not borne out, however. Bright children, average children, and stupid children all learn to talk. They are all successful at mastering a linguistic system that is virtually identical to that of their models, one which is neither distorted nor deficient. Regardless of general intelligence, a child succeeds in mastering a complex system of rules and underlying representations that specifies an infinite set of sentences. Children may vary on minor points such as volubility or size of vocabulary, but they do not vary with respect to the significant structural features of linguistic organization. If the role of learning is minimal, serving only to activate the innate system and to fill in some details at the structural fringes, it is impossible for radical structural errors to arise.

The abstractness and structural complexity of languages is a fourth strong argument in favor of the rationalist view. We know a great deal about language, but despite centuries of serious investigation, we would be at a complete loss to describe exhaustively the structure of any language, even the most intensively studied. But this is essentially what the child does. He masters the entire set of lexical items and structural principles that constitutes a linguistic system. He does this on the basis of indirect and fragmentary evidence, and at an age when he is not yet capable of logical, analytical thought. This remarkable phenomenon can be explained in terms of the rationalist view, but hardly in terms of the empiricist position. If linguistic structure is genetically transmitted, its tremendous complexity does not pose a problem for the child. His learning task is the relatively simple one of narrowing down the range of innately specified possibilities until he arrives at the right one. It is not a matter of building up the entire linguistic system from scratch, but only of filling in some peripheral details.

The empiricist claim, however, is that the entire linguistic system is indeed built up from scratch on the basis of the child's general intellectual capacity. The child is purported to discover, not just some structural details, but the entire scheme of linguistic organization as well. Born without any linguistic expectations or predilections, he is supposed to make, at a preintellectual age, a series of linguistic discoveries that far surpass the cumulative results of the efforts of all those scholars who have ever investigated language!

This would not seem to be a reasonable claim. It is important to remember that the linguistic system that is acquired can never be directly observed. The structure of this system must be discovered on the basis of the very indirect evidence of linguistic performance. Even if the child learned to talk at an age when he was capable of analytical thought, therefore, he would still not be able to master the principles of linguistic organization if they were not part of his genetic endowment. Any number of structural hypotheses can be conceived that will account for the finite set of linguistic observations that the child has available to him as evidence; to take one example, he would have no reason not to believe that a language was just a finite list of utterances that had to be memorized. With no inborn structural principles to guide him, the child could hardly be expected to discover the nature of the linguistic system that partially underlies the verbal activity of the people around him. He would have no basis even for suspecting the existence of this system. Furthermore, its abstractness and complexity puts it well beyond the possibility of being discovered by trial and error.

LANGUAGE UNIVERSALS

We have seen that, in the rationalist view, linguistic structure is innately specified in considerable detail. The same inborn structural framework underlies all languages, and the function of the child's exposure to language is more to activate his linguistic capacity than to shape it.

If this view is correct, then all languages must be structurally very similar to one another. If the same genetically transmitted structural framework underlies all languages, then languages can differ from one another only with respect to the peripheral structural features that the child learns through experience. Despite their surface differences, all languages must be alike in most respects. They must constitute variations on the same structural theme.

To put it another way, the claim that language is innately specified implies that all human languages must fall within a fairly narrow range of structural possibilities, as illustrated in Figure 9.1. This range of possibilities, represented by the solid lines, is imposed by the innate linguistic specifications that make it possible for the child to acquire a language in the first place. The learning task that the child is faced with, then, is that of narrowing down this range of possibilities still further, until he has in effect

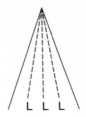

FIGURE 9.1

discovered which particular language L, of all possible languages, is the one spoken around him. Of all conceivable languages, only those that fall within this narrow range of possibilities can be acquired by the child in a natural, spontaneous fashion.

A structural feature that is common to all languages is called a **language universal**. By and large, we may equate language universals with those structural features of languages that are innately specified; if all languages share a certain property, it is probably because this feature is part of our genetic endowment as human beings.

The claim that all languages are very much alike is often met with skepticism. After all, when we compare linguistic systems—in learning a foreign language, for example—we are struck by the differences between them. No one will deny that languages differ from one another in a multitude of details. On the other hand, we must realize that surface peculiarities are much more likely to attract our attention than underlying structural principles, while it is in the latter that we would expect to find language universals. By now it should be clear that surface linguistic diversity often conceals underlying uniformity.

All languages exemplify the same basic organizational scheme. More specifically, every human language comprises an infinite set of sentences, each of which manifests, in phonetic form, a conceptual structure. A complex series of syntactic rules serves to connect conceptual structures with surface structures, which are linear strings of lexical items grouped hierarchically. A series of phonological rules connects the surface structure of each sentence with its phonetic manifestation on the basis of the underlying phonological representations of its lexical items. Each individual lexical item consists in the association of semantic, syntactic, and phonological properties, the relation between its semantic and phonological

241

properties being arbitrary in most cases. Phonologically, a lexical item is represented as a linear series of segments, each segment specified with respect to distinctive phonological information.

There are simply no exceptions to this organizational scheme. No one has ever found a human language lacking syntactic rules, phonological rules, or discrete lexical items. No one has found a language in which lexical items were not composed of linear sequences of sound segments. Out of all conceivable ways in which a language could be put together, actual human languages are unanimous in picking this particular way. Linguistic systems differ somewhat in structure, but they vary only within the confines of this common framework.

In outlining this common organizational scheme, we have barely begun to point out the universal characteristics of language design. Languages have much more in common than simply this general framework, so the range of variation among them is restricted still further.

Before a linguist starts to investigate a new language, therefore, he already knows a great deal about its structure. On the basis of his experience with other languages, he has acquired a substantial body of expectations, whether or not he has ever tried to formulate them explicitly. He has noted the existence of apparently universal linguistic traits, even if only in the back of his mind, and he would be very much surprised to find a language that violated his tacit predictions.

He knows, for example, that in the new language it will be possible to pose questions, to give commands, and to express negation. He knows the language will have an unbounded set of complex sentences involving embedding, conjoining, or both. There will be demonstratives of some sort, words expressing quantity, pro forms, nouns, and verbs. In all probability, there will be agreement phenomena of some kind. The linguist also does not have to be told that he will encounter many complex lexical items that are constructed from simpler ones. He will find idioms, as well as cases of metaphorical extension in the use of simple lexical items. The lexical items of the language will fall into classes on the basis of their behavior with respect to grammatical and phonological rules, and these classes will overlap. The linguist will expect the language to have vowels, stops, fricatives, nasals, liquids, and perhaps glides and affricates. No morpheme will contain nine consecutive vowels or nine consecutive stops. If the language should be a tone language, it will not have more than a half dozen distinctive tones, and probably fewer.

We could continue this enumeration of shared linguistic traits at great length, but there would be little point in doing so. Rather, we will examine somewhat more carefully the nature of syntactic and phonological rules in order to further illustrate the claim that, out of all conceivable ways in which a language could be put together, human languages are unanimous in choosing one particular way.

Syntactic rules apply to abstract sentence structures and modify these structures in some way, connecting them with structures that are less abstract (that is, more like surface structures). However, there are very severe restrictions on the ways in which they can do so. In language after language, the kinds of modifications that syntactic rules effect turn out to be very similar, and these occupy only a very narrow band in the spectrum of conceivable modifications.

One thing that syntactic rules do is to insert semantically empty morphemes as trappings on sentences. The *to* of *I want to go*, for example, is inserted by a syntactic rule of English; *to* is apparently devoid of semantic content, but various verbs, among them *want*, require that this morpheme accompany an embedded clause. In similar fashion, a syntactic rule inserts the semantically empty morpheme *that* after *know*, producing sentences like *I know that he is rich*.

Another function of syntactic rules is to mark agreement. A rule of English, for instance, marks verbs to agree with their subjects in number and person; on the basis of this syntactic specification, phonological rules give verbs their proper phonological form. French has a similar rule, as well as one that marks an adjective to agree with the noun it modifies in number and gender.

Syntactic rules also serve to reduce constituents, by deleting them completely or by replacing them with a pro form, and to change the order of constituents in a sentence. Both deletion and permutation are involved in the derivation of English possessives such as *Peter's hat*, which come from abstract structures like *the hat of Peter's*. *The* and *of* have to be deleted by syntactic rules, and the possessor noun phrase, *Peter's* in this example, is transported and placed before the preceding noun. Another permutation rule of English applies to verb particles and places them after a following noun phrase. From the structure underlying *The mayor hurriedly looked up the number*, this rule produces the structure manifested as *The mayor hurriedly looked the number up*.

Further examples of deletion and permutation are provided by possessive expressions in Aztec. *In conetl ical* 'the child's house' consists of the article *in* 'the'; the noun *conetl* 'child'; the possessive prefix *i*, meaning 'his'; and *cal* 'house.' The structure underlying *in conetl ical* can be manifested in various other ways as well; the variants *in ical conetl, conetl ical,* and *ical conetl* mean the same thing. Two optional syntactic rules produce the variants. One permutes a noun phrase containing a possessive prefix such as *i* with a preceding noun, and the other deletes the article *in*. The former yields *in ical conetl,* and the latter produces *conetl ical*. When both rules apply, the result is *ical conetl*.

For each of these types of rules that are exemplified over and over in human languages, we can conceive of indefinitely many other *a priori* possible rules that simply never occur. Of all the syntactic rules that we can formulate on the basis of general intelligence, the rules children do in fact master when learning to talk constitute an extremely restricted subset. It is common for a rule to insert a semantically empty form in one particular spot in a sentence, as in the derivation of *I know that he is rich*. But in no human language will we encounter a rule that inserts two semantically empty morphemes after every word. A rule producing *I that that know that that he that that is that that rich that that* would be a linguistic impossibility. Similarly, no actual syntactic rule has the effect of adding to a sentence a string of morphemes equal in number to the words already present; such a rule would translate *I know he is rich* into *I know that that that that that he is rich,* and *I know Robert never tries to start trouble* into *I know that that that that that that that that Robert never tries to start trouble*. No one has ever found a language in which a syntactic rule served to insert a copy of each word directly after it, producing sentences like *Tennis tennis is is a a demanding demanding sport sport*. It should be apparent that there is no limit to the number of rules of this type that could be invented but which are in fact never used in human languages.

Agreement and reduction rules are similarly restricted. In no language, for example, will one find a rule that marks all verbs of a sentence, except that verb which has the first noun phrase of the sentence as its subject, to agree with the first noun phrase in number and person; in English, this rule would produce sentences like *I be looking for the book which Helen am disappointed with and George like very much*. Nor will one ever encounter a syntactic rule that makes an adjective agree with any arbitrary noun in the sentence except the one it modifies. No language has a syntactic rule deleting every second morpheme or every third word. If a complex sentence is formed by conjoining two simpler sentence structures, the first of two identical noun phrases in the conjoined structures will never be pronominalized, but always the second. Sentences like *John came to visit and he stayed a month* are therefore possible, where *John* and *he* are taken as referring to the same person, but one does not find languages in which the Pronominalization rule operates instead on the first noun phrase, yielding sentences like *He came to visit and John stayed a month*.

Likewise, there are severe restrictions on the ways in which permutation rules can modify sentences. A rule that ordered the words of a sentence according to how many sound segments they contained would be a linguistic impossibility. No language contains a syntactic rule that optionally reverses the order of all the words in a sentence, allowing, for instance, *Night tomorrow dinner to coming are Boston from men old blind three* as a variant of the sentence *Three blind old men from Boston are coming to dinner tomorrow night*. Nor will we ever find a rule that reverses the members of each successive pair of words, yielding things like *Blind three men old Boston from coming are dinner to night tomorrow*.

Similar observations can be made in reference to phonological rules. Phonological rules add segments, delete segments, modify or further specify the identity of segments as given in underlying phonological representations, and so on. Within these boundaries, there is a very wide range of structural possibilities, but relatively few of these possibilities are ever exploited in human languages. Let us consider just two kinds of phonological rules, those that insert segments and those that change the identity of segments.

Certain kinds of segment insertion rules are found fairly commonly in languages of the world. In starting to investigate an unfamiliar language, for instance, a linguist would be well prepared to encounter a rule that inserted a glottal stop to separate any two adjacent vowels or to begin any word that would otherwise begin with a vowel. He would not be surprised to find a rule that inserted a vowel between two identical or similar consonants (as for English *judges* [ǰʌǰəz]). Nor would he be surprised to find a rule that inserted a vowel at the beginning of a word that would otherwise begin with a consonant cluster.

On the other hand, no linguist would expect to find a rule that inserted [a] after every second segment in a sentence; such a rule would be a linguistic impossibility. Nor would a linguist be prepared to find a rule

245

that separated any two adjacent voiced stops in a string by inserting a voiceless stop between them, or which added [čpl] to the end of any word that would otherwise end in a nasal consonant.

In the same way, phonological rules that change the identity of segments tend to be similar in languages all over the world. Many of the same phenomena turn up in language after language, while others never seem to occur at all.

For example, there would be nothing out of the ordinary in a rule that changed [ɪ] to [i] in word-final position, or which made stops voiceless in this position. It would not be at all surprising to find a language in which [f] was manifested as [h] at the beginning of a word, or in which a voiced stop showed up as a voiced fricative intervocalically. Assimilation rules also tend to be similar from language to language. It is very common, for instance, for a vowel to be at least partially nasalized before a nasal consonant. Consonants occurring adjacent to one another are frequently assimilated in voicing, so that either they are all voiced or they are all voiceless. An assimilation rule labializing a stop before [w] is in no way unusual. And so on.

But no linguist expects to find a language in which a consonant is made voiceless if it occurs between two voiced consonants. It is fairly certain that there is no language containing a rule that changes [a] to [t] before a nasal. No language seems to have a rule that manifests a glottal stop as a nasal vowel, or that changes [č] to [m]. Out of all conceivable rules serving to change the phonological characteristics of individual segments, only a highly restricted class is found to be operative in human languages.

CONCLUSION

People have studied language for many different reasons, but our discussion has concentrated on two that are probably the most significant. On the one hand, we have viewed the investigation of language as an attempt to explain linguistic creativity, to find out how it is possible for a speaker to create and understand a potentially unbounded class of sentences that are completely novel to his experience. On the other hand, we have looked to linguistic investigation as an avenue that will allow us ultimately to fully comprehend language acquisition.

We found that the unbounded character of language can be traced to the nature of human conceptual powers. As human beings, we are in principle capable of conceptualizations having any desired degree of complexity (although there are of course limitations on the complexity of any thought that we can form and operate with at any given moment). From any one of an infinite number of possible conceptual situations, a surface structure can be derived by the choice of appropriate lexical items and the application of syntactic rules. Phonological rules connect each of these surface structures with a phonetic manifestation. The abstract linguistic system thus specifies an infinite set of phonetic sequences, each of which is paired with a conceptual structure.

Because he possesses an abstract linguistic system of this type, a speaker controls an infinite number of sentences that he can draw upon in speaking and understanding. By studying the structure of these systems, we are therefore progressing toward an explanation of linguistic creativity. We will completely understand linguistic creativity when we completely understand the structure of linguistic systems, the way these abstract systems are used in actual verbal performance, and the psychological processes that produce conceptual structures.

We concluded that children learn to talk because language is built into them. The contention that the capacity for language is innately specified finds support in various quarters. The view that linguistic experience serves more to activate language than to shape it accounts for the fact that language is species uniform and species specific. It explains the relative perfection of language acquisition, and enables us to understand how, at a preintellectual age, a child is able to master a system of remarkable complexity and abstractness. Furthermore, the hypothesis that linguistic structure is innately specified is consistent with the observation that all languages are similarly designed. It explains the fact that all known languages fall within an extremely narrow range of structural possibilities, one that is far more restricted than the range of possibilities we can conceive of on the basis of general intelligence.

Even if we accept the hypothesis of innate specification, we are left with many interesting questions that must be answered before our understanding of language acquisition is complete. For example, precisely which aspects of linguistic structure are not innately specified but must be acquired through experience? How does this learning take place? What stages does a child go through in discovering the structure of his language and in learning to use it? On what kind of data is language acquisition crucially dependent? To what extent are language universals determined by general psychological constraints (constraints that affect other cognitive phenomena as well), and to what extent are they determined by our special inborn linguistic capacity? It should be apparent that these questions can be answered satisfactorily only in the context of an adequate theory of linguistic structure and an adequate theory of general psychological organization, neither of which is presently available.

Thus, linguists are far from knowing everything there is to know about language. The positive results of linguistic investigation are extensive and significant, but they are small when measured against the amount we still have to learn. Language is difficult to study because it is a psychological phenomenon, one that is intimately associated with other aspects of psychological structure. It is for precisely the same reason, however, that an understanding of language is of such great importance. The study of language just might provide the key to understanding ourselves.

Selected Readings

Anderson, Wallace L., and Norman C. Stageberg, eds. *Introductory Readings on Language*, rev. ed. New York: Holt, Rinehart and Winston, 1966

Bach, Emmon. *An Introduction to Transformational Grammars*. New York: Holt, Rinehart and Winston, 1964

Bloomfield, Leonard. *Language*. New York: Holt, Rinehart and Winston, 1933

Bloomfield, Morton W., and Leonard Newmark. *A Linguistic Introduction to the History of English*. New York: Alfred A. Knopf, 1963

Boas, Franz. *Introduction to the Handbook of American Indian Languages*. Washington, D.C.: Georgetown University Press, Institute of Languages and Linguistics, 1966

Brown, Roger. *Words and Things*. New York: The Free Press, 1958

Cherry, Colin. *On Human Communication*. New York: John Wiley & Sons, 1961

Chomsky, Noam. *Syntactic Structures*. The Hague: Mouton and Co., 1957

———. *Cartesian Linguistics*. New York: Harper & Row, 1966

Denes, Peter B., and Elliot N. Pinson. *The Speech Chain*. New York: Bell Telephone Laboratories, 1963

Dinneen, Francis P. *An Introduction to General Linguistics*. New York: Holt, Rinehart and Winston, 1967

Fodor, Jerry A., and Jerrold J. Katz, eds. *The Structure of Language: Readings in the Philosophy of Language.* Englewood Cliffs, N.J.: Prentice-Hall, 1964

Gelb, I. J. *A Study of Writing.* Chicago: University of Chicago Press, 1952

Gleason, H. A. *An Introduction to Descriptive Linguistics,* rev. ed. New York: Holt, Rinehart and Winston, 1961

Hockett, Charles F. *A Course in Modern Linguistics.* New York: The Macmillan Company, 1958

Hudson-Williams, T. *A Short Introduction to the Study of Comparative Grammar (Indo-European).* Cardiff: University of Wales Press, 1961

Hudspeth, Robert N., and Donald F. Sturtevant, eds. *The World of Language: A Reader in Linguistics.* New York: American Book Company, 1967

Jakobson, Roman, C. Gunnar M. Fant, and Morris Halle. *Preliminaries to Speech Analysis.* Cambridge, Mass.: M.I.T. Press, 1952

Jespersen, Otto. *Growth and Structure of the English Language.* Garden City, N.Y.: Doubleday & Company, 1955

————. *Language: Its Nature, Development and Origin.* New York: The Macmillan Company, 1949 (available in paperback)

Ladefoged, Peter. *Elements of Acoustic Phonetics.* Chicago: University of Chicago Press, 1962

Lehmann, Winfred P. *Historical Linguistics: An Introduction.* New York: Holt, Rinehart and Winston, 1962

Lenneberg, Eric H. *Biological Foundations of Language.* New York: John Wiley & Sons, 1967

Malmberg, Bertil. *Phonetics.* New York: Dover Publications, 1963

Pedersen, Holger. *The Discovery of Language.* Bloomington: Indiana University Press, 1931

Reibel, David A., and Sanford A. Schane, eds. *Modern Studies in English.* Englewood Cliffs, N.J.: Prentice-Hall, 1969

Samarin, William J. *Field Linguistics: A Guide to Linguistic Field Work.* New York: Holt, Rinehart and Winston, 1967

Sapir, Edward. *Language: An Introduction to the Study of Speech.* New York: Harcourt, Brace & World, 1921 (available in paperback)

Saussure, Ferdinand de. *Course in General Linguistics.* New York: Philosophical Library, 1959

Smalley, William A. *Manual of Articulatory Phonetics,* rev. ed. Tarrytown, N.Y.: Practical Anthropology, 1963

Stern, Gustaf. *Meaning and Change of Meaning.* Bloomington: Indiana University Press, 1931

Sturtevant, E. H. *Linguistic Change: An Introduction to the Historical Study of Language.* Chicago: University of Chicago Press, 1917

Waterman, John T. *Perspectives in Linguistics.* Chicago: University of Chicago Press, 1963

Wilson, Graham, ed. *A Linguistics Reader.* New York: Harper & Row, 1967

Index

2
3
4
H 5
I 6
J 7